Computers and Personnel Management

Computers and Personnel Management

A practical guide

M. L. Gallagher

HEINEMANN : LONDON

William Heinemann Ltd
10 Upper Grosvenor Street, London W1X 9PA

LONDON   MELBOURNE
JOHANNESBURG   AUCKLAND

First published 1986

British Library Cataloguing in Publication Data
Gallagher, M. L.
  Computers and personnel management
  1. Personnel management – data processing
  I. Title
  658.3'0028'5   HF5549

ISBN 0 434 90645 X

Printed in Great Britain by
Redwood Burn Ltd, Trowbridge

Contents

Preface   viii

Acknowledgements   x

1 Computer-based personnel systems   1
Introduction – Traditional approaches – Recent developments –
Definition of a CPMIS – Scope of the personnel management
information system – The best approach

Part I The electronic environment   11

2 The electronic office   12
Introduction – An historical perspective – Types of computer –
Word processing

3 Hardware   18
Introduction – The central processing unit – Peripherals –
Backing storage devices – Input/output devices – Data
transmission

4 Software   38
Introduction – Operating systems – Application systems –
Processing techniques – Data files – Utility programs – Job
control language – Fourth generation languages

5 The data processing organization   56
Introduction – Typical organization structures – Head of function
– The systems analyst – The programmer – Systems programmer
– Database administrator – Computer operations manager

6 The systems development process   63
Introduction – Methodology and standards – Investigation and
feasibility – Specification of requirements – System proposal –

System specification – Programming – System testing –
Implementation – System Review

Part II The personnel management information system 73

7 **Feasibility study** 74
Purpose – Cost–benefit analysis – Scope of the system –
Approaches available

8 **Specification of requirements** 86
Importance – Format and scope – Part I – Part II – Appendices

9 **General requirements** 103
Introduction – Security – Resilience – Query language and report
generator – Flexibility – Response time – User-friendliness –
Support

10 **Specific requirements** 124
Introduction – Personnel records – Salary records – Absence

11 **Pension records** 144
Actuarial requirements

12 **Recruitment** 152
Competitions – Job applicants – The system in operation

13 **Budgets and establishment** 161
Post file – System outputs – Management information

14 **Training** 170
Training courses – Training aids

15 **Word processing and letter production** 178
Stand-alone word processing – Advantages of word processing –
Disadvantages of word processing

16 **Manpower planning** 185
Manpower planning defined – Aims of manpower planning –
Stages in manpower planning – Computer modelling – Reports –
A manpower planning model

17 **Query language and report generator** 203
Principles of operation – A simple system – DATATRIEVE –
Desiderata of a query language

18 **Other features and peripheral applications** 218
Conditions of service – Accidents on duty – Facilities booking –
Industrial relations information – Disputes information –
Graphics – Diary facilities – Telephone directory – Labels

19 **Proposals for hardware and software** 227
Seeking proposals – Proposals from whom? – The invitation –
Evaluation of proposals – The recommendation – Format of
recommendation report

20 Signing the contract   237
Avoiding problems – General Clauses – Specific clauses –
Summary

21 System implementation   251
Involvement and participation – Data protection legislation –
Preliminary work – Impact on the organization of the personnel
function – The project team – Hardware installation – Systems
testing – Training – Procedures – File set-up – Implementation
policy – The live system – Test version of the system – Post-
implementation review

22 Glossary of terms   276

Index   283

Preface

In recent years developments in computers and in the electronic office in general have begun to have a more significant impact on the personnel function. This has happened in two main ways

1 Personnel professionals have been involved in the negotiations and agreements covering the introduction and use of computer-based technology.
2 The electronic office is becoming a reality within the personnel department.

Traditionally, personnel professionals have had limited exposure to computers and computerization of the personnel function has generally been regarded as a low priority. If it featured at all in corporate systems development plans, it was well down the list compared with the organization's general ledger, payroll, stock or production control system. Meanwhile, computer systems were developed for planning and controlling the maintenance of the organization's plant and equipment and substantial effort was also devoted to developing systems to aid classification and record-keeping of the balance sheet assets of the organization. The need for the latter was boosted by inflation accounting which emphasized the increased cost of asset replacement.

However, just as an organization's most valuable asset – its skilled and experienced workforce – does not feature in the balance sheet, neither has there been a corporate appreciation of the need to use proper systems to monitor this valuable resource and to assist in utilizing it most effectively.

In comparison with other professions, training and education of personnel officers has not placed much emphasis on computer systems and procedures and, while more has been done recently in this area, an amount of ground has yet to be made up.

This book is divided into two parts. Part I describes, very much in outline, the development of computers over the years, the hardware and software involved, the organization of the data processing function and the systems development process. In doing this the relevance to the personnel function is emphasized.

Part II is concerned with the application of computer technology to personnel management – the approaches which are available, how to go about determining which is most appropriate, the scope of the system and how implementation should be handled.

The book should be useful to three categories of reader

1 Professional personnel staff who need to have a basic understanding of computers and the development of computer systems from a labour relations point of view.
2 Professional personnel staff who want to take advantage of the developments in computer technology in order to provide a more effective and efficient personnel management service. It is hoped that it will be particularly useful to the person within the personnel management function who is given responsibility for investigating the computer options available and for eventually implementing a system. In this context, systems ideas and approaches cannot be regarded as being of universal application but they should help to stimulate thinking as to what a computer-based personnel management system should embrace and how the project should be approached.
3 Computer professionals or management services staff who wish to have an appreciation of the elements of a personnel system.

Acknowledgements

I am grateful to the many people in RTE who assisted me in writing this book – to senior management for its encouragement and to the staff in both Data Processing and Personnel who were involved in implementing the personnel management system.

I would like to thank Digital Equipment Corporation (DEC), Dorset County Council, G. C. McKeown & Co. Ltd and International Computers Ltd (ICL) for their cooperation and assistance. I would also like to thank Hewlett Packard, IBM, and WANG.

Grateful thanks are due to Órla Fagan for coping with the manuscript and finally to my wife, Anne, who was a tremendous source of encouragement and help at every stage of the projects.

Michael L. Gallagher

1 Computer-based personnel systems

Introduction

Since the latter half of the 1970s there has been an increased emphasis on the need for computer-based personnel management systems – systems which will enable personnel management to manage more efficiently and effectively and to provide a more positive service to the organization.

In the past, those responsible for the development of a corporate data processing strategy tended to ignore or failed to appreciate the need for such a system. Personnel management was also slow to appreciate the benefits which such a system could yield. Very often the only contacts between management services/data processing staff and the personnel function related to such matters as

- the establishment of clerical procedures to interface with the computer-based payroll system
- the clarification of conditions of employment in as far as they related to the calculation of pay by the computer
- production of *ad hoc* reports from the payroll system
- negotiations on the introduction of computer technology in other departments.

The appreciation of the need for a Computer-based Personnel Management Information System (CPMIS) has come about because of four main influences:

1 In the generally prosperous 1960s and the pre-oil crisis years of the early 1970s most organizations were expanding, employment was increasing and pay and conditions were improving. This scene has changed dramatically. The emphasis now is on increased productivity from the work force, freezes on recruitment, short-term working, temporary lay-offs and redundancies. This has highlighted the need to have more information about the organization's most important

resource. Such information will help determine the most appropriate manpower and personnel policies and allow them to be implemented effectively.

2 The increasing demands made by labour legislation which relates to personnel practices, and by increasing requirements for statistics by government departments and other agencies.

3 The rate of development of computer technology. There has been a considerable move away from the traditional approach of a large main-frame processing mainly batch-type applications, to on-line applications both on main-frame and on distributed or local computers. The progress being made in terms of processing power and capacity of the micro-computer has also increased the opportunities for applying the new technology to personnel management.

4 The increased availability of computer-based systems for personnel. While computer hardware has become readily available it is useless unless appropriate application software is available. There is still a relative scarcity of personnel management systems but more packages are becoming available and software development aids are allowing for the quicker development of custom-built systems.

Despite the appreciation of the need for a CPMIS it is not easy for the personnel function to appreciate fully what a computer can do for it or how it should go about specifying its requirements. In order to achieve a good CPMIS there has to be a greater understanding of the personnel function by the management services function and then together they can combine to harness the technology most effectively.

Traditional approaches

While there has been a scarcity of computerized personnel systems, many organizations have had a certain amount of personnel data held on the payroll system. Generally these consist of

Employee number
Employee name
Salary scale and point
Grade
Date of birth
Date of joining the organization
Date of entry to pension scheme
National Insurance number and classification
Contract expiry date
Cost centre
Status/category
Sex
Increment date

By their nature payroll systems lend themselves to batch processing techniques. However, it is feasible to provide on-line access to the file.

This would allow access to the records of individual employees and should be of benefit to the personnel department. While the latter may be beneficial, access to a good query language would indeed be even more useful.

A query language provides the facility to retrieve information easily and quickly from a computer-based system without having to pre-define the specific requirement at the system design stage, or to have a special program written.

A number of retrieval systems are currently available which are easy to use and which enable the user department as distinct from the data processing department, to use a computer terminal to process its own *ad hoc* queries and obtain answers either on a visual display unit (VDU) or via a printed report. See Chapter 17 for a description of query languages.

Provided the data in the system are kept up to date, this approach can be a very useful precursor to a proper personnel management system. There can be a tendency to neglect data which does not directly influence an employee's pay and if this happens, reports produced by the system may be incorrect, the system will get a bad reputation and the deterioration in the quality of the data will accelerate.

The accessibility of this data is a major factor in determining its usefulness. If the organization uses a computer service bureau to process its payroll, it may be difficult and expensive to respond to requests for information. In this situation what normally happens is that a number of standard reports are automatically produced at periods which correspond to the payroll processing cycle – weekly, fortnightly or monthly. If a special report is required, there may be a delay in having it produced and this practice may be discouraged because of the costs involved.

If the payroll system is processed in-house the position may be somewhat better. The computer department should be in a position to respond to requests for *ad hoc* reports and this is particularly so with the availability of query languages and report generators which enable such requests to be serviced with minimum effort. The basic data from the payroll system can be of considerable help to an organization which is about to embark on a full scale personnel records computerization project. If the data is already held on magnetic media it will speed up considerably the file set-up in any new system.

Other benefits which will accrue from this approach are

1 The personnel staff will have become acquainted with computers. They will have obtained some benefits from using the system and, having become aware of its shortcomings, will be in a better position to consider what their real requirements are.

2 The use of the system will have required the formalization of certain administrative procedures which may be of benefit in designing the new procedures which any CPMIS will require. These will include the use of codes for grades, staff categories etc.

3 It will have encouraged the use of a single identifier for each employee. In many organizations there has been a tendency for employees to

have a payroll number, a different personnel number and perhaps a variety of other identifiers. It is highly desirable that there should be just one such identifier and that this should be the unique personnel number allocated by the personnel function to a person on joining the organization. This number should be used at all stages, for example when an employee leaves and subsequently returns.

Another approach which may have been used by the personnel department is the use of a time-sharing system. For some years systems have been offered which use the facilities of large main-frame computers with access via telephone lines. Organizations have tended to input a limited amount of data for each employee and have found these systems useful for providing various statistics and reports from the data held and also to use it as input to a model to assist in the evolution of alternative manpower strategies.

Recent developments

The evolution of the micro-computer
Recent developments in the micro-computer area have affected the personnel function in three ways

1   Its popularity for both home and business use has given rise to a lot of interest in the application of computer methods in areas which were previously largely immune to the impact of computers. Personnel people are coming into constant contact with people from other functions who have made use of the developments and now wish to consider their application within personnel management.
2   Micros are being used for certain discrete activities within the personnel management function – using spread-sheets to model the impact of wage and salary increases, using database systems for mailing lists, sick leave statistics or the analysis of industrial accidents.
3   The availability of personnel packages on micros or the use of application generators on micros to develop a tailored system has provided a boost, although it is difficult to be precise about the size of organization which can be well serviced by a micro because it depends on
    • the characteristics of a particular micro, e.g. power, size of memory, disk capacity, networking ability
    • the scope of the package or the specific requirements of the organization.

However, as a general rule, if an organization employs more than 500 people the claims of a micro to provide the personnel function with a good service would have to be examined very critically.

The availability of packages
An application package is a ready-made system or suite of computer programs designed in such a way that it will meet the requirements of a

variety of users. The implementation of a package in an organization involves the customization of the package to reflect the particular needs of the organization and this is largely done by setting up various parameters within the system. Since the mid-1970s the number of packages has increased considerably, but there is still very little choice in comparison with the variety of packages available for the more traditional computer applications. Such packages are now available on micros, mini-computers and main-frames.

Appreciation of the need

In recent years the emphasis on productivity, rationalization and keeping staff numbers down has highlighted the need for computer systems to monitor the manpower resource and to assist in manpower planning. This has had the effect of a greater budget allocation to personnel management in the corporate computer development plan.

There may also be a tendency to de-emphasize the direct savings – in terms of reduced staffing of the personnel function – and to concentrate on the less immediately quantifiable benefits of having better management information. The head of the personnel management function will be aware of the developments in computer-based systems within other functions and will also come under increasing pressure to provide results as quickly as the Production Director or Finance Director can. Management colleagues will expect almost instant answers to questions such as: 'How many engineers did we recruit last year?' or 'How many staff are due to retire over the next ten years?' Instant answers will be expected as to the cost to the organization of wage agreements being negotiated, and once they have been negotiated delays in implementing the new agreements are no longer tolerated.

The availability of systems development tools

In recent years there have been significant advances in systems development aids, sometimes known as fourth generation languages, which allow for faster development of new systems. Some of these are based on substantial user involvement. This is a necessary element in the development of any new system but traditionally it tends to be disjointed. There is substantial involvement at the stage where requirements are being defined, a lower level of involvement during the system definition stage and then there is a gap while the system is being developed until the system testing is ready to start. With the new development aids there is more constant user involvement, the development cycle is shorter, and the user has greater scope for changing his/her mind about requirements as the system develops. Because of the way in which the system comes into being, system testing is a less onerous task and so the user is allowed to get on with planning the actual implementation of the system.

Definition of a CPMIS

A CPMIS can be defined as a computer-based information system which is designed to support the operational, managerial and decision-making functions of the personnel division in an organization. A management information system has been compared with a pyramid in which the base consists of data or information for transaction processing in an operational environment. The next level up consists of information which is used to support day-to-day management. The third level consists of information which is used at the next level of management for tactical planning purposes. The top level consists of information which is used by top management for strategic planning and policy development. This is illustrated in Figure 1.

The nature of a CPMIS will be viewed differently by each type of user. At the operational level those involved will be primarily clerical personnel. They will want to know how the system will perform and how they will be expected to provide it with basic data.

- Will it replace the existing manual records?
- Will it do away with the need for diaries of upcoming increments, service pay entitlements and retirements?
- Will it make work more interesting, less interesting, or more demanding?
- Will it smooth out the unbearable workload which occurs during peak recruitment periods?
- Will it cover external training courses as well as internal courses?
- Will it produce letters to staff and job applicants – increment advice,

Figure 1   *The computer-based personnel management information system*

promotion advice, acknowledgement letters, letters calling applicants for interview, and letters of rejection?
- What will replace the 'Green Book' or 'Black Book' of salary scales and allowances?
- Who will do the coding of input for new employees?
- How will an employee's salary history or absence record be found?

First level managers or supervisors will expect the system to perform existing tasks more efficiently.

- To be more up to date then the manual system.
- To replace the various diaries and notebooks which are an essential part of the present system.
- To do away with a lot of the headaches associated with such matters as the implementation of a general salary increase or dealing with the response to a recruitment drive.
- To be able to provide information in response to requests from up the line. These often require a lot of research and the answers are always 'required yesterday'.
- To get reports on how up to date the work in the section or department is.

Departmental and senior management will expect information from the system which will enable them to develop personnel plans and policies. This will include

- Profiles of the staff by age, qualifications, experience and mobility.
- Projections of the expected staff profile 5, 10 or 15 years hence.
- Regular summary reports on salary levels, absence, training activity and recruitment activity.
- Regular reports on staff numbers, vacancies, and comparisons with establishment figures.
- The ability to respond to *ad hoc* enquiries.
- How much it will cost to increase the basic overtime rate for all operational grades by 15 per cent.

Scope of the personnel management information system

There are personnel management packages on the market which have the facility to hold basic data about employee such as name, address, phone number, salary, grade, sex, allowances, date of birth, date joined organization, date left organization.

They provide a number of standard reports and some limited facilities for adding new fields or altering the sequence of the reports. Any personnel management professional recognizes that this is not a complete personnel records system, but unfortunately to a great extent it has been the data processing person's view of what constitutes such a system. Each organization will have its own particular requirements but any CPMIS introduced should be as comprehensive as possible. It should be capable of keeping track of all employees from the initial application for employment through the employee's working life and into retirement. It should ideally hold all records about the employee other than matters which for convenience or confidentiality are more appropriate to the employee's personal file.

The following should be an integral part of any good CPMIS.

Personnel records

This relates to identification data, current and historical salary and allowance data and various employee attributes such as grade and key dates.

Training records

Data relating to each employee's qualifications, skills and experience. The system would also hold details of internal and external courses and course attendees.

Establishment

Establishment relates to the setting up of budgets for appropriate staff levels and grades throughout the organization. The system should encompass these budgeted posts and report on variations between actual staff numbers and the budgeted numbers.

Absence

The system should allow for the recording of various absence types, e.g. sick leave, annual leave or special leave without pay. Input to this subsystem should be automatically reflected in the establishment subsystem.

Industrial relations and manpower planning data

The system should hold data to assist management in negotiations and in planning for alternative strategies. Much of this would be held for normal administrative purposes so what is required is the facility to extract the data in meaningful terms, to be able to project forward and to test the impact of applying various rules and scenarios.

Pension records

The system should maintain all details of service entitlements of employees, contributions by both the employee and the organization to the pension scheme, details of dependents – spouse and children, data required for actuarial purposes to verify the viability of the scheme, and details and entitlements of employees who have become pensioners.

Recruitment

Details of all vacancies and applicants should be held by the system. These should show the status of each vacancy and of each applicant and should perform as much as possible of the administrative process. This will generally mean that the system should interface with a word processing system.

The best approach

There is no single 'best approach' which can be applied in all circumstances. The best approach is the one which is most appropriate to a particular organization. This will be determined by

- the nature of the organization: manufacturing, distribution, transport, public service etc.
- the organization structure: centralized or decentralized; where responsibility for payroll processing rests
- the state of systems development within the organization generally
- the budget available.

The system must, however, meet a number of basic requirements. These are

1 It must be an on-line system.
2 Confidentiality of data must be safeguarded and there must be a comprehensive security system employing the use of passwords.
3 The emphasis must be on screens (VDUs) rather than on paper.
4 The design of the system must ensure as much flexibility as possible.
5 The system must be easy to use.
6 The system should include an effective report generator/query language.
7 Data within the system must be easily accessible. Essential keys for retrieval are: 'personnel number' and 'employee name'.
8 Information must be displayed in as meaningful a manner as possible e.g. by use of description rather than codes on screen.

Part I The electronic environment

2 The electronic office

Introduction

The term 'the electronic office' is generally understood to refer to the impact which the merging of electronic technology relating to computers, word processors and telecommunications has had on the business office. It may also be extended to embrace facilities such as electronic mail, digital photo-typesetting, document reproduction, facsimile transmission and information retrieval from microfilm. These technologies are used for performing normal office operations – creation, storage, processing, receipt, editing, reproduction and dissemination of information.

An historical perspective

The main phases in the evolution of computer technology are known as 'generations', with the first generation computers being those which became commercially available in the early 1950s. The US Bureau of the Census is generally credited with having installed the first commercial computer in 1951.

First generation

This generation lasted until the end of the 1950s and computers in this era had their basis in wired circuitry and thermionic valves. Their outstanding features were:

- Very expensive
- Quite large and, because they generated a lot of heat, required special housing
- The medium of internal storage was magnetic drum.

Second generation

The second generation, which covered the first half of the 1960s, saw the introduction of printed circuits and the replacement of valves by transistors. Typical computers were the ICT (ICL) 1300 and the IBM 1401. The outstanding features of this generation were

- In comparison with the previous generation they were smaller in size and generated less heat
- Internal storage capacity was increased and processor speeds started to be measured in microseconds rather than milliseconds i.e. millionths rather than thousandths of a second
- Core storage took over from magnetic drum as the main medium for internal storage
- Machines started to evolve as series rather than as stand-alone processors.

During this period punch card machines became popular and with hardware available to manipulate the cards, many systems which were the forerunners of today's computer-based accounting systems were developed. The hardware consisted of

- *key punch* which punched holes in the cards to represent the data
- *verifier* which by means of a rekeying operation, checked the accuracy of the original punching of data
- *calculator punch* which accepted cards which had already been punched, carried out some specified calculations and automatically punched the result on the card.
- *tabulator.* This essentially was the processor and printer. The punched cards were sequenced (sorted) and then read by this machine which listed them on the printer and could also accumulate and print totals
- *sorter* which, by sorting one column at a time, placed the cards in the desired sequence
- *collator.* This machine had two functions: to *merge* two batches of cards e.g. an employee pay rates file with a time-sheet file or batch; to *match* two batches of cards e.g. to identify only employees for whom there is a time-sheet
- *reproducer* which took the data as punched in one batch of cards and reproduced it in another batch. It also had facilities for 'gang punching' e.g. punching a common time-sheet date on all cards.

Third generation

The arrival of the third generation in the mid-1960s proved to be an important milestone in the evolution of computers. The advances over the previous generation were very significant and although relatively expensive allowed an increasing number of organizations to reap the undoubted benefits which computerization could bring. Because of the high costs involved and the need to get maximum utilization from the machine the computer service bureau business was spawned. This in itself was important in that it allowed smaller companies to avail themselves of the new technology and to take advantage of the continuing developments. Many of the computers acquired by companies during this period are still in use.

The following are the outstanding features of this generation

- further reductions in size
- the cost/performance factor has improved significantly
- increased internal core memory capacity
- increased emphasis on the use of disk as a backing store medium and substantially reduced cost per megabyte
- processor speeds are rated in nanoseconds i.e. one-thousandth of a microsecond
- ranges of computers came into being e.g. IBM360, ICL1900. Models within these ranges were designed to be 'upwards compatible' thereby enabling systems developed for the lower models in the range to move up the line with limited modification
- the use of high-level languages became common e.g. COBOL, FORTRAN and PL/1
- limited communications facilities became available.

Fourth generation

The fourth generation of computers arrived in the mid-1970s. The distinguishing marks were the introduction of standard architecture which provided for greater mobility of systems, the introduction of micro-technology and significant software developments.

The IBM4300 and ICL2900 ranges coincided with the start of this era. Micro-technology gave rise to the availability of micro-computers, word processors and intelligent terminals.

The outstanding features of this generation are

- further reductions in the size of the hardware
- better price/performance
- hardware which in many cases will operate in a normal office environment
- core storage, based on small rings of ferromagnetic material, has been replaced by semiconductor memory based on the silicon chip. This has led to great expansion in the amount of memory available typically 8 megabytes (8,000,000) as against, say, 256 kbytes (256,000) in the previous generation
- cheaper and bigger backing storage devices. Typically single disk drives with a capacity of 500–1000 megabytes as against about 10 per cent of that figure previously
- sophisticated systems software. Operating systems such as ICL's VME and database management systems such as IDMS
- the availability and enormous popularity of personal and home computers

Types of computer

Business computers are generally divided into three classes: main-frames, mini-computers; and micro-computers. Because of the rate of technological development in the computer industry it is not easy to give a definitive description of each. A desk-top micro can now have substantially more memory available to it than a third generation main-frame computer, and many micros have left some of the earlier minis far behind. However, there will always be a place for all three classes – it is very much a case of 'horses for courses' and in order to highlight the differences, typical configurations and typical applications are described below for each type.

Main-frame computers

A main-frame computer is a large expensive machine of great power, significant processing capacity in terms of speed, a large amount of backing store and fast printers. It operates in a custom-built environment and is supported by a typical data processing organization.

A large main-frame computer may be used to meet the main data processing requirements of the organization as a whole or a number of different functional areas. It is particularly relevant where there is close interrelationship between the information requirements of various functional areas. Some applications require the power and facilities of a main-frame in order to be viable: examples are airline booking systems, broadcasting advertising sales systems, centralized payroll systems and large integrated production planning and control systems.

Mini-computers

A mini-computer in terms of cost and processing power lies between the micro-computer and the main-frame. It is in fact a scaled-down version of a main-frame and in many cases will have been developed by main-frame manufacturers specifically to address a section of the market for which this level of processing power is appropriate. Typically the peripherals are also scaled-down versions, for example, line printers are still appropriate but perhaps at a speed of 300 L.P.M. instead of 1500 L.P.M. A mini-computer configuration would normally occupy a dedicated room and would be looked after by a small, specialist data processing staff. In some cases mini-computers are used in a distributed data processing environment. In this situation local processing is done on the mini but the computer is in communication with a central main-frame which then processes summary or planning data or provides the mini with access to centralized data. Early minis such as the DEC PDP11 were often associated with 'non-business' systems such as process control, quality control and environmental monitoring.

Typical mini business applications are those which do not impinge on the organization as a whole, but in smaller companies a mini may service the same applications as a main-frame would do in larger companies. Typical applications would be maintenance stores, personnel records and library systems.

Micro-computers

A micro-computer is a small, low-cost computer with a processor based on a single silicon chip. The dividing line between the micro and the mini is becoming increasingly blurred especially with the advent of multi-user, multi-tasking micros. At the other end, the line between the home computer and the business micro is also becoming blurred.

More and more software is becoming available to cater for a whole range of business applications. A small organization will have a choice of many packages capable of handling all of its accounting requirements – general ledger, creditors, debtors, sales analysis, bank reconciliation, order processing, stock control and payroll etc. Apart from application packages a number of general packages are also available. Two important categories of the latter are

1 Database systems which allow for relatively easy development of systems and range from basic easy to use facilities through to more complex systems – CARDBOX, dBASE III and DBMS are examples.
2 Spread-sheets, which are a computer version of the paper spread-sheet divided into rows and columns. These packages are described as modelling systems, allow for the manipulation of data input to and held in the spread-sheet and are generally easy to use. Common spread-sheets are SUPERCALC, MULTIPLAN and LOTUS.

Word processing packages such as WORDSTAR and WORD are also readily available for micros.

Word processing

Whereas data processing (DP) is concerned with the processing of data, word processing (WP) is concerned with the efficient processing of words or text. The technique is designed to provide a more efficient way of meeting the typing needs of a business and typically is used for the production of standard letters and for preparing reports and documents which are subject to change before they are finalized. As disk storage has become cheaper the word processor is being increasingly used for all correspondence originating in an office and copies are then stored electronically rather than in hard copy.

Word processing is available in three forms

1 Dedicated word processors. These are special purpose computers which are built so as to act efficiently as word processors but generally are not suitable for other computing applications. They can be single user, twin user or multiple user (cluster) systems. In the case of the latter all users share a common disk storage and sometimes share a

common processor (shared logic systems).
2 Use of a standard word processing package on a general purpose micro (where a dedicated system cannot be justified). There is a wide variety of WP packages available – they vary in terms of the features which they offer, in their style and in ease of use. Since these packages are usually designed to operate over a wide range of micro-computer types, they cannot always efficiently use the special function keys available on the keyboard. This leads to a combination of keys being used when a single designated key would suffice. Although the system documentation will refer to these key combinations it is sometimes possible to tailor the system to particular micros.
3 On minis some manufacturers provide a word processing package which can be used from any terminal in the system. It is generally based on the text editor available to programmers of the system and while it will not generally constitute a fully blown WP system, it can meet many of the needs in a general office environment. This facility is seldom available on main-frames.

Word processors are of most value where there is

- a high volume of routine correspondence
- a requirement to send personalized letters to people on mailing lists – staff, customers, suppliers, members etc.
- a need to produce documents which contain large sections of standardized text e.g. legal documents, specifications or proposals
- a lot of drafting, editing and revision.

A dedicated word processor normally uses a high quality daisy-wheel printer, whereas the printer attached to a micro may be aiming at speed rather than quality.

A typical single-user dedicated word processor would have the following facilities

- document creation, storage and retrieval
- automatic word wrap, page numbering, centring, underlining, overtyping and reformatting, right justification, proportional spacing
- efficient search
- automatic correspondence
- global search and replace
- forms handling
- spelling check
- file extract and file merge
- sort facility
- column handling
- graphics (usually limited)
- records management
- help facility
- calculation
- column addition
- password security

3 Hardware

Introduction

There are two basic types of computer

.1 The *analog* computer, in which the basic data is handled in a con tinuous form. This type of computer measures physical magnitud such as voltage, resistance, temperature, speed, flow-rates and pres sure. A typical use of an analog computer is patient monitoring ir hospitals. Main applications are in the industrial, scientific researcl and engineering fields.

2 The *digital* computer in which the basic data is represented in discret form. The term digital relates to the way the computer functions – b taking discrete numbers and performing mathemetical calculations o them.

Computers are also either special purpose or general purpose. Specia purpose computers are specifically designed to do one particular type o work while the latter, as the name suggests, are designed to be of genera use. In the personnel management context, the only relevant compute type is the general purpose digital one.

This chapter describes the main characteristics of the hardware tha goes to make up such a computer and examines them in terms of

- basic components or elements
- peripheral equipment
- input/output methods
- transmission of data.

The central processing unit

The heart of any computer is the central processing unit (CPU). Thi consists of four elements

18

The control unit.
The arithmetic/logic unit.
The internal working memory unit.
The input/output control unit.

The *control unit* directs operations within the computer and so is in overall control. It tells the arithmetic unit what it has to do and where, within the computer's memory, the data on which it has to act is situated. In effect it acts as a coordinator for the other units and acts as the switching centre for the computer.

The *arithmetic/logic unit* is the slave which does the work. It performs all of the mathematical operations and the logical operations such as comparisons, matching and decision making.

The *internal working memory unit*, which must be distinguished from external or backing storage (such as disks), is used for storing software such as operating and application systems. Internal memory is directly addressable and is accessed in a random fashion (RAM).

Internal memory is sometimes referred to as 'core memory' because ferrite core was in use until the mid-1970s. This has been replaced in modern computers by semi-conductor memory – MOS (metal oxide semi-conductor). Internal memory in a computer system is expressed in terms of bytes or words – these terms indicate the number of bits (binary digits which can have either of two states, usually designated by 0 and 1) in a unit of storage. Numeric and alphabetic data is stored in a sequence of bits which are grouped together. The most common unit for storing a character is the 8-bit byte. Other arrangements consist of 12, 16, 24 or 32 bits – known as *words*. This can be quite confusing. Main-frame computers tend to operate on a 32-bit word, equivalent to 4 bytes. Smaller computers (micros) tend to operate on an 8 or 16-bit word. In recent years there has been an enormous expansion in terms of the size of memory available on all types of computer. In the early days of the micro the memory range was generally 4k to 64k bytes – the abbreviation 'k' is used to denote 2^{10} or 1024. Memory of a megabyte – one million bytes – is now common on business micro-computers.

The *input/output control unit*, as the name implies, governs the data input and output operation. This involves the interface between the processor and the outside world of VDUs, printers and other peripheral devices.

Peripherals

A computer is not of much value to the personnel management function unless it is capable of receiving input such as employee details, providing output such as staff listings, and storing data about employees and the organization. This is done by connecting a variety of peripheral devices to the processor. The cost of CPUs has reduced enormously relative to processing power and memory size, and, while peripherals have also experienced this phenonomen because of the relatively high mechanical

content, they are still expensive. It is likely that the cost of periphera
equipment on a dedicated personnel management computer will excee⊂
the cost of the processor. Peripherals are now considered under tw⊂
headings

• backing storage devices
• input/output devices.

Backing storage devices

The main backing storage media in use are magnetic tape, and magneti⊂
disk.

Magnetic tape

Magnetic tape is similar in principle to audio tapes or video tapes used i⊂
domestic recorders/players and there are both reels and cassette⊂
cartridges in use. Magnetic tape is popular both as a medium of backin⊂
store and as a medium for inputting transaction data to the system. Th⊂
most common type of tape is the ½ inch reel-to-reel version on whic⊂
data is stored on either seven or nine tracks. In the personnel manage⊂
ment context it is a handy and relatively cheap medium for holdin⊂
security copies of files and for the transfer of data from one computer t⊂
another, for example for transferring details of salary changes from th⊂
personnel computer to the payroll computer, or earnings data in th⊂
other direction. The main drawback of tape is that it is a serial mediun⊂
This means that it is necessary to search continuously through the whol⊂
of the tape until the required item is found. If data relating to 500⊂
employees is held on tape in employee number sequence and employe⊂
number 2500 is required, the system will have to search through half o⊂
the data on tape before the employee is found.

This highlights the fact that it is not a suitable medium for storag⊂
where random access is required, such as an enquiry from a terminal. A⊂
a medium for holding master files it is suited to a batch processin⊂
environment where there is a high transaction hit rate and where th⊂
transactions being processed are presented to the program in the sam⊂
sequence as the master file. To update information stored on magneti⊂
tape it is necessary to create a new file on another tape on another driv⊂
as shown in Figure 2.

The features of a magnetic tape unit are

1 It has two reels – the second one being the 'take-up' reel.
2 It has read/write heads for transferring the data to and from mai⊂
 storage.
3 A write-protect ring can be put on the tape as it is loaded and this wi⊂
 prevent the unit over-writing the tape.
4 The tape moves past the heads at speeds of up to a few hundred inche⊂
 per second.

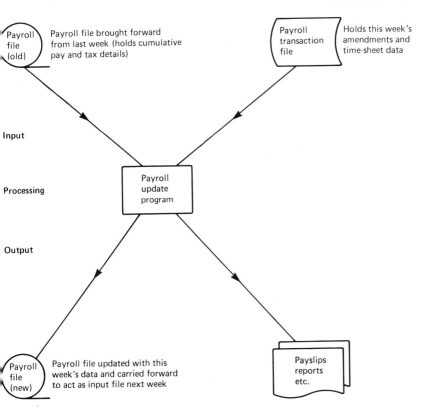

Figure 2 *Flow chart of a payroll update using magnetic tape*

The magnetic tape itself has the following features

1 It is possible to record up to 6250 bits per inch. This is known as the packing density of the tape.
2 The tape is ½ inch wide and reels come in various lengths up to 2400 and 3600 feet.
3 The tape has a plastic base and is coated on one side with material which is capable of being magnetized.
4 There are either seven or nine tracks on the tape and the data is coded in such a way that one character is coded across the tracks.
5 Each reel has leader and trailer tape which cannot be used. This is useful for threading the tape through the unit; the start and finish of the recording surface is indicated by means of special markers.
6 The speed at which data can be transferred to the processor is determined by the speed at which the tape moves past the read/write heads and the packing density of the tape used. At the top end – fast drives normally associated with main-frames – transfer rates of over a million characters per second can be achieved. In the case of a

dedicated personnel computer the practical rates are probably closer to 100k characters per second.
7 The capacity of a tape using high packing density can be up to 50 million characters.
8 Magnetic tape is re-usable.

The advantages of magnetic tape are

1 It is a relatively inexpensive medium and has large storage capacity.
2 It is widely used, so it is often possible to transfer data between computers, for example to obtain employee PAYE details from the income tax authorities, or transfer payroll details to the banking system.
3 It can operate at a very high data transfer speed.
4 It is a very convenient medium for back-up storage – including off-site storage.
5 It can be a useful medium for recording transactions off-line, for example in tape-encoding data preparation machines or as the final output from a key-to-disk system. This is more relevant in a batch processing environment and may only be relevant in the case of initial file set-up in the CPMIS context.

The disadvantages of magnetic tape are

1 Only serial access to data is possible – this requires that *all* records are read until the one required is found.
2 Input transaction data must be sorted to the same sequence as the master file before it can be processed.
3 Because of the two previous points it is not a suitable medium where an on-line system is concerned.
4 Updated information cannot be written to the same location on the tape – another tape must be used and the whole file must be copied until the appropriate location is reached.

Cassettes and cartridges are devices which operate basically in the same way as ½ inch tape but have smaller capacities and are slower. Cassettes are generally associated with home computers and with a number of older business computers. The cartridge, also known as streamer tape, is a very useful facility on a micro or mini-computer for holding back-up copies of files. They have a capacity of up to about 90 million characters and are particularly useful for backing up Winchester disks. This process takes about five minutes.

Magnetic disk
At the present time disk storage is probably the most suitable form of backing store available. This is especially true in the on-line environment and in many computer installations disk is overwhelmingly used for both on-line use and back-up. In such installations the use of magnetic tape is restricted to providing a means of accepting data from, or providing data

for, other computers. Disks as we know them today may be replaced eventually by optical disks which are currently being developed laser technology.

Three types of disk are considered below

1 Hard disks – fixed and exchangeable.
2 Winchester disks.
3 Floppy disks or diskettes.

All of the types of disk described below can be termed 'random access storage devices'. This means that the required item of data can be retrieved without searching through all of the data until it is found. This contrasts sharply with magnetic tape. Information is stored in the form of tracks on the magnetic surface of the disks and the read/write heads operate on the disks as they rotate at high speed. The heads operate very close to the magnetic surface but do not touch it.

Access to data is effected via an addressing system. The address of a required item of data is established and then the heads are instructed to move to that address or location and the contents of the address are retrieved during the next revolution of the disk. The same addressing system is used when data has to be written to the disk. Because of this addressing system and because of the random nature of the storage units, it is not essential to store data in a predefined order as it is on magnetic tape.

In batch processing only records on the master file which are affected by transactions need to be accessed by the update program. Records for which there are no transactions present remain unchanged and there is no need to re-write them as there is with a tape-based system.

In recording data on *hard disks* the cylinder concept is used. To understand this it is necessary to look at the structure of the disk pack and the read/write mechanism (see Figure 3). A disk pack is equivalent to six LP records stacked on top of each other with a spindle holding them together and providing enough space for the read/write heads to access all sides except side A of the top record and side B of the bottom one. This gives rise to ten recording surfaces and each surface has 200 tracks. All of the read/write heads are fixed to a single mechanism. They appear like a comb and when the access mechanism moves all heads move together in formation across the disk surfaces. Accordingly, whenever the access mechanism halts each head will be positioned over the equivalent track on each of the ten recording surfaces. This physical structure is considered when the storage of data on disk is being organized. The first record is written on the disk starting at track 1 of surface 1, then track 1 of surface 2, track 1 of surface 3 to track 1 of surface 10. In this way it is easy to visualize the concept of the cylinder. The disk can then be regarded as comprising 200 cylinders. This concept is an important consideration in physical system design so that the access mechanism movement can be kept to a minimum and the data retrieval process is speeded up.

Hard disks can be divided into two types, exchangeable and fixed.

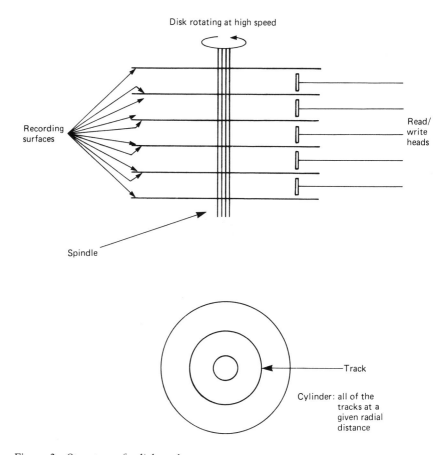

Figure 3   *Structure of a disk pack*

Exchangeable disks are so called because the disk packs can be removed from the disk drive and exchanged for others which are required for processing. In a personnel records system, salary history over three years old might be deleted from the live system and archived. The archiving process could transfer the data on to an exchangeable disk which would not normally be on-line but would be 'loaded' whenever access was required to the data.

The features of an exchangeable disk system are

1 Disk packs are loaded as and when required.
2 The disk revolves at a speed of several thousand revolutions per minute.
3 All arms on the read/write mechanism move together as one when accessing a surface on the disk.
4 Exchangeable disks hold up to 300 million characters.

5 Typical access times are 40–50 milliseconds (thousandths of a second) and data transfer rates are in the region of between ½ and 1¼ million characters per second.

The features of fixed disk systems are

1 The disk unit contains disks which are fixed rather than removable.
2 The data is constantly on-line.
3 Some fixed disks have a capacity which has to be expressed in gigabytes (10^9 characters) and can achieve data transfer rates of up to 3 million characters per second.

A *Winchester disk* is a hard fixed disk which operates within a hermetically sealed compartment so as to avoid contamination from dust or other agents. They are very robust devices and can operate satisfactorily in dusty conditions such as warehouses. These hard disks have significantly greater capacity than floppy disks (diskettes) – generally within the range 5–40 megabytes – and are proving to be a very attractive alternative to floppies on micros. The rotation speeds are high and this results in a fast data transfer rate. When floppies are used rather than hard disks it is easy to establish copying and back-up procedures since one floppy can be copied directly on to another floppy. The capacity of a floppy disk is seldom much in excess of a megabyte. Accordingly, copying of files for security purposes from hard disk to floppies can be an extended procedure, and special attention has to be paid to drawing up security copying procedures. Streamer tape (cartridge) can prove to be a convenient medium for holding back-up copies, since the capacity of cartridges can be equivalent to disk capacity.

Diskettes are also known as *floppy disks* or *floppies*. They acquired the name because of their non-rigid construction, being made from flexible material and look very different from conventional hard disks (see Figure 4). They store anything from about 100,000 bytes to around 1,000,000 bytes. Their capacity is determined by

• the use of one or both surfaces for data recording
• the recording density used e.g. single, double or quad
• the diskette size – the standard sizes are 3½ inches, 5¼ inches and 8 inches.

Diskettes can withstand a fair amount of handling and can be sent through the postal service with limited risk. The surfaces are not exposed since they are encased in a cover. Although essentially the use of diskettes is restricted to small micro-based systems they can act as a useful medium for data collection and distribution.

Magnetic disks have the following advantages

1 The file organization systems supported by disk allows any item of data to be accessed directly.
2 They provide fast access and high data transfer speeds.
3 They provide the background facilities required for on-line operation.
4 They provide access to very large volumes of data.

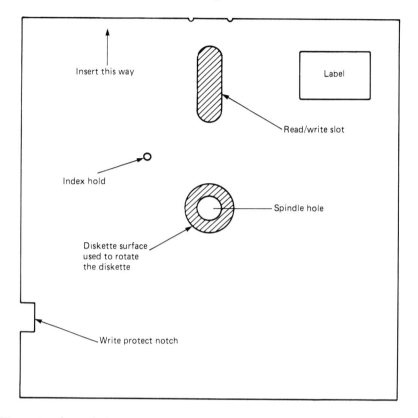

Figure 4   *Floppy disk (diskette)*

5 Updating in place is possible, whereas tape requires the creation of a new file.
6 Disk packs are re-usable.

The disadvantages of magnetic disks are

1 As a storage device they are quite expensive.
2 They are more sensitive to the environment than tapes and require care and attention.
3 Proper procedures must be designed and adhered to in order to avoid serious loss of data when problems such as a head-crash occur where, because of minute particles of dust, the heads come into direct contact with the disk.

Input/output devices

There is a great variety of ways by which data can be captured and input to a computer and by which information can be produced by the computer. The choice of input media will depend on a number of factors such as the type of business and the location of branches. Some input devices are relevant only in particular industries e.g. bar code readers in stores or supermarkets. Other media which were important in previous years are significantly less so now, e.g. punched cards and punched paper tape.

Computer input devices or media are

- keyboard devices – VDUs and consoles
- document readers – OCR (optical character recognition) and MICR (magnetic ink character recognition)
- magnetic media – magnetic tape encoders, key-to-disk systems and floppy disk systems
- data capture devices – data recorders, direct input devices and POS terminals (point of sale)
- media recorders – punched card readers, paper tape readers, punched tag readers and badge readers.

A number of these devices can also be used for output but the normal output devices/media are

- printers
- VDUs
- magnetic tape
- COM (computer output on microfilm)
- graph plotters.

The following section examines briefly some of the various input and output methods available with particular reference to those which are relevant in the context of personnel management.

Punched input

The punched card was at the heart of many of the earlier computer-based systems. In today's environment it is not so important from a CPMIS point of view but it is worth examining as a method of input because it is a useful way of explaining the principle of data representation and it will help to explain some of the features of inputs to existing batch system – especially payroll-associated personnel systems. The most popular type of punched card has been the 80-column variety. There have been, and still are, other sizes of cards and punched input also exists in the form of punched paper tape and punched tags – as used in the clothing business.

The 80-column card

The punched card is a rectangular piece of high-quality card approximately 19 cm × 8 cm. In its basic form the rows and columns are identified on it and one of the top corners is cut away in order to assist in making sure that all cards are facing the right way when they are being placed in the card reader. Data is represented on a punched card by means of holes punched in the card which form a code which can be interpreted by the computer. The card consists of 80 columns and 12 rows. The rows consist of 10 rows representing the digits 0–9 and 2 rows known as 'zones'.

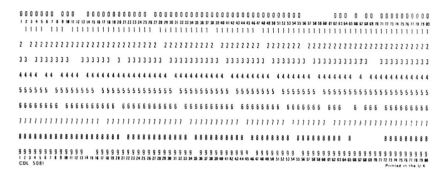

Figure 5   *A punched card with data encoded on it*

Card code	Employee number	Surname	First name	Start date			Salary	Date of birth			
				dd	mm	yy		dd	mm	yy	
01											

| 1 | 2 | 7 | 30 | 50 | 56 | 64 | 70 | 80 |

Figure 6   *Typical input document to punched card-based system*

A single numeric character can be represented by a single hole in any of the 10 numeric rows, and alphabetic and special characters can be represented by a combination of holes in the numeric rows and the two zone rows (see Figure 5). The cards are input to the computer via a card reader – they are fed into a hopper/stacker and a photo-electric reader senses the holes in the card. The data encoded on a card can be interpreted and printed on the top of the card as it is punched (see Figure 5).

Input documents for use in a punched card-based system usually show the card columns on the form (see Figure 6). The data is initially punched on to cards by an operator using a key-punch machine. Then a second operator verifies the original punching. This is done by feeding the punched cards into a second machine called a verifier. The operator then re-keys the data and the verifying machine draws the operator's attention to any variations. In this way very accurate input data can be achieved (see Figure 7).

Key-to-disk input

Data can be coded directly on to disk by means of an independent computer system consisting of a processor, disk unit, tape unit and a

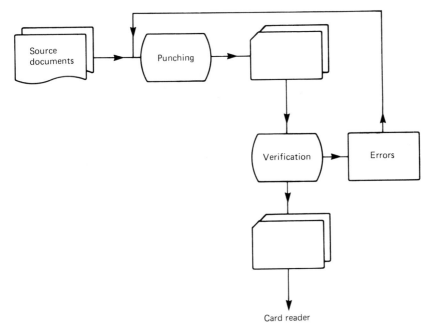

Figure 7   *Punched cards – the data preparation process*

number of key-stations. Such systems are designed to cater efficiently for large volume data preparation work and extremely high throughput rates can be achieved by the keyboard operators. The process is essentially the same as for punched cards – it provides for data verification and since the final output is not on cards, the 80 character limit per record is no longer a restriction. The data is held on disk and when it is completed and verified it can be output to magnetic tape or diskette for processing by the computer or it can be transmitted over the telephone line (see Figure 8). A single key-to-disk system can have up to about 60 key-stations or VDUs. Key-to-tape and key-to-diskette systems are also available.

A key-to-disk system can provide a very fast, efficient and accurate means of inputting high volume data to a CPMIS. This is especially relevant during the initial file set-up phase if good manual records are in existence or at the stage when salary or absence history is being input. Many data preparation bureaux provide a key-to-disk service and can output magnetic tapes from the system in a variety of formats to suit the various types of computer.

VDUs

A VDU (visual display unit), also commonly referred to as a terminal, consists of two devices

1 The keyboard which is used for input.
2 The screen which displays what is input via the keyboard and also

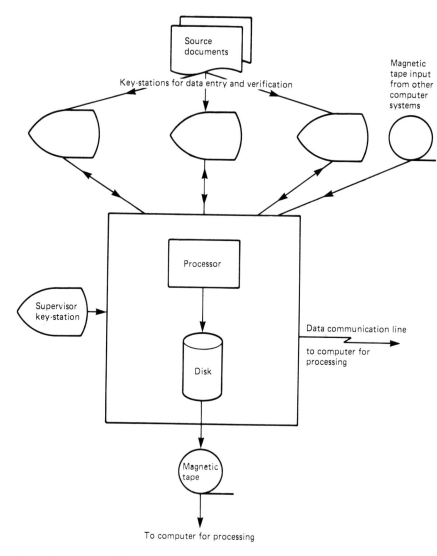

Figure 8   *A key-to-disk system*

displays the messages received from the computer.

The term 'terminal' is an all-embracing one, and it is possible to identify several types of terminals, of which the VDU is only one. Other types are

- teletype (teleprinter or telex)
- cash dispensing terminal at a bank
- supermarket checkout
- remote batch
- portable.

The VDU (see Figure 9) is the one which is most relevant in the personnel

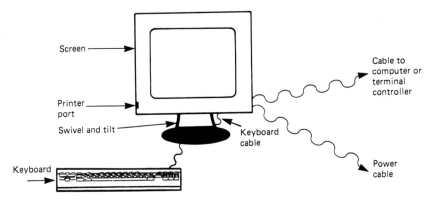

Figure 9   *Elements of a VDU*

management context. It provides a very fast and convenient means of interacting with a computer: the screen can display 1920 characters in 24 lines with 80 characters per line. The majority of VDUs make use of CRT technology – cathode ray tube as used in television sets, although some, especially portable ones, utilize LCD technology – liquid crystal display as used in calculators. The LCD screens have tended to be limited in terms of the number and length of lines displayed but full-size displays are now coming on the market.

The keyboard part of the VDU is similar to the familiar QWERTY layout of the typewriter. It also has several additional keys which perform specific functions (function keys). Examples of these are delete, insert, backspace and print. There are also other keys aimed at making input more efficient. The prime example is a numeric block, normally on the right-hand side, which facilitates the input of purely numeric data. Screens can be either colour or monochrome, and their displays generally utilize one of two modes

1 Scrolling, in which lines appear at the bottom of the screen and move up the screen.
2 Paging, in which one full or complete screen is replaced by another complete screen.

VDUs use a cursor to indicate the position of the next input/output character. The cursor is a character-size symbol – usually a small block – which can be moved around the screen by means of special keys on the keyboard. In a screen display catering for the modification of employee details the application system will normally place the cursor at the start of the first field which can be modified. It is then moved to the field which the user desires to modify by a key such as ⎡ TAB ⎤ or ⎡ → ⎤ and if the user moves the cursor too far it can be reversed by the ⎡ BACK TAB ⎤ or ⎡ ← ⎤ keys.

Some VDUs have a certain amount of in-built intelligence – they have the control facilities available locally by means of a micro-processor. These terminals are of the intelligent or stand-alone variety. Other terminals are 'dumb' but local control facilities are provided by means of a cluster controller. In the case of the latter a number of VDUs would be linked to the controller which is then linked to the computer rather than a direct VDU–computer link. VDUs also operate in either teletype mode or block mode. In the case of the former each character is transmitted to the computer as it appears on the screen. In block mode, data is transmitted to the computer in blocks e.g. a screenful of data at a time. Since the VDU is a very important constituent of a personnel system and since it provides the means of allowing the user to communicate with the system, the choice of the right type of VDU is important. The main things to look for are

1 Size and attractiveness of the unit
2 Facilities for moving and tilting the screen. Some VDUs still have the keyboard attached to the screen. This results in a lack of flexibility and it is better to be able to move both parts independently.
3 The colour of display. For high usage a monochrome display is usually better than a colour display. The options to be looked at then are generally black and white, green, or variations on bronze.
4 The quality of the display. This concerns resolution, size of characters and effectiveness of contrast. The finish of the screen is also important as regards glare.
5 Special features such as
   • inverse (or reverse) video i.e. black on orange instead of orange on black
   • two levels of brightness
   • blinking displays
   • availability of a printer port – this enables a printer to be attached directly to the VDU for either or both screen printing and local printing
   • ability to display 132 characters on screen
   • graphics capability – facilities to output graphs, histograms, pie charts etc.

Some VDUs also provide facilities such as touch sensitive screens, and the ability to use light-pens or a 'mouse' which can be used as a pointing device and for controlling the cursor.

Printers
There are many types of computer printer but the main types associated with personnel control systems are the line printer, the matrix printer and the daisy wheel printer.

Line printer
This is the type of printer normally found in a main-frame computer environment. It is also used with mini-computers for large volume printing. It is an impact printer which outputs a line of print concurrently and typical printing speeds range from 300 lines per minute to around 1500 L.P.M. The quality of print is normally good and it is the system

normally found on computer-produced documents such as income tax certificates and bank statements. Where high-volume print output is required laser printers have been replacing line printers. These are extremely fast non-impact printers which use laser technology for the formation of characters.

Matrix printer

A dot-matrix printer is an impact printer in which each character is formed by the combination of a number of pins from a matrix of pin print hammers. The most popular matrices are 9 × 7, 9 × 9 and 7 × 5. This type of printer is common with micro-computers and as 'local printers' operating off a larger computer. The print output is easily recognized by the dots which make up the characters.

The print speed is quoted in characters per second – normally within the range 80–400. Some of these printers have a facility to produce higher quality output by using a greater concentration of dots. This is known as near letter quality (NLQ). It reduces the printing speed to about one third of its normal speed. This print quality is suitable for almost all requirements. It can be quite appropriate in a personnel environment since it can function as a good printer for letters to employees and job applicants or for word processing and can then be used in normal mode for other printing jobs.

Daisy wheel printer

This is also an impact character printer but by using a daisy wheel print-head it can produce fully formed characters comparable to a good typewriter. This is known as letter quality and is suitable for word processing applications. Print founts are changed by changing the daisy wheel. Print speeds are generally less than 100 C.P.S. and these printers are normally more expensive than dot-matrix printers.

With a CPMIS it is common to have character printers in close proximity to the staff. While ink-jet printers, which create characters by directing a jet of ink at the paper, are relatively quiet, they are also expensive. To avoid upsetting staff, local impact printers will in general have to be silenced. This means fitting an acoustic cover on each printer. These can reduce the noise level by up to 90 per cent. Some models are less than aesthetic in appearance especially where they have to cope with a sheet feeder and this should be considered in deciding on the equipment layout plan.

In deciding on a suitable computer configuration on which to run a CPMIS it is easy to underestimate the printing requirements because of the desire to reduce the amount of paperwork to an absolute minimum. Generally what is required, especially if the personnel division is not located in a single site, is the facility to produce small volume prints quickly and conveniently – very often simply a print-out of what has been viewed on screen.

The price of printers is dependent on five main factors

- quality
- impact or non-impact
- width of line
- number of characters in the print set
- printing speed.

Frequently an inexpensive, slow, 80-character printer, attached to a printer port on a VDU and capable of producing screen prints will fulfil many needs.

In general impact printers represent the least reliable link in the data processing chain. In comparison with other components they can be prone to mechanical problems, especially with paper feeding and ribbons, and require relatively frequent maintenance.

Graph plotters

Graph plotters are devices which are able to draw diagrams such as graphs and pie charts by using a special mechanism to control the use of pens. A plotter can be a very useful resource in a personnel management system. Histograms, trend curves etc. can get the message across more succinctly and effectively than voluminous reports and tabulations.

Some VDUs have the facility to display graphical output which is useful, but less so than hard copy. Another recent development is the use of printer/plotters which are now being used with micro-computers.

COM

COM (computer output on microfilm) relates to the process of converting data directly from computer format to microfilm output without going through any intermediate printing stage. The microfilm output can be in the format of rolls, cartridges or microfiche. It is a very useful medium for storing the equivalent of large print-outs and is particularly relevant for 'historical' items, such as salary history records, which have been removed from the live system. Some organizations provide a COM bureau service. The bureau will take a magnetic tape produced by the computer and within a matter of hours return it with the microfilm output formatted as if actual print-out had been input to the microfilming process.

When planning the CPMIS consideration should be given to the desirability of incorporating microfilm into the integrated plan, dealing not just with the computer system but with its impact on procedures and operations.

Microfiche is sheet film, of which each sheet can hold about 100 A4 pages. It is a very convenient format since access to a particular record or page is easily obtained. Each fiche has an easily read index as to what it contains, e.g. 'employees Acorn to Davis'. It also has a detailed index showing the contents by frame. Comparison of access to fiche and access to film is almost equivalent to comparing disk with magnetic tape. Once

he fiche is produced it is relatively cheap to get additional copies and
iche readers are cheap in comparison with film readers. It is therefore
easible to provide convenient access at a number of locations.
Particularly suitable for microfiche are

Manual records which will be replaced by the computer system e.g.
Kardex. This data can be microfilmed in the normal way. What is
important is to ensure that the same output format is used for both
this material and subsequent material: use film cartridge or fiche – not
a combination.
Audit trails which require only occasional access.
Reports which need to be sent to branch offices etc.
Archival data.
Input documents such as absence returns.

Data transmission

Data transmission is the movement of data by telecommunications
ystems. It is becoming more common because of the increase in the use
f computers and the need for decentralized computer systems to
rovide input to or to access corporate databases. Where a dedicated
ersonnel computer needs to have access to employee earnings on
nother computer this can be provided by transferring data between the
wo computers using data transmission facilities. In the case of multina-
ional corporations there may be a need to access personnel data on the
eadquarter's computer from a number of countries. The use of large
ime-sharing computers for modelling will involve the use of data
ransmission facilities perhaps even involving satellites.

On-line data transmission

In the case of on-line data transmission the computer or a communica-
ion processor is connected to the communications lines and is constant-
y scanning them to determine if they are in a position to send or receive
ata. As soon as the line is ready transmission begins. Local terminals
re connected either directly to the computer or via a terminal cluster
ontroller (see Figure 10). In the case of terminals which are not local,
elephone lines are often used to link the computer and the terminals or
luster controller. In this case a modem must be used to convert the
igital signal from the terminal to an analog signal which can then be
ransmitted over the telephone line. At the computer end of the line
nother modem must be used to convert the signal back into digital
ormat.

Data comunications use either parallel or serial techniques. In parallel
ransmission a number of bits are transmitted simultaneously whereas
n serial transmission the data is transmitted one bit at a time. In
ddition data can be transmitted in three ways: first, in one direction
nly (simplex); second, in both directions, but only in one direction at

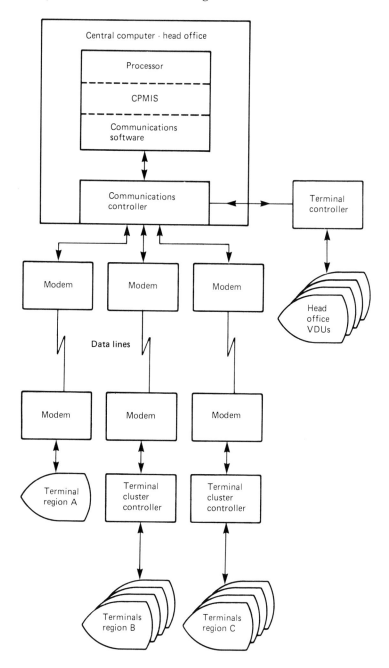

Figure 10   *Data transmission – regional access to HQ computer*

any given moment (half-duplex); and, third, in full duplex mode which allows data to move in both directions simultaneously.

Data transmission speeds will vary over a range of 300 bits per second to 50,000 bits per second. Normal speeds are generally within the range 2400–9600 bits per second.

4 Software

Introduction

When someone in the personnel department switches on a computer terminal it responds by displaying a message something like

WHICH FACILITY DO YOU WISH TO USE?

and lists the various facilities which are available. The person selects access to the personnel system and the screen then identifies the facilities available within the personnel management system and invites a further selection, user identification and a password. When a user is conversing with the computer in this way, he or she is not conversing with the hardware, but is talking to a program which was written by a computer programmer. Without the program the terminal or computer would be of no use and without a whole series of other programs, the program which handled the dialogue would also be worthless. This program must use other programs in order to get the message on screen and to receive replies from the user and as soon as a facility within the personnel management system is chosen further programs will be called upon to provide this facility.

These programs are collectively known as software which is usually defined as program support which enables computer hardware to operate effectively. Another definition of software describes it as all programs including operating systems, compilers, translators, interpreters, assemblers, utilities and application programs. It can also be argued that the term embraces all documentation such as operating manuals and system and program specifications.

Basically software can be divided into system software and application software. System software is usually supplied by the computer manufacturer and consists of the programs which are concerned with the control and performance of the computer system itself. Application software on the other hand relates to the systems which are run on the computer. Some application software may be supplied by the computer manufacturer but generally it is provided by the computer user either by developing new systems to meet specific requirements or by acquiring an application package from a software supplier. A CPMIS is a good example of application software which may be either custom-built or a package which will meet the needs of various organizations.

Operating systems

The operating system in a computer is the master control program. But, while all operating systems must perform the basic functions, they vary significantly in terms of facilities and user interface. The operating system controls multiprogramming on larger computers and assigns resources to the various programs on a priority basis. It also controls transfer of data between the various peripherals including terminals.

The primary tasks which an operating system performs will be influenced by the type of computer on which it is run and, accordingly, operating systems are usually categorized into the following types

- single-user
- multi-user
- multiprogramming
- concurrent multi-tasking multi-user
- time-sharing
- foreground – background
- TP (transaction processing).

In addition general purpose systems combine a number of features from the types listed above.

Over the years operating systems have become increasingly sophisticated in terms of facilities offered and their efficiency. In larger installations they are taking over more and more of the tasks which were previously handled by computer operators.

Functions of an operating system
The normal functions performed by an operating system are

1 Scheduling and loading of jobs so as to maximize processing.
2 Control over the selection and operation of peripheral devices (input/ output).
3 Supervision of the multiprogramming operation.
4 Communicating with the computer operator via the console.
5 Maintaining a complete log of computer operations.
6 Drawing the operator's attention to peripherals that deserve attention.
7 Providing error-correction routines.
8 Control over file handling procedures.

Application systems

Application systems consist of the various programs which cater for particular business or user needs. Examples are

- CPMIS
- hotel booking system
- payroll system
- stock control system
- airline booking system
- general ledger system.

Application systems may be divided into two categories: custom-built systems and application packages.

Custom-built systems are developed by a user, or for a user, to perform specific tasks. Traditionally this has been the area in to which organizations buying a computer have had to put much effort and money. The bulk of the staff in a computer systems and programming department is involved in building and maintaining such systems.

The principal advantage of a custom-built system is that it should meet the exact needs of the organization including the need to interface properly with the organization's other systems. The main disadvantages are the time, manpower and financial resources required to develop it. The timescale has to take account of program and system testing and substantial user department involvement in the development process.

Application packages are generalized systems designed to address a common computer application area in order to avoid unnecessary duplication of computer-based systems by many users – payroll processing being a very good example. Packages can come complete with programs on magnetic media and full documentation covering the setting up and use of the package. There may also be regular training courses available describing the facilities of the package. Generally the more comprehensive packages or those dealing with a complex business function will require substantially more involvement by both the supplier and the customer. Some systems which can be classified as packages may still require many person-months of system investigation and implementation support by the supplier before they can be implemented fully.

The advantages of using an application package are

1 It saves on systems development effort and expense on the part of the user.
2 The timescale required to get the system up and running is considerably shorter than for a custom-built system.
3 The system should already be tried and tested. Since it should be 'bug-free' it will enable the user to get on with the task of implementing the system.
4 It is generally possible for a user to see the system in operation before a decision is taken to computerize.

5 Maintenance should be minimal although the package will have to keep step with changing requirements, such as taxation changes affecting payroll systems.

There can be certain disadvantages attaching to the use of a package.

1 It may not meet the requirements exactly so a certain degree of changing the requirements may be necessary in order to fit the package.
2 The use of a package may not fit in with aspects of corporate systems strategy.
3 Control of the development and maintenance of the package rests outside the organization. The system may not be capable of maintenance if for any reason the supplier goes out of business.
4 Some packages can be expensive both in terms of the initial cost and the annual service charge.

Processing techniques

Batch
The essence of batch processing is that information about individual transactions is collected over a period of time, the data is coded, an off-line data preparation process takes place, the input file on tape or whatever is sorted into the same sequence as the main file (master file), and the transaction file is then matched with the main file and processed at fixed intervals of time – daily, weekly or monthly. Most businesses have high volume routine data processing requirements which are particularly suited to batch processing. For these applications it can be a highly economic manner of processing, and indeed some of them will not be suited to any other processing method. Batch processing is characterized by turn-around times of hours or days, data preparation activity operating against very tight deadlines, and large numbers of printed reports. Batch processing is unsuited to fast moving data and situations which require an instant response.

Batch processing necessitates the passing of the job through many people and stages before it is completed. It is worth taking the payroll example shown in Figure 11 and tracing it through its various stages.

1 It is concerned with the processing of weekly time-sheets for a week which ends at midnight on Sunday and the production of pay-slips and cheques which are issued to employees every Friday.
2 Time-sheets arrive in the wages department from all operational areas throughout Monday and up to the deadline of the mid-morning postal delivery on Tuesday. As they arrive they are checked and extended and assembled in batches. A batch consists of up to thirty time-sheets and a batch slip is attached to each showing the number of time-sheets in the batch and the total number of hours on time-sheets in the batch. The batches are then logged in a batch book and as they are ready they are sent to the data preparation department. The final deadline for receipt of batches of timesheets in data preparation is 14.30 in Tuesday.

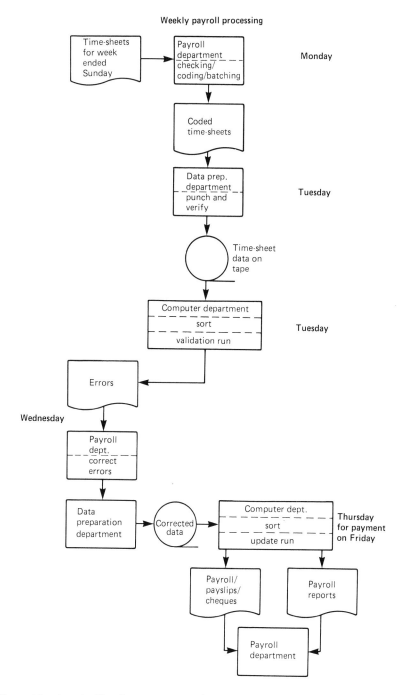

Figure 11   *A typical batch processing application*

3 In the data preparation department six or seven staff enter the time-sheet data on the key-to-disk system and subsequently verify the data. This activity starts on Monday morning and the magnetic tape, along with a run control sheet, is sent to the computer department at 17.30 on Tuesday evening.

4 In the computer department the tape is received by the data control clerk who logs its receipt and sends it on to the computer operations section. The tape is then loaded on a tape drive, the data is sorted into batch number sequence and the validation run is done. This checks the accuracy of each time-sheet and batch and produces a validation report in batch number sequence which highlights any errors.

5 On Wednesday morning the data control clerk gets the tape and the report from the previous night's run and sends them to the wages department. The wages department checks the validation report against the batch book to ensure that no data has been mislaid and then proceeds to identify the errors.

6 As soon as the error conditions have been resolved the corrections are sent to data preparation where a new tape is produced and sent to data control on Wednesday evening.

7 The same procedure as for the validation run is observed. In the overnight processing the file of valid time-sheets is sorted into employee sequence for processing against the employee file in the update run which produces the payroll, cheques and various management reports.

8 On Thursday morning the data control clerk despatches the output to the wages department.

9 On Friday employees receive their pay and on the following Monday the whole process starts again.

In a situation such as this, the processing is done by the computer when most of the users of computer terminals have gone home. Thus the load on the computer is spread more evenly and the load imposed on the computer in processing the payroll does not impinge on the service to on-line users.

On-line

In the case of an on-line system, the transaction data is captured on terminals which also receive computer output. The terminals may be either general purpose VDUs or special data collection terminals such as factory terminals or point of sale terminals in supermarkets. In an on-line system the input transactions may update the files or database or they may be stored in a transaction file for subsequent updating of the database in batch mode. User departments can get the data to the computer more quickly than by going through a separate data preparation process. The main advantage is that transactions can be recorded as they occur and the data once input to a transaction file on the computer can be enquired on until it is processed. It is particularly suited to situations where real-time update is not necessary but processing still needs to take place relatively frequently, for example daily or twice daily. The terminals can usually be used for access to the main files or database for enquiry purposes. This can be very beneficial as long as it is realized that the data is only as up-to-date as at the end of the last update run.

In the payroll example above (page 42) it might be beneficial to hold the payroll masterfile on disk and to provide on-line enquiry to it from VDUs in the wages department. This would show the earnings and other data for an employee as at the last update. On Thursday, enquiry would show the up to date position but an enquiry on the following Wednesday would still show the same situation.

Real-time

Real-time systems are somewhat similar to on-line systems but they have one important characteristic – the files or database are updated as soon as the transactions are input to the system. The term 'real-time' refers to the technique of updating the database with transaction data immediately the event to which it relates occurs. In this way the state of the database should reflect the real world which the system is designed to portray. When a person makes a reservation for a hotel room the booking is immediately updated on the computer and the room cannot be booked by anyone else unless the reservation is cancelled. Initially real-time systems were associated with application areas such as airline bookings, banking, television advertising and production control systems but in recent years they have become much more common and the vast majority of personnel systems being installed now are real-time systems.

The main benefits which tend to accrue from the use of a real-time system are

1 Paperwork is reduced. Batch systems have a tendency to generate a lot of paper at both the input and output ends of the system.
2 Some tedious tasks may be eliminated or reduced, so jobs may become more interesting and rewarding.
3 The business operation and the computer system become more integrated than in a batch processing environment. A worker with a VDU on the desk can have access to all the information required to perform the duties of the post.
4 Data in the system is more accurate and up to date, leading to better management information.
5 A better service is provided to a more satisfied customer: the employee who has a pay award processed promptly or the personnel manager who is in a position to get last week's absence statistics is in receipt of a better service.

Data files

A computer file can be defined as a collection of related records. Each record is composed of a number of fields and each of these fields is in turn made up of one or more characters. Figure 12 attempts to explain this concept by way of an extract from a personnel master file.

The complete file has a record for every employee. Every employee record has a number of fields which hold attributes relating to each employee – number, first name, surname, title, date of birth etc. These fields are made up of a number of characters which may be alphabetic, numeric or in some cases special characters may be used – such as the full stop in the title field, e.g. Mr.

There are three main types of files: master files, transaction files and reference files. Master files are those which are of a relatively permanent nature, and one of the outstanding features is that it is regularly updated. This normally consists of both data which is relatively static by nature and data which will change each time a transaction is processed. In the case of a payroll master file the static data would also include the fields shown in Figure 12 and the changing data would be balance fields such as gross pay to-date, tax paid to-date and net pay to-date. Changing data in the personnel file would include absence to-date and uncertified sick leave in the past year.

Transaction files, also referred to as movement files, consist of records corresponding to transactions or documents which are then processed against a master file. Such files are of a temporary nature and are generally not held on the system for long. Usually they are replaced by a transaction file covering a new time period. A typical example of a transaction file is the time-sheet data in the payroll system. In this case

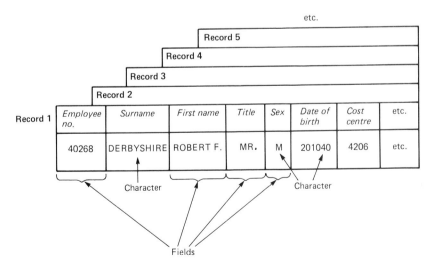

Figure 12   *File elements – personnel master file*

the file is replaced by the following week's time-sheets.

Reference files, like master files, are of fairly permanent nature. They are files which contain reference data which are accessed by a system during processing. Typical examples are price lists, income tax rates or discount terms. In the personnel management context the parameter file and the descriptor file described in Part II are reference files.

File organization

Records are held on a file in various manners or sequences. There are three main systems of file organization

1 Sequential or serial.
2 Indexed sequential.
3 Random (direct access).

Sequential files

Files on both tape and disk can be organized in this manner. The records are physically stored in ascending key sequence and accordingly it is not necessary to have any special index or formula to locate a particular record. A good example is a payroll master file where the records are held in employee number sequence. This is the only type of file organization which can be used on magnetic tape. As mentioned it can also be used with disk, but records still have to be accessed serially and accordingly it does not avail of the direct access capability of this medium. It is a type

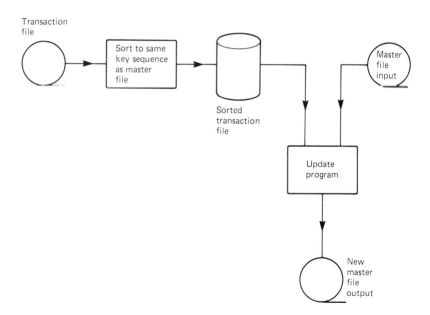

Figure 13   *Sequential file processing*

of file organization which is suited to batch processing where there is a high hit rate – that is a high proportion of the records on the master file have a matching transaction record. It is not suitable for on-line access to the file.

A typical example of a sequential file process is shown in Figure 13. This shows a transaction file coming into the system, being sorted into the same sequence as the master file which is also an input to the update program. This program reads a record from the master file, processes any transaction for that record and creates a new record on the new output file – regardless of whether there was a matching transaction.

Indexed sequential
This form of file organization is applicable to disk rather than tape and is used in both batch and on-line applications. The records are still stored in ascending key sequence, so sequential processing is still possible. Its distinguishing feature is that an index or table is maintained which defines the actual location of the record on the direct access device. This makes the updating of records substantially simpler than with sequential (serial) files. The transaction key is obtained and the program quickly finds the relevant record, updates it in place and ignores the other records. Accordingly there is no need to transfer all of the records on to a new file as in the sequential file update process. Back-up in the sequential process is achieved by holding on to the input master file and the transaction file. However this is achieved with indexed files by 'dumping' or copying the files to tape or disk.

New records are inserted into an overflow area and the sequence of records is maintained by a system of chaining. The file is then periodically reorganized and this re-creates the normal sequence. If the payroll master file is organized in an indexed sequential manner the provision of an on-line enquiry facility is possible.

Random
With random organization algorithms are used to define the relationship between the record key and the actual location of the record. In this way individual records may be located without the need to search through the file. There is no direct relationship between contiguous records and new records are added at the end of the file.

Database systems
There are certain disadvantages associated with conventional data file systems and database systems are designed to help overcome these (see Figure 14). The main disadvantages of file-based systems are

1 There is a tendency to have duplicate data.
2 Inconsistency may arise because all files which contain a particular item of data may not be updated simultaneously e.g. an employee's grade or cost centre may be changed in the personnel file but not in the payroll file.

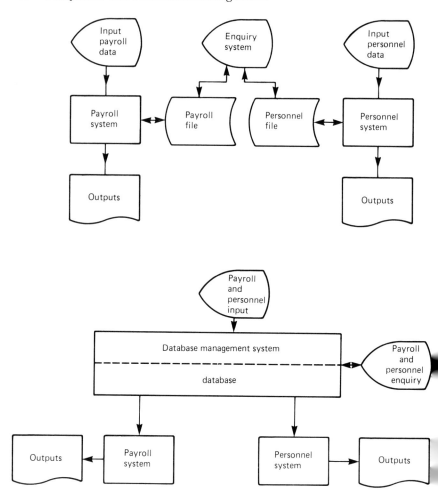

Figure 14   *Comparison of conventional and database approaches*

3 A change in the structure or contents of a file will have widespread repercussions for programs.

Database systems aim to overcome these problems and provide a number of other benefits as well. A database is defined as a collection of structured data supporting the whole business or important elements of the business and which can be easily accessed and used. The essential features of a database system are

1 Data should be input only once.
2 Duplication of data can be avoided.
3 The structure should be flexible and it should be possible conveniently to add new data items and structures.
4 It should provide facilities for

- controlling access (users and passwords)
- both batch and on-line processing
- recovery and restart
- a comprehensive audit trail.

Once a database has been created, it can be used for many applications, some of which may have only been at a very preliminary stage when the database was designed initially.

The terminology associated with database systems is quite different to that associated with conventional files. The following are some of the terms used.

Data item   Also known as fields or data elements, this is the smallest unit of data in a database, e.g. personnel number or employee category. A record is composed of a number of data items.

Set   A set defines a relationship between a number of records and enables the system conveniently to access a group of related records. 'Owner' and 'member' are terms used to describe relationships between sets.

DDL   Data description language defines the basic functions necessary in the management of a database and allows for the specification of data relationships.

DML   Data manipulation language provides statements which can be included in an application program and which allows the program to process the database as required.

In complex systems the task of writing an application program is substantially easier with a database than with conventional files. If a number of files is involved the programmer's task of retrieving or processing the data required is a complex one and if any change is made to the file structure, such as a new file or new field being added to a record, the program change necessary will take some time to make and test. With a database system the application programs are largely independent of the database structure; the job of data retrieval is done by the database manager and so is largely transparent to the programmer.

High level languages

A high level language can be defined as any programming language which allows the programmer to concentrate on the problem to be solved by using a format with which the programmer is familiar. The format includes instructions in English which can be understood to some extent by anyone looking at the program, and mathematical equations and relationships.

The following are the main features of a high level language

Programs are written using an extensive vocabulary of words, symbols and sentences in accordance with rules governing format and syntax. Programs written in the language are translated into machine code by translators or compilers.

3 Since the language is problem orientated, the programmer is allowed to work on the problem to be solved and to some extent can do this independently of a particular computer – the resulting program should be capable, at least in theory, of being run on other types of computer.

The process of translation is shown in Figure 15. When the programmer has understood the requirements and has designed the structure of the program, the program statements are either input directly to the computer or are written on sheets which are then transcribed on to an input medium such as magnetic tape, diskette or punched cards. At this stage the language is sometimes referred to as the source language and the program is known as the source program. The source program is then input to the compiler for the language in which it is written. As a first step the compiler examines the program for errors. It obviously cannot locate errors in program logic so the errors highlighted are those statements which breach the syntax or grammatical rules of the language. The compiler produces a listing of the source program and a listing of errors with references to individual statements within the program. The programmer then corrects the errors and reinputs the program to the compiler. As soon as the errors have been cleared and the program has reached what is known as the 'clean compile stage', the compiler produces the object program. The object program is the source program converted into machine language and this is the version of the program which can be run. At this stage program testing can commence using test data. This is when the programmer finds out if the program will produce the expected results.

A program seldom produces the correct results on the first run and as soon as the programmer ascertains what statements in the program are causing the problems, or what additional statements are required, the changes are made to the source program and the process is repeated until the right results are produced. At this stage the programmer is satisfied but still to be tested are how the program interfaces with other programs in the system and how the user's expectations match those of the programmer. These questions will only be answered when system testing starts.

Some languages or versions of languages use an *interpreter* rather than a *compiler*. The interpreter is different in that it converts a source program on a line by line basis into machine code at run time i.e. it is not converted into an object program prior to execution.

The following are high level languages

- ALGOL
- BASIC
- COBOL
- FORTRAN
- PL/1
- RPG

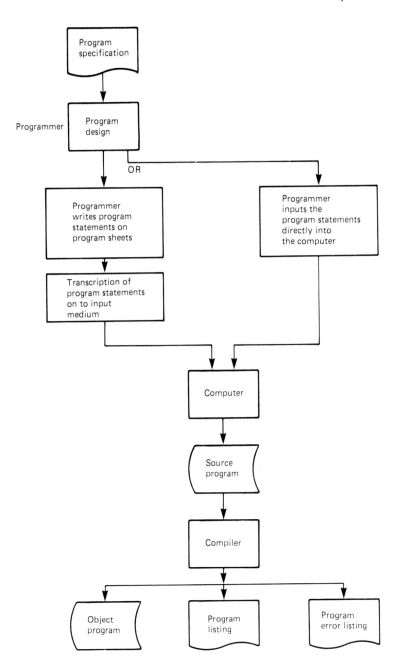

Figure 15   *Program compilation process*

Writing a program in COBOL

COBOL is a good example of a high level commercial programmin
language. It is widely used and is typical of the type of language used i
developing a CPMIS – especially in the larger computer environment.
was envisaged initially that any program written in COBOL should l
capable of running on any computer. Over the years a number ‹
variations of COBOL have evolved and this has made the transfer ‹
programs between different types of computer more difficult. It is sti
relatively easy to move COBOL batch systems between computers bι
on-line systems can prove to be much more difficult – and this has litt
to do with the programming language used. Versions of COBOL aι
available to run on most computers from micro to main-frame.

Divisions

A COBOL program is divided into four divisions

1 *Identification division*   This part of the program contains informatiο
  which identifies the program, such as program name or title, th
  author, the date written and a remarks section which can be used ·
  provide a description of what the program does.
2 *Environment division*   This division specifies the particular hardwaι
  configuration under which the program runs. Requirements for boι
  source and object versions of the program can be specified e.g. tł
  computer series and model. The input–output section provides a liι
  to various files that are used by the system.
3 *Data division*   All items of data to be used in the program aι
  described in this division. The division is divided into two sections: fi
  section and working-storage section. The former contains a descri
  tion of each file and its constituent record types which the progra
  will use in either input or output mode. An example would be tł
  personnel file with its different types of records, e.g. personnel mastι
  record, employee absence record and employee training record. Tł
  contents of each record would then be described by taking each fie
  and describing its characteristics – name, size and the format in whiι
  held. The entry EMPNO PICTURE 9 (5) might describe a five-digι
  (numeric) personnel number.
     The working storage section is used to define temporary work fielι
  which the program itself uses. A program designed to list all eι
  ployees and their annual salaries and to provide a total for the numb
  of employees and the total of their salaries would require to have
  least two fields defined in this section. One of these would be i
  cremented by one for every employee record read and every annuι
  salary would be added to the contents of the other field. Whι
  processing is complete these fields would be printed.
4 *Procedure division*   This is the division which does the work.
  contains all the program instructions required to solve the particul
  programming problem. The division consists of a number of statι
  ments written in accordance with the rules of COBOL and using tł

data names defined in the data division. The following are examples of statements appropriate to this division

File handling:

OPEN PERSONNEL-FILE
READ PERSONNEL-FILE AT END GO TO FINISH-ROUTINE

The first statement will make the personnel file available and the second statement causes a record from the file to be read into memory. When all records have been read the program will branch to a special routine.

Arithmetic:

MULTIPLY SICK-DAYS BY DAILY-RATE GIVING SICK-PAY
ADD SICK-PAY TO CUMULATIVE-SICK-PAY

Branching:

GO TO PROCESS-SALARY-CHANGE.
IF CUMULATIVE-SICK-DAYS GREATER THAN 150 GO TO PRINT-SICK-NOTICES

The first statement is an unconditional branch while the second branch is conditional on the employee having more than 150 days cumulative sick leave.

Data handling:

MOVE INPUT-CATEGORY TO OUTPUT-CAT.

Utility programs

Certain functions are common to all computer installations and computer manufacturers supply utility or service programs, in conjunction with the operating system, designed to meet these general needs. Types of utility programs are

1 *Sort* A sort program is designed to arrange records in a predetermined sequence. The sequence required is specified to the program as a series of parameters such as the sort key(s) and the required sequence e.g. ascending or descending.
2 *Merge* A merge program is frequently part of a combined sort/merge facility. A typical merge program would combine two files such as an absence file and this week's absence transaction file to produce a new composite file in employee number sequence.
3 *Editors* Every programmer has to have a convenient method of making changes to programs and this is achieved through the use of an on-line editor. This facility is used to replace, delete or insert individual characters or whole lines in a program. It is achieved by viewing the text on screen and using a series of commands or special keys on the keyboard.

4 *Copying*   The copy facility provides the programmer with a means of copying data either on the same device or to alternative devices. An example is the copying of the personnel files to disk or tape for off-site security storage. This can be done for individual files or for all data on a particular device e.g. copying the entire contents of one disk pack to another one.

5 *File maintenance*   These routines cater for such items as reorganizing disk files periodically to eliminate or tidy up overflow conditions and housekeeping routines such as disk initialization, blocking and de-blocking of records and the writing of header and trailer labels on magnetic tape.

6 *Program testing aids*   These facilities improve productivity by providing ways of assisting in the debugging process.

Job control language

Job control language (JCL) or system control language (SCL) is concerned with controlling the running of jobs on the computer. It is the link between the application system or program and the computer's operating system. It allows for inputting to the system job names, files to be used and peripheral devices to be used. It also caters for allocating priorities, for specifying interdependence of jobs in a job stream, and for taking back-up copies.

Although the heading of this section is job control language it could, perhaps more correctly, be replaced by 'command languages'. This is a broader classification which could then be subdivided into interactive command languages, batch command languages and operating system control languages. Some computers have separate languages for each function e.g. one for batch work and another for interactive work.

Fourth generation languages

Fourth generation languages, known as '4GLs', are expected to result in substantial improvements in productivity on the part of systems development staff. They are the latest in the line of software development aids which started with assembly languages. The shift in effort in systems development from analysts and programmers to the computer itself is shown in Figure 16. Although this figure is not to scale, the productivity increases of systems development personnel have nevertheless been enormous.

It is difficult to provide a precise definition of a 4GL since it can mean slightly different things to different people and there is a wide divergence between the facilities provided by a number of systems available, all of which are claiming 4GL status. In the micro-computer market there are systems available which perform many of the functions of a 4GL but in larger computers a 4GL may indeed relate to a family of software products revolving around an application generator. Application generators operate on the same principle as report generators but go a lot

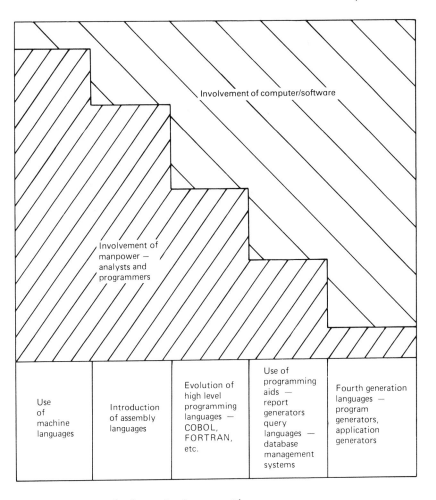

Involvement of computer/software

Involvement of
manpower —
analysts and
programmers

| Use of machine languages | Introduction of assembly languages | Evolution of high level programming languages — COBOL, FORTRAN, etc. | Use of programming aids — report generators query languages — database management systems | Fourth generation languages — program generators, application generators |

Figure 16   *Impact of software development aids*

further. They are flexible tools which allow systems designers and programmers to create the application structure – the files or database and provision for all inputs and outputs. The idea is that the user is more closely involved with the analyst. Between them they define the system inputs, outputs and the processing required. All of this data is input to the computer and it in turn generates the system/programs to handle the application.

Promoters of the system claim enormous improvements in productivity over conventional methods. They also claim that there should be an improvement in the quality of systems because of the increased user participation in the analysis and design process. The subsequent maintenance of the systems should also become easier.

5 The data processing organization

Introduction

Personnel management will have regular dealings with data processing personnel. This contact may arise for any of the following reasons

1 Personnel management matters in relation to the DP staff, e.g. job specifications, job grading, interviews for job vacancies.
2 Negotiations with user department staff on the introduction of new computer-based systems and procedures.
3 The introduction of new systems which may interface with the personnel management function, e.g. payroll or staff rostering.
4 The introduction of a CPMIS. In this case the contact may arise because

   • the DP department is designing and installing a custom-built system within the personnel department
   • the DP department is providing advice and assistance on the selection and installation of a personnel package
   • the personnel department wants to do its own thing against the wishes of the DP Department.

Because of this contact it is worthwhile that personnel department staff understand what the DP department or division does and appreciate the nature of the jobs of the analysts and programmers. These are members of the staff who are likely to have an average age less than that in the organization as a whole, are well above the average salary for their age group and show themselves to be a very mobile group. In installing a CPMIS the personnel department staff should understand the difference between the various types of computer person they will meet while the system is being implemented – systems analyst, database administrator, analyst/programmer, systems programmer, application programmer, maintenance programmer, computer operator and data control clerk.

The structure of the data processing function and its place in the organization varies from one organization to another. The factors which influence this structure are the size of the organization, the nature of the business, the way in which the function has evolved, the state of computer systems development and the emphasis which the organization places on the need to be at the forefront in terms of the use of computer-based technology. Accordingly job titles and functions will vary. This chapter aims to describe the functions using the most common types of structure.

Typical organization structures

In parallel with the move towards corporate management information systems, the use of databases which cross functional boundaries and the convergence of information technologies, there has been a trend towards higher level executive status for the person in charge of the data or information processing function. It is not unusual to find the management services director reporting directly to the chief executive alongside the heads of the finance, production, sales and personnel functions. This type of structure is shown in Figure 17.

Alternatively the function can reside within one of the major functional areas. In this case the finance function is likely to be the controlling one. One of the reasons for this is that traditionally the accounting systems were among the first to be computerized. As a reporting arrangement this can work very well in certain organizations but the main dangers are that there will be an emphasis on the development of accounting or accounting-related systems, that other areas will either be neglected or may be given systems which have an accounting bias (e.g. no personnel system or one which is tagged on the payroll system), or that organizational politics may inhibit the development of systems which cross functional boundaries.

Similarly when the controlling function is production or engineering the emphasis will tend to be towards applications in these areas. This often results in the growth of parallel and often competing data processing departments. In this type of situation it is common to have a computer steering committee, which develops the policy, indicates priorities, approves the development plan and in general terms monitors achievement.

The function may be a broad one which embraces management services such as organization and methods, work study and operations research as well as data processing. In dealing with the function here the emphasis is on data processing.

A variety of organization formats are used, but the most common ones are those reflecting either a functional or project orientation. In the project organization each project has a project leader who is allocated a number of analysts and programmers for the duration of the project. The main advantages of this format are the normal ones associated with project teams, *viz.*

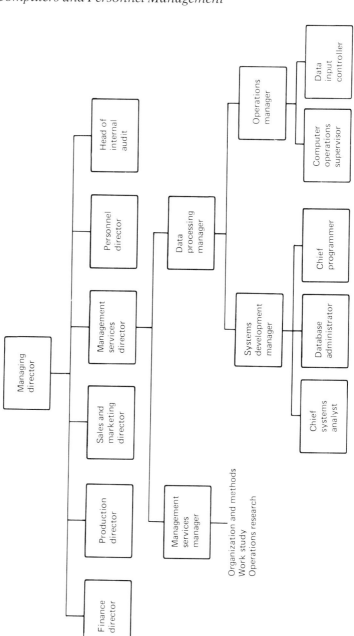

Figure 17   *Organization chart*

- communications difficulties are minimized
- responsibilities are focused on a single group
- team spirit and a sense of competition are fostered.

In the functional organization, systems analysts and programmers are split into separate groups under a chief systems analyst or systems manager and a programming manager respectively. A systems project is handled initially by the analysts who pass it over to the programming group as soon as the appropriate stage has been reached. The advantages of this format are the degree to which specialization can be obtained and the flexibility offered in terms of training and supervision.

Head of function

As already indicated, the title of the person responsible for data processing will vary but for the purposes of this section the title data processing manager (DPM) is used. The DPM will have responsibility for three main areas – systems development and maintenance, computer operations and technical support or systems support.

The following are the main duties of the DPM

1 Development of, or assistance with the development of, a data processing policy for the organization and the subsequent maintenance of the plan.
2 Execution of the defined data processing policy.
3 Management of the data processing function – assessing performance of staff, staff motivation etc.
4 Liaison with the user departments and working with management to identify problem areas or opportunities for further systems development.
5 Ensuring that proper systems development, systems maintenance and computer operating standards exist, are kept up to date and are adhered to.
6 Ensuring that proper security and back-up arrangements are in existence and are tested regularly.
7 Ensuring that relevant and effective systems are designed, implemented and documented efficiently.
8 Ensuring that proper post-implementation evaluations are carried out.
9 Providing suitable development and training for data processing staff.
10 Coordinating all activities within the department to ensure the smooth development and running of systems.
11 Resolving conflict between sections e.g. between programmers who feel restricted by procedures designed by the group responsible for setting and policing standards or by the computer operations section.
12 Providing guidance and advice on data processing problems.

The systems analyst

There is a number of variations on the role of the systems analyst. The emphasis may be on the user and the business problem to be solved by the computer, or on how the computer will actually do the job. At the user end the term business analyst is often used while as the system moves towards a definite computer solution the analyst may be called a systems designer or an analyst/programmer. The latter title emphasizes the close link between the role of the analyst and that of the programmer. The analyst/programmer title is a very useful one in that it provides for a degree of flexibility which is particularly useful in smaller data processing departments.

The following are the main duties of a systems analyst

1 To examine the feasibility of potential computer applications and to consider all of the various approaches to computerization which are available.
2 To perform a proper analysis of user systems and requirements.
3 To develop a proper cost–benefit analysis in conjunction with the user.
4 To design systems which take into account not just the computer procedures but the clerical and other procedures around the computer system.
5 To specify the checks and controls to be incorporated into the system – this will usually be done in conjunction with the audit staff.
6 To specify the most appropriate processing techniques to be used, e.g. micro, mini or main-frame; batch system or real-time system.
7 To estimate the loading of the proposed system on the hardware proposed – this involves estimating transaction levels, file sizes, processing requirements, run times, print-out volumes etc.
8 To ensure that there is proper communication and clear hand-over instructions at each stage of the project, e.g. program specification, file set up procedures, operating instructions, back-up procedures.
9 To ensure that the system is properly tested and documented.
10 To provide the environment for proper system testing, pilot running and parallel running as appropriate.

The programmer

After systems design the programmer becomes involved. Using program specifications produced by the analyst or system designer the job of programming can commence. The program specification for every program in the system will consist of

1 The inputs, outputs and files relevant to the program. These will be described in full showing file and record layouts, field description and report or screen layouts.
2 A flow chart or other diagram indicating the main logic of the program and the modules that go to make up the program.

3 The processing rules for manipulating the data.

It is the programmer's job to convert this specification into a working program and this process involves breaking the task down into its elements. This can involve the use of detailed flow charts, followed by coding, inputting to the computer and testing.

The main duties of the programmer are

1 To reach an understanding of what each program is expected to do and to clarify any problems with the analyst/systems designer.
2 To design the structure of the program in accordance with the installation standards.
3 To produce a working and efficient program using the installation standards and within the budgeted time allocated.
4 To test the program thoroughly both as a unit and in relation to other programs.
5 To provide the required program documentation.

These duties relate to the applications programmer. This is the title given to the programmer who is responsible for writing the initial programs for a computer application. Sometimes a distinction is made between an applications programmer and a maintenance programmer. In many computer installations as soon as a system becomes operational responsibility for correcting any subsequent problems, for amendments and improvements is handed over to a maintenance programmer.

Systems programmer

The systems programmer specializes in non-application programs, i.e. systems software, such as operating systems, data management systems, data communications. This post may also be titled software programmer or technical support programmer. Liaison with the computer supplier to keep abreast of new releases of the operating system, TP monitor or DBMS software is the responsibility of this person. Support is also provided for the analysts and programmers in regard to queries on system software performance and features, statistics on computer usage and backing storage transfer volumes. The systems programmer also assists the applications programmer in interpreting program dumps and in resolving problems which appear to be caused by the systems software rather than application software. Another person who may be involved in this area is the network controller. This person manages the links catering for the transfer of data from terminals to the processor and between various computers.

Database administrator

The database administrator carries responsibility for controlling the corporate database. Sometimes the term data administrator is used, which indicates that the scope of the post is broader and includes all data, both database and non-database systems. This is a relatively new but important post in the DP hierarchy and its presence recognizes the value of data as a corporate resource. The duties of the post may include

1 Control of the data dictionary.
2 Setting of standards in relation to the use of the data dictionary.
3 Designing the logical structure of the database and advising on physical storage strategy.
4 Devising security, integrity and access control systems.
5 Organizing archival storage arrangements.
6 Ensuring that proper recovery and back-up arrangements are in existence.
7 Participating in the formulation of systems development plans.

Computer operations manager

The computer operations manager is responsible for the operation of the computer and ancillary equipment in an installation. He or she will control a number of sections, such as the following

1 The computer room where the computer operators look after the running of the computer and the various peripheral devices.
2 The library where all reels of tape, disk packs, and manuals are stored.
3 The data preparation section which prepares input for the computer by transferring data from input documents to tape, disk, or some other input media.
4 Data control which is responsible for the coordination of all computer processing operations and ensuring that there is a smooth flow of work through the computer room. This section is the main link between the user departments and the computer – especially in a batch-processing environment. It receives data for processing, logs its receipt, ensures that it is processed, retrieves the output from the computer, performs the necessary control checks, arranges for the preparation of output e.g. bursting and trimming of print-out, and logs the despatch of the output to the user departments.

Other duties of the computer operations manager are

1 The development of operating schedules or timetables and ensuring that these schedules are met.
2 Maintaining a log of machine utilization and down-time.
3 Arranging to have regular preventative maintenance carried out on all equipment.
4 Reporting faults to suppliers and ensuring that they are cleared quickly.
5 Controlling stocks of supplies – paper, preprinted stationery, tapes, disks etc.
6 Ensuring that security and fire precaution arrangements are observed.

6 The systems development process

Introduction

Over the years the computer business has had its share of failures in terms of systems which were not completed on schedule, cost substantially more than the original budget, were less than successful in meeting the users' requirements or which collapsed. This is not just what happened in the past; failures and disasters still occur. The most likely casualty is the first-time user and since many personnel departments are likely to be first-time users it is worth considering how these problems can arise and also the stages which a system must pass through from the time the initial seed is sown through to a review of how well the resulting system is performing.

Various factors can be identified as contributing to unsuccessful systems development and among the most important are

- the failure to establish clearly what the system should do – not finding out the true requirements of the user
- the lack of top management involvement with the system, leading perhaps to the failure to take proper policy decisions
- inaccurate or unreasonable original estimates of the development effort required and the costs involved – computer people (in particular computer salespeople) are notoriously optimistic when it comes to proposing implementation timetables
- the lack of proper systems development methodology and standards
- the lack of proper project control and reporting procedures
- the lack of proper communications between everyone involved in the system
- the lack of appropriate training and procedures.

These matters are covered in Part II. In this chapter the stages in the development process are described and the importance of having a defined methodology and set of standards to facilitate the process is emphasized.

Methodology and standards

The format of a systems development methodology and standards will vary from organization to organization and indeed within the organization the procedures must be flexible enough to allow for a certain amount of adaptation to cater for the characteristics of individual systems. Basically it provides a framework within which the data processing staff operate but the framework should not be so rigid as to unduly restrict the creative talents of the staff.

The standards relate to every stage in the system life cycle as shown in Figure 18. Every computer-based system goes through the same process whereby the application is conceived, developed, implemented and maintained. If any one phase is neglected, there may be serious consequences for the system. Standards are introduced for each phase to ensure that this does not happen and they form a code of practice covering

- systems development methodology
- communications/documentation
- project control
- system design philosophy
- programming (structure of programs and programming rules and regulations)
- testing requirements
- change control
- operating procedures

Within system development, the standards should provide the analyst with a method of working and describe the output required at each stage. They should clearly identify the respective responsibilities of data processing staff and users – in particular in relation to the definition of requirements, system testing and control of requests for modifications. They should also clearly identify the stages in systems development, the involvement of senior management and users at each stage and the arrangements for moving from one stage to another, which might involve authorization by senior management or agreement or signing-off by user departments. This process is shown in outline in Figure 19. In this chart the involvement of the internal or external auditors might also be relevant at key points.

Investigation and feasibility

This is the first phase and consists of a brief survey of the area involved and will result in taking the project into the next phase, postponing development for a period or recommending that no further action be

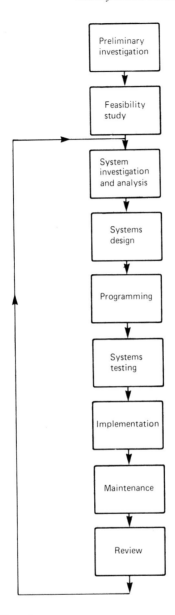

Figure 18   *The system life cycle*

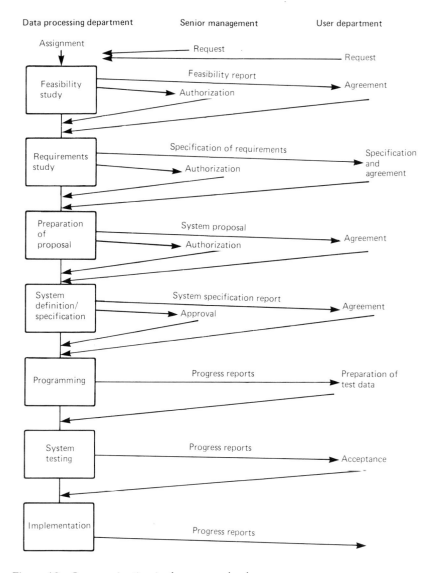

Figure 19 *Communication in the systems development process*

taken. Sometimes it is subdivided into a preliminary investigation followed by a more detailed feasibility study.

The phase is initiated by management, who perceive the need because of changes or expected changes in the business environment, limitations or failure of existing systems, or the awareness of technological advances relating to the particular area involved in particular systems which competitors are developing.

The objectives of this phase are

1 To determine the feasibility of computerization of a particular system or area of operation.
2 To define clearly the objectives, scope and limitations of the project.
3 To establish a good working relationship between the user department and the DP department.
4 To acquaint user management with the approach and method of work in systems development.
5 To estimate the resources required for systems development, live running and maintenance.
6 To identify the likely benefits which should accrue from the introduction of the system.

During this phase, which should be as short as possible, the analyst will be concerned with

- how the present system works
- the staffing levels involved, their grades and duties
- the volume of work: statistics on the various types of transaction, level of overtime working, employment of casual staff etc.
- any current backlog of work and any seasonal influences on the workload
- the time taken to process data through the system, delays in issuing management reports etc.
- lists of all documents, files and reports associated with the system
- interfaces with other systems.

The output from this phase is a formal report called a *Feasibility Report* or *System Study Report*. This report may contain

- an introduction which puts the report in perspective and perhaps quotes the terms of reference
- the objectives for the system
- a commentary on how the present system achieves or fails to achieve those objectives
- interfaces with other systems and the implications of these interfaces
- present operating costs and conditions including organization structure and staffing levels
- a first estimate of systems development time and a related draft implementation timetable
- a schedule of the hardware and other requirements e.g. availability of system at weekends
- expected benefits which will accrue from the use of a new system
- a cost–benefit projection
- conclusions and recommendations.

The report would normally be supported by working papers and flow charts. It is then up to senior management to decide whether the system should advance to the next stage.

Specification of requirements

This is a crucial stage in the development of a computer-based system and during this phase responsibility for ensuring that all requirements are clearly defined rests primarily with the user. The fact that the report from this stage may be produced by an analyst from the DP department does not absolve the user from this obligation. Every user will feel that there is no problem attached to specifying what the system will have to do, but in practice failure to identify all requirements at this stage is probably the major reason for subsequent dissatisfaction with a system.

The first task in this phase is to provide a comprehensive description of the present system and operations. This helps significantly in defining what the new system should do. Throughout this phase much time will be spent in discussions with staff at all levels in both the main user area and in other areas which will interface with the system. The output from this stage is the *Specification of Requirements Report*, the format and contents of which are described in detail in Part II. The next stage cannot commence until there is confirmation that this statement represents the views of all concerned. There should also be acknowledgement of the reasons as to why any peripheral requirements may not have been included. Senior management should also be given an opportunity of examining the report.

System proposal

A system proposal is the formal response of the DP department or external supplier to the specification of requirements. It outlines the nature of the proposed solution, how the system will operate, the costs involved and an implementation timetable. Regardless of its source it should be regarded as a firm commitment to provide a computer-based system and so is an integral part of the contract.

In some in-house systems, particularly a smaller system, there may not be a separate system proposal. The proposal may in fact be part of either the system study or the system specification.

A system proposal would normally contain

1 A description of the proposed system showing how it should operate in practice.
2 The costs of the system, the benefits which may be expected and an implementation timetable.
3 The amount of development effort which will be required and how this will be staffed – who will be working on the system.
4 The approach envisaged with regard to system testing, file conversion, parallel running, staff training, system documentation and implementation.

System specification

As soon as the system proposal is accepted by the user, work can start on preparing the system specification. This phase takes the requirements as agreed and the work which has led up to producing the proposal and develops the system to the level of detail necessary to prepare the way for programming. At this point the analyst is concerned with the detail of input and output, the processing required, and the way in which the system will operate on a day-to-day basis. Depending on the level of complexity of the system and the amount and quality of work done at the earlier stages, this phase can take many months of hard work. It is concerned with the computer-orientated design of the system – the detail of the input transactions, the detail of the printed reports, screens and other outputs, the file or database structure, the contents of records, the processing required and the efficiency of the system from a computer processing point of view.

A typical system specification will contain

1 An introduction covering the relevance of the document and how it has evolved from the previous phases.
2 A description of the system. This is usually an outline in a narrative form with accompanying flow charts, procedure charts, run charts, data-flow diagrams or data models.
3 Detailed descriptions of inputs, outputs and files, for example: document layouts (input), screen layouts, report layouts, file/record layouts, database schemas.
4 A description of the controls which operate within the system. This includes control over input and processing, restrictions on access (e.g. passwords) and control on output (e.g. numbering of cheques).
5 Processing required. This may in fact be handled by specifying generally what each program in the system is expected to do and by backing this up with individual program specifications issued separately.
   Arrangements for testing may also be described in this section.
6 Implementation considerations – arrangements for converting existing files, checking parallel runs, production of user procedures and production of computer-related procedures.
7 A detailed development and implementation timetable. This section should list all of the tasks to be done, including individual programs, showing the interrelationship between each task and the planned start and completion date for each task.
8 A back-up plan. This should describe the procedures to be developed for taking security dumps of files, for ensuring system resilience (e.g. duplexing) and for running the system at an alternative site in the event of the computer not being available.

It is at this stage that the first reliable estimate of the amount of computer programming effort required can be produced. Up to this point the estimates are to a large extent informed guesses and what comes out at the end of this exercise may be quite frightening compared with the previously available estimates. This is a valid reason for ensuring that senior management continue to have an approval role at the conclusion of this stage.

Estimates produced now have a firm basis and if they are substantially at variance with the original estimates it is still not too late to review the viability of the development. The choice now lies between

- abandoning the system
- continuing as planned
- shelving the system for a period
- modifying the aspirations for the system.

All of these options are available for an in-house development, although it is generally felt that by the time this stage is reached the commitment is irreversible. Where an external supplier is involved the options may be restricted by the nature of the contract between the parties. A variable price contract should provide a formula for opting out in such circumstances. A fixed price arrangement protects the customer from upwardly moving prices, but a substantial error in estimating may tempt the supplier to cut corners.

Programming

The system specification provides the basis on which programming of the system can start. The document gives the programmer a clear description of the system, its purpose and objectives, the programs involved and the interrelationship between them. In this way the programmer can see the relevance of a particular program or program module within the context of the overall system. This report provides the programmer with the layouts required – these may also be available as part of the data dictionary – and this is the back-up to the actual program specifications. Program specifications may consist of a low level description of what the program should do, flow charts, decision tables and structure diagrams.

The programmer should have to adhere to programming standards which relate to both the structure of the program, coding rules and regulations and items such as checkpoint/restart procedures and file labels. Programming standards ensure that all programmers in the installation adhere to a particular format which makes program maintenance by programmers other than the author a less difficult task.

Program testing is also the responsibility of the programmer who must ensure that programs work and provide the required interface with other programs.

System testing

The objective of system testing is to ensure that all individual programs are working as expected, that the programs link together to meet the requirements specified and to ensure that the computer system and the associated clerical and other procedures work together. The initial phase of system testing is the responsibility of the analyst who determines what conditions are to be tested, generates test data, produces a schedule of expected results, runs the tests and compares the computer-produced results with the expected results. The analyst may also be involved in procedures testing. When the analysis is satisfied that the system is working properly, he or she hands it over to the users for testing. The importance of system testing by user must be stressed. Ultimately it is the user who must verify the system and give the go-ahead.

Parallel running is often regarded as the final phase of system testing. Since the parallel operation of two systems is very demanding in terms of user resources it should only be embarked on if the user is satisfied with the results of testing – it should not be started if problems are known to exist.

Implementation

As the system is tested it starts to move into the implementation phase. Ideally the system should be completed and fully tested before implementation gets under way but unless a package is being installed this seldom happens. Normally what happens is that parts of the system which are required for file set-up are completed first and this process gets under way. Conversion programs may also have to be available which allow data from another system to be used in setting up the files. Once this data is set up it must be kept up to date and thus the first use is made of the new system. This may be followed by a period of parallel running and then a decision is made to drop the old system.

As soon as the first phase of implementation – file set-up – starts all system documentation should be available *viz.* user manuals, procedures manuals, computer operating instructions and security procedures. The system then passes from the development staff to the computer operations personnel and once the system is live strict procedures should be enforced governing programmers' access to programs and files. Procedures should be established to control all requests for system and program changes, from the request by the user to the implementation by the programmer.

System review

This last phase of the development/implementation process is the review of the system or 'post audit' as it is sometimes known. This is usually carried out by a group consisting of a representative from the user department, internal audit and data processing. Its basic purpose is to see if the system has met the objectives set for it. This will comprise a comparison of actual costs and benefits against the original estimates, a review of how well the system is performing generally, a review of requests for changes and an examination of documentation, control and security procedures and back-up arrangements.

Part II The personnel management information system

Part I provided a brief introduction to computers in general – to the hardware and software and to the systems development process. It is now appropriate to examine in some detail the personnel management application.

The approach taken is broadly to follow the systems development process starting with the feasibility study, looking at the options available, going on to define requirements in some detail, getting proposals, signing the contract or getting firm commitments and implementing the system.

7 Feasibility study

Purpose

The initial systems investigation/feasibility study is carried out in order to

- examine why a CPMIS should be introduced
- determine what the scope of the system should be
- specify the requirements in broad detail
- describe the relationship between the proposed CPMIS and other systems either existing or planned
- describe how it is envisaged that the above interface will be achieved
- define and quantify the benefits which are likely to accrue from the use of such a system.

The likely benefits might include

- reduction in staff numbers within the personnel function
- reduction in overtime or employment of casual staff e.g. at peak recruitment periods
- providing a better service to line management
- better control e.g. better records on sick leave
- better management information e.g. for use in negotiations with trade unions or for forward planning
- better staff relations because of the ability to update records more quickly e.g. speeding up the payment of a general salary increase
- less pressure and more rewarding work within the department
- improved image of the department
- determine the various computer options available and recommend the most appropriate
- provide an estimate of the likely costs
- provide an approximate implementation timescale.

The report arising from this study should set the boundaries of the system – what it will do and (equally important) what it will not do. It is not uncommon for managers who have not been involved in the detailed work of initiating a system to expect it to do things which were never envisaged. The best way to avoid this situation is to be very precise at this stage about the scope of the proposed system and to ensure that this is understood by everyone involved. Where it is decided not to computerize some aspect, it is worth enumerating the reasons for this decision.

The study forms the basis for a decision to go ahead with the project, to modify the approach or to drop it altogether. If the modifications proposed are significant a revised report should be produced. The cost–benefit analysis in the report should spell out clearly the implications of the system since this is likely to be the major factor in influencing the decision.

The estimated costs should form the basis of the budget for the project. Any significant cost increases which are identified at a later stage should result in a new cost–benefit report. Estimates of cost savings should be based on discussions with those responsible for achieving these savings and ideally should not be imposed but should be their view on how the system will affect existing costs. It is important to retain relevant working papers so that facts and commitments are available to clarify any confusion when eventually the time comes for 'the cheque to be cashed'. In order to get realistic commitments on savings from department managers they must be fully aware of what the system will do and how it will affect work practices. Since it is not uncommon to find managers from within the same department with widely different views of what the impact of computerization will be, it is important that all managers be educated in the use of computer-based systems during this phase. This can be done by having them attend appropriate courses on computers but more importantly by exposing them to how computer technology can be related to the personnel management function. One very effective way of doing this is to visit organizations which have introduced computer-based systems – especially if it is envisaged that a package solution may be appropriate.

Cost–benefit analysis

It is more difficult to put figures on benefits to be expected than it is to quantify the costs associated with a new system. In the case of a CPMIS most of the benefits may be of such a nature that it is difficult to attach a monetary figure to them e.g. better management information, a more effective department. It is likely that the project will require the approval of some management committee or steering group made up of representatives of the main functions within an organization. The introduction of a CPMIS is unlikely to have a major impact on activities within their individual areas of responsibility. Accordingly their support cannot be counted on unless the case stands on its own merits which effectively means that the quantifiable benefits must outweigh the costs.

Because of the facilities for better monitoring of staffing levels and of the use of casual staff, members of the committee may even see the system as a threat to operational flexibility. The finance director may even feel that the quicker implementation of pay awards may adversely affect cash flow. The proposal is also likely to be competing for a scarce resource, whether it is money or manpower, so to have any chance at all, cost savings are of paramount importance.

Costs

The cost structure will vary depending on whether a bureau is used, or a package running on a dedicated personnel computer, or corporate computing resources. In the case of the latter the costs will be influenced by the organization's policy in regard to charging for the use of these resources, both the initial development charge and the support charges. The following is a checklist of cost headings. They will not of course all be appropriate to a particular approach.

Initial costs
Hardware costs
- processor/console
- disk drives/tape drives
- printers
- VDUs
- disk packs for back-up cycle
Installation Costs
- delivery and installation
- electrical work e.g. provision of a clean power supply
- environmental work e.g. air conditioning, fire precautions
- cabling for main installation, VDUs and local printers
Communications Costs
- modems
- data lines
Manuals (hardware and system software)
Training courses
Sundries
- acoustic covers for printers
- furniture – tables or desks for printers and VDUs
- improved lighting
- window blinds
- microfilming of records from old system
Software costs
- package costs
- modifications to package
- development costs
- system software – operating system, utilities etc.
- word processing, query language etc.

Implementation costs
- casual staff/temporary assistance
- file set up – data preparation
- overtime
- special conversion software
- travel and subsistence

Development charge by corporate DP department

Recurring costs
Hardware Maintenance
Consumables
   disk packs
   magnetic tapes, tape casettes
   paper
   printer ribbons
Insurance including consequential loss
System software licence
Application software maintenance
Application software/package licences
Service charge by corporate DP deparment

It should also be remembered that the introduction of a computer-based system requires that the staff should be suitably trained to operate the system. This may lead to

- the need to upgrade staff because of the additional skills which are acquired
- recruitment of expensive experienced personnel from outside the organization
- having to provide trained staff to back up key personnel in the new environment
- a continuing investment in staff training.

Benefits
The following is a checklist of the benefits which may arise from the introduction of a CPMIS.

Staff savings
These will depend on

- the nature of the system being introduced
- the type of system which it will replace
- the efficiency with which the existing system is operated and the manner in which the new system will be used
- the commitment to realizing these savings which may involve some restructuring within the personnel department.

In costing staff savings, elements such as the company's contribution to social insurance and pension funds should be taken into account.

Overtime and employment of temporary help
The system would be expected to assist in coping with peaks and so reduce the need for overtime or temporary staff.

Cessation of direct costs of running the existing system
This includes existing hardware and software maintenance charges and computer service bureau costs.

Organizations tend to have a recommended approach to the form of cost–benefit statement for capital projects. This may involve the use of a desired rate of return on investment (ROI) and its use in preparing a discounted cash flow (DCF) statement. DCF is used to measure the ability of an expenditure proposal to reimburse the initial expenditure and provide, in addition, an adequate rate of interest on the money used. Where the purpose of a capital project is to generate revenue in the future the DCF method is invariably used but with computer projects a case can be made for adopting a more straightforward approach as shown in the following example.

Cost–benefit example	
Initial costs	£
Hardware costs	35,000
Personnel package	12,000
System software	3,000
Installation costs	2,000
Implementation costs	3,000
Total initial costs	£55,000

A 20 per cent annual depreciation rate is not unusual for computer hardware. This represents a five year write-off period, which is a reasonable term for amortization of software as well. In this example this would give rise to an annual charge of £11,000. Since this does not reflect the cost of money, the write-off period should be adjusted to reflect this for the purpose of the exercise. A useful way to do this is to relate it to current leasing rates. If a repayment rate of £22 per month per £1,000 is taken, the equivalent of the capital cost is spent in a period of 3.8 years:

$$\frac{£1,000}{£22 \times 12} = 3.8$$

Instead of an annual charge of £11,000 the charge is now £55,000 ÷ 3.8 or £14,470.

Initial costs annualized over 3.8 years		£14,470
Annual charges		
hardware maintenance	3,000	
software maintenance	1,000	
consumables	1,800	
software licences	1,300	7,100
Total annual costs		£21,570

Annual savings

1 typist – personnel administration	£10,000	
1 senior clerk – personnel admin.	15,000	
1 secretarial assistant – recruitment	11,500	
Annual overtime budget reduced by	3,500	
Temporary assistance – no longer required	6,000	
Total annual savings		£46,000
Net annual savings arising from project		£24,430

Scope of the system

There are varying views as to the scope of the CPMIS. These can range from the narrow view that it should be a straight replacement for an existing manually maintained basic record, through to an all-embracing personnel or human resources database system supporting payroll processing and staff rostering. While there are strong arguments for having as comprehensive an approach as possible this may not always be appropriate. The scope of the system is largely determined by

- the state of systems development within the organization and corporate policy in regard to integrated systems development
- senior personnel management's view of what the system should do
- the nature of the organization and the significance of personnel data for use by other systems.

A factor which has a major impact on both the scope of the system and on choosing the most appropriate hardware and software is the structure of the organisation. By this is meant the degree of centralization or decentralization and the extent to which the organization is an integral unit. There is very little point in considering a comprehensive central personnel management system if individual companies within the group have total responsibility for local personnel administration. A situation like this would obviously call for some form of decentralized processing with the means of communicating with head office for purposes of consolidation to provide summary data for corporate personnel planning.

Approaches available

Micro-computer

Systems available on micros are geared towards the smaller organization – those with hundreds of employees rather than thousands – or very basic systems which provide a limited service for a larger number of employees. The latter can satisfy a need within a section of the personnel management function such as training or pension administration.

The advantages are its low cost and little computer expertise is required. There are three main types of system available on micro

1 A generalized database package. In this case the background software

or structure is available and the system is developed around it. This software, in its most basic form, is used in applications such as mailing lists, but some of the packages available can be used to develop quite sophisticated systems.

2 A custom-built system or package using conventional programming techniques and either standard file structures or a database system for data management and retrieval.

3 A spread-sheet. This approach does not provide a personnel system – it is generally used for calculations and modelling.

Micro-computers or personal computers have generally been regarded as single-user computers but the technology has been developing very rapidly. The original 8-bit micro-processors have been superseded by 16-bit processors which have removed the limitations on primary memory size and have improved program execution speeds. Facilities which help to get over one of the main inconveniences of micros – the security copying of hard disks – are becoming available. There have been significant advances in providing multi-user and networking facilities but it is not valid to expect the same level of performance from a micro as from the more expensive mini or main-frame.

Because of the low cost – especially for a single user system – and the ease of installation, a micro solution has many attractions. However, it should be remembered that you get what you pay for and, while a micro-based system may provide a very worthwhile solution in some instances, the larger organization is unlikely to find that a micro-based system will meet its requirements. The range of facilities provided by any system must be assessed against the cost of these facilities and the use which will be made of them.

Payroll associated
All payroll systems are of some benefit to the personnel department even if it is only to produce listings such as

- all staff with annual salaries between £15,000 and £20,000
- staff in each cost centre
- all staff who have been paid over £3,000 in overtime so far this year.

Some payroll systems go further and hold a lot of data which facilitates the production of regular personnel reports. Such data includes

- salary history
- grade history
- absence e.g. sick leave and annual leave
- home addresses
- next-of-kin details
- pension fund details
- annual allowances.

The use of a payroll-associated system has its limitations but can be a useful launching pad for a future comprehensive personnel system. It has the following advantages.

1 It allows personnel staff to become familiar with computer-based systems.
2 It may introduce certain procedural discipline and streamline the relationship between personnel and payroll departments.
3 It allows for the holding of personnel data on magnetic medium and it can subsequently be used in the basic file set-up of the CPMIS. One of the big problems in setting up a personnel system is to get good initial data. Home addresses, home telephone number, next-of-kin etc. will often not be completely reliable in a manual system but if they are maintained on computer they can be verified from time to time and in particular prior to transfer to a new system.
4 Experience in using the system helps personnel management and staff to specify their requirements for a new system. Invariably the best users of computer-based systems are second-generation users and the best input to the definition of requirements and design of a new system comes from users who have had prior experience of using computer-based systems.

However, there are disadvantages in using a payroll system as the basis of a personnel system.

1 Payroll systems tend by their nature to be batch systems. This usually results in
   - transcription of basic data on to input forms
   - tight inflexible deadlines because of the need to fit in with data preparation and payment deadlines
   - delay in updating files because of having to fit in with the normal payroll processing cycle.
2 The primary purpose of the system is to produce the payroll. Personnel data may be looked on as of secondary importance. Responsibility for the system rests with the payroll department which normally resides within the financial function rather than the personnel function.

The main advantage of linking personnel and payroll requirements is that a certain amount of duplication of data is avoided. Apart from the duplication of effort involved, in maintaining similar data in two systems, a certain amount of effort will of course be devoted to reconciliation of data held in the two systems. In practice the argument for using a common database are stronger in the larger organizations and in the smaller micro-based systems than in the medium-sized systems.

This is an alternative which should be considered but because it involves the close cooperation and sometimes diverging requirements of two functions – personnel and finance – the organizational climate and structure will need to be right if a satisfactory implementation is to be achieved.

Mini-computers

For many organizations a package running on a mini-computer has many attractions. There are probably more packages on the market capable of running on a mini than on either micros or main-frame. This choice increases the prospect of finding a package which has the features and facilities required. A comprehensive package running on a mini should be capable of coping efficiently with about 10,000 employees.

In a medium-size organization it allows the personnel function to 'do its own thing' especially if a suitable package is available. It may avoid the problem of the personnel department having to wait until the DP department is in a position to slot in work on a personnel management system which will run on the main-frame, or until the payroll department is convinced that it should scrap its existing system. The inevitable further delays which result from developing a system or trying to find a package which will meet both sets of requirements are also avoided.

To be successful it must be a corporate decision rather than solely a personnel decision. Because of frustrations with what appears to be neglect by corporate data processing management, and the fact that in recent years personnel managements at conferences and exhibitions are being presented with systems which run on minis and micros there has been a tendency for the personnel department to declare UDI. This is not a good thing from the corporate viewpoint and management services or data processing staff should be involved from an early stage (see also page 241). In this way the system can take account of relationships existing or which will exist between this system and other systems and provision can be made for this. Of course, for this joint approach to be feasible, the DP function will have to be seen to have a positive and open-minded approach to computerization and the electronic office in general. In far too many organizations DP departments continue to emphasize traditional approaches and have a tendency to put everything on the mainframe regardless of the suitability of other solutions.

Word processor

Some personnel departments which have been using word processors for normal work such as general correspondence, preparation of reports, minutes of meetings and drafting of agreements have also used them to hold basic personnel data. This data can then be retrieved and listed in various sequences. To use a word processor in this way has little to recommend it and the result cannot be regarded as a personnel management system.

In some circumstances it may be appropriate to have a word processor-based recruitment system completely separate from the personnel system proper. This can be a very valid approach where recruitment activity is significant and the majority of job applicants are from outside the organization.

Main-frame computer
Where an organization already has a large investment in a main-frame computer this must be the first option to be investigated. There are many advantages to a main-frame system

1 It utilizes a valuable corporate resource.
2 The personnel system can be designed to interface with other systems.
3 The personnel people have access to in-house expertise initially during the development and implementation of the system and subsequently when the system is operational.
4 Access is available to powerful processing capability and storage capacity.
5 VDUs situated in the personnel offices may also be able to access other relevant systems e.g. personnel budgets in the financial systems.
6 The system will have access to devices which may not be available on a dedicated mini e.g. laser printers.
7 It is usually possible to provide additional VDUs more easily, since the use of a local computer may impose restriction on the number of VDUs which can be used.

There are three main options available when using the organization's main-frame

- a package
- a stand-alone system which interfaces with other systems
- a personnel database which services all systems which relate to the organization's personnel resources.

Package
If a suitable package is available it offers a relatively fast solution. The difficulty is that there is a scarcity of CPMISs which run on main-frame computers. There are various software directories available which classify packages by application area and computer manufacturers. Having found a CPMIS which runs on the corporate machine the analyst must then check that it runs under the operating system and with the transaction processing system used by the organization. At that stage the facilities offered by the package can be examined and related to the requirements.

Stand-alone systems
This is a custom-built system designed to meet the specific needs of the personnel function. Its main attraction is that it is designed to do exactly what is required, unlike a package where some requirements may either have to be dropped or modified in order to fit the package.
 The main problem with this approach is the effort required to develop the system. This effort has to come not just from the analysts and programmers but also personnel staff on whom the main burden of system testing will fall.
 The availability of more powerful application generators, or fourth-

generation languages, which allows for building of application systems within relatively short timescales will make this an increasingly viable and attractive option.

Personnel database

This again is a custom-built approach designed not just to meet the needs of the personnel function but to take a corporate view of personnel data. The database design would allow for all personnel-related applications, e.g. payroll, travel and subsistence or staff rostering, and the database is frequently referred to as the 'human resource database'.

Theoretically this is the preferred approach. In the case of a new organization an ideal opportunity exists for designing a personnel database. A similar opportunity arises where the time has come to redevelop an organization's personnel-related systems. In both cases a corporate approach to systems planning is possible and users can be convinced of its practicality. Generally what happens is that payroll and other systems are running satisfactorily and their redevelopment is either not justified or is resented by the user departments. The design of the database and the development of the systems to maintain and use the database can be a very big job and the timescale quoted often frightens user departments away from this approach.

The disadvantages associated with a main-frame solution are

1 A CPMIS has to share the resource with many other applications. A number of these may have a higher priority than a personnel management system, so it may be well down the list when resources are required to provide enhancements to the system. In the event of occasional hardware problems the CPMIS will have to give way to the systems which are crucial to the operation of the business.
2 There may be a feeling that once data is held outside the personnel department there may be confidentiality problems. This is generally ill-founded and frequently the nature of the data held is no more confidential than other data held, for example in the payroll files.
3 The personnel function will feel that it has no control over the operation of the system. This may be true in certain circumstances but today systems are almost completely under the control of the user department.
4 In the event of industrial action being taken by data processing staff the personnel department would be left without a system. This may be important since the personnel department is normally staffed during an industrial dispute.
5 Integrated word processing is generally regarded as an essential feature of a CPMIS, but is not a strong point with main-frame computers.

Bureaux

Computer service bureaux came into being in the mid-1960s and the business peaked in the first half of the 1970s. Their primary role was to provide a relatively cheap service to organizations at a time where it was very expensive to install an in-house computer. When more powerful mini-computers came on the market their importance diminished and this process has accelerated as the price/performance ratio on minis has improved and as the micro has become more powerful.

The bureau still has a role to play in the case of certain types of application – for example where larger files are required, where batch processing is appropriate and where large volumes of printed output are involved. Most of the systems run at bureaux have been around for a number of years and the amount of systems development work on new bureau applications is relatively small. Payroll processing is an application which is particularly suited to a bureau – in fact it is probably the main bureau function and even where an organization has substantial in-house computing facilities, the payroll may still be processed at a bureau.

When organizations first considered computerization, payroll was a natural choice. Having developed a few payroll systems the benefits of having a single flexible system capable of handling the requirements of all organizations became obvious. In this way each bureau tended to develop its own payroll package and some packages were developed which were capable of servicing the needs of many bureaux. Payroll processing can be very efficient and the service can be provided at very competitive rates. Operations staff are geared up to stationery changes for cheques, payslips and credit transfers. Arrangements are in operation with banks for the transfer of payment data on magnetic medium. The bureau will also have systems and programming staff familiar with the detail of the system and available to respond instantly to legislative changes affecting income tax and national insurance.

Bureaux have also responded to the changing technology by introducing new services. Whereas initially bureaux invariably offered a batch service, many now offer on-line input of data (not necessarily real-time updating of files) and on-line enquiry. It may also be possible to take summary data from the payroll system back to the in-house computer.

Bureaux can offer four types of service to the personnel department

1 Custom-built system.
2 Access to a payroll/personnel package.
3 Access to personnel package.
4 Access to special features.

Today any bureau-based personnel system would have to be an on-line one. The development of a custom-built system is likely to prove expensive and it is likely that more cost-effective solutions are available, such as relating the requirements to an existing bureau package. Some of these packages are quite comprehensive and are well worth pursuing. It is also worth considering this method on a short- or medium-term basis as a means of getting established with the first phase of computerization, especially if personnel management has had no previous experience of computer-based systems. Computer bureaux can also offer access to modelling facilities which may not be available within the organization.

8 Specification of requirements

Importance

In the development of a CPMIS the most crucial phase is that dealing with the definition of requirements. The output of this phase is a formal specification of requirements. This document should be the outcome of discussions and agreement involving everyone within the personnel division and representatives of the organization's management services or systems development function. It is important that all managers within the personnel division are involved at this stage and staff generally should be informed of the plans, and given the opportunity to express their view on the various discussion drafts of the report before it is finalized. Such discussion with the staff must be meaningful, and not simply issuing copies of draft reports with limited follow-up in order to be seen to be involving everybody. It sometimes happens that a manager 'feels' he knows what goes on in his department and what the procedures are, but because he is operating at a distance from the day-to-day activities may unwittingly gain a false picture of what the true requirements are.

It must be remembered that the staff who currently run the old system are the people who will run the new system and if it is deficient when compared with some of the facilities provided by the previous one they will not be very happy working with it.

It is the specification of requirements which defines the scope of any future system. This will be influenced by a number of factors, and it is important that everyone involved in its preparation realizes what is to be included and what is being left out, together with the reasons for deciding that certain requirements are not included, e.g. the expected cost, difficulty of getting reliable input data or impracticability. Having come through the feasibility stage, the decision as to whether a micro mini or main-frame is most suitable will probably have been taken. However, there will be functions which the likely solution may not be able to cope with e.g. word processing on a main-frame. These functions plus any marginal requirements should also be included. They may subsequently be dropped as requirements, but will prove useful in deciding between alternative proposals.

It is highly unlikely that this phase will finish without a number of spirited meetings on what the system should embrace. There are also likely to be various drafts of the report before a final agreed version is available.

The agreed specification of requirements is the 'bible' from then on. As the system develops, modifications may be appropriate but these should always be suitably documented and distributed. This is the only way in which it will be possible to answer questions in the future such as

- 'Why doesn't the system handle the booking arrangements for training facilities?' or
- 'I thought the system would automatically calculate and apply the rates which apply under the new shift-working agreement!'

Format and scope

An organization may have its own systems development standards which specify the format of the report. If this is the case these standards may dictate the content and layout, but it is still appropriate to list what the report should contain and to suggest a layout.

The report should clearly identify the main requirements, the secondary or peripheral requirements and provide as much concrete data as possible, *viz.* data elements, codes to be used etc. To achieve this in as clear a manner as possible it is suggested that the report be broken down into two main parts plus appendices. *Part 1* should describe the main record processing system envisaged, embracing, for example, record maintenance, training information, recruitment subsystem, establishment reporting and the pension fund subsystem. *Part 2* should describe aspects which, while important in themselves, are somewhat on the periphery or independent of the basic record processing system, e.g. information on industrial accidents or the recording and retrieval of information on industrial disputes.

Part 1

Introduction
This section should state the purpose of the document and how it has been structured. How the document will be used to evaluate system proposals should be outlined and any major areas where other options may be considered should be highlighted. For example, it might say

> In the document the requirements in relation to *recruitment* have been described as if this function should be part of an integrated personnel information system. This does not completely preclude considering this function as a stand-alone word processing type application.

In order not to close off certain options a statement along the following lines should be included.

This document is not a definitive statement of requirements. Requirements will be defined more precisely during the next phase. The final definition will be influenced by the availability of existing software and the cost of developing a system to meet specific requirements. Coding systems described in this document are included for explanatory purposes only.

The personnel management function

This section describes the personnel management function as it operates within the organization. The purpose of including a section such as this is to ensure that the management services or data processing staff involved in the project understand the nature of the function and how it is organized, and to help any outside agencies, such as software houses, to gain a similar understanding.

The section outlines the organization structure, the functions of each department or section and the interrelationship between them. It should also list the benefits which each department expects the system to provide.

The division as a whole can expect considerable benefits from computerization. These benefits will fall into two categories

1 The availability of up-to-date information in an intelligible and easily accessible form throughout the division. Although, for reasons of confidentiality, certain restrictions will have to be imposed on access to information, the staff can expect to become more involved in the total work of the division. This should lead to greater job satisfaction and a greater awareness of each person's contribution to the operation of the division.
2 Unnecessary duplication should be eliminated and repetitive time-consuming procedures should be reduced. This will enable the division to provide a better, more professional service to the organization. Some departments or sections will benefit more than others from computerization. In the organization structure shown in Figure 20 the personnel administration department will have to play the main role in inputting data to the system and the industrial relations department, which will have limited input to the running of the system, will be a major beneficiary in terms of use of the database.

System summary

This section should provide an overview of the existing system and what the new system will be expected to cover. The following is typical of the content of this section.

The organization's personnel records system, which copes with 3500 permanent staff, 500 casual staff and 1000 pensioners, is primarily based on a Kardex system. Certain personnel information is also available from the payroll system

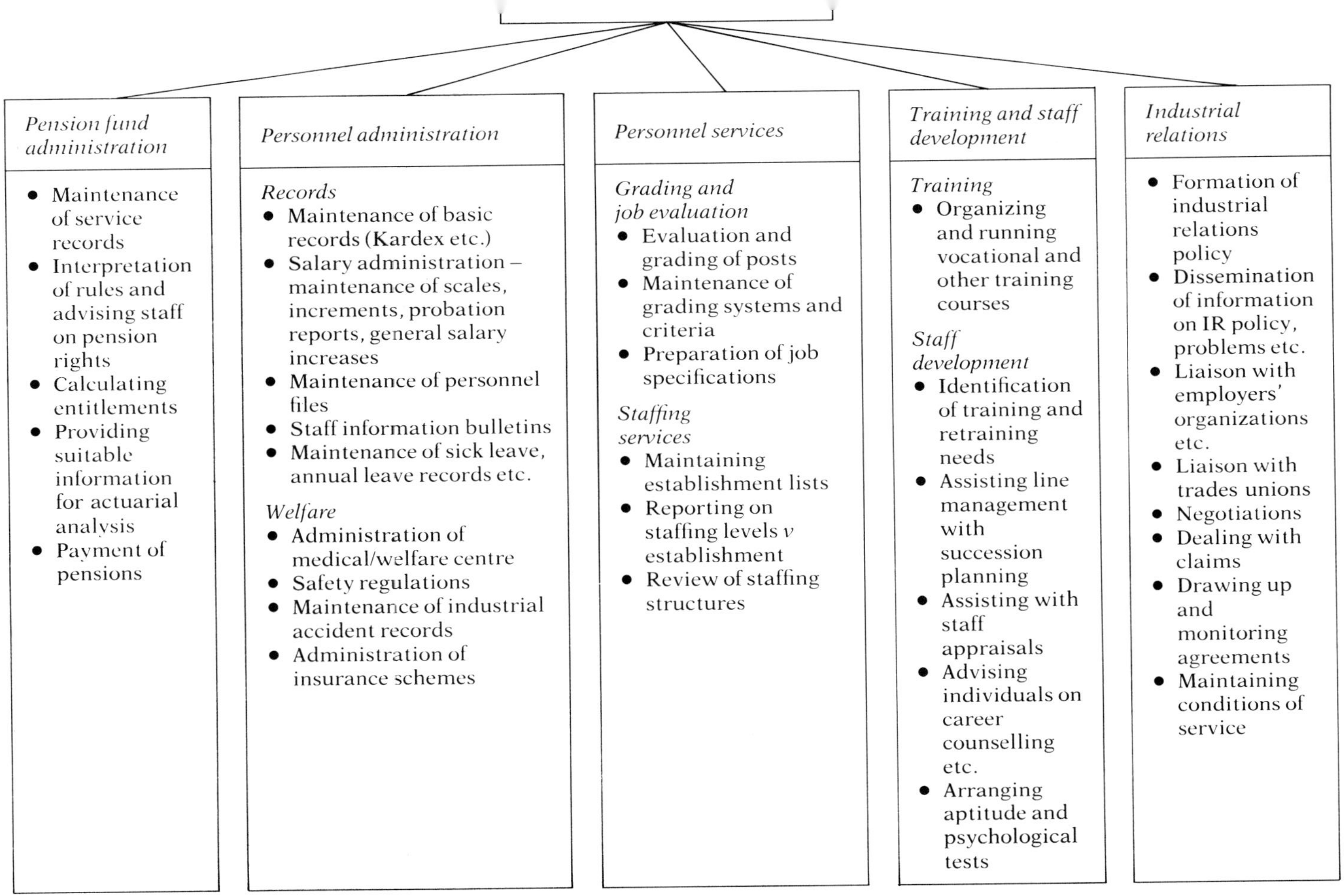

Pension fund administration	*Personnel administration*	*Personnel services*	*Training and staff development*	*Industrial relations*
• Maintenance of service records • Interpretation of rules and advising staff on pension rights • Calculating entitlements • Providing suitable information for actuarial analysis • Payment of pensions	*Records* • Maintenance of basic records (**Kardex** etc.) • Salary administration – maintenance of scales, increments, probation reports, general salary increases • Maintenance of personnel files • Staff information bulletins • Maintenance of sick leave, annual leave records etc. *Welfare* • Administration of medical/welfare centre • Safety regulations • Maintenance of industrial accident records • Administration of insurance schemes	*Grading and job evaluation* • Evaluation and grading of posts • Maintenance of grading systems and criteria • Preparation of job specifications *Staffing services* • Maintaining establishment lists • Reporting on staffing levels v establishment • Review of staffing structures	*Training* • Organizing and running vocational and other training courses *Staff development* • Identification of training and retraining needs • Assisting line management with succession planning • Assisting with staff appraisals • Advising individuals on career counselling etc. • Arranging aptitude and psychological tests	• Formation of industrial relations policy • Dissemination of information on IR policy, problems etc. • Liaison with employers' organizations etc. • Liaison with trades unions • Negotiations • Dealing with claims • Drawing up and monitoring agreements • Maintaining conditions of service

Figure 20 *Structure of a typical personnel division*

which is run on the in-house computer. Other personnel-related systems also run in-house are the travel and subsistence system, staff cars system and staff rostering system. Pensions are paid monthly via a payroll package run at a computer service bureau. The system envisaged will provide the personnel division with a personnel administration system which will embrace personnel records, absenteeism recording, recruitment, training, pension fund adminis-tration and establishment reporting and which will provide significant and up-to-date management information.

This section should then list certain basic requirements which must be met. These requirements should include the features which any good system should have as listed in Chapter 1 (page 9).

Other items which should be mentioned here are

1 The number of users or terminals which the system is expected to handle. The location of all VDUs and printers should be specified. This is important since the geographic location of users determines the appropriate configuration and influences the decision as to whether communications hardware and software will be required. Even the location of users within the same complex or campus should be specified since certain types of computers have difficulty in serving users more than a few hundred feet away from the processor.

2 While most of the data will probably be input by one section, which will effectively control the system, other sections will have to be able to input data which relates to their particular area of activity e.g. recruitment or training. The system design will have to allow for this to be done in a convenient manner, in a way which is controllable and which preserves confidentiality. The training section should, for example, be in a position to update details of courses attended, qualifications attained etc. without having access to the individual's salary details.

3 Any needs to interface with existing or future systems. The main requirement here is that a stand-alone personnel system should interface efficiently with the payroll system.

4 Where well-established reporting mechanisms are already in exist-ence, the system must produce outputs which are at least equivalent to that which managers already receive. This can be the case where regular reports on establishment versus actual numbers serving are produced regularly.

5 Since the system should, as far as possible, replace all manually maintained records, it must be seen to cope with matters such as records of salary and grade history, increments, employment con-tracts about to expire and forthcoming retirements. In effect it must provide a continuous employment history for each employee.

6 The need to cope with rules and regulations which may be specific to the organization, for example as regards sick leave.

7 The ability to cope efficiently with general salary and wage increases.

8 There should be archiving procedures built into the system so that the

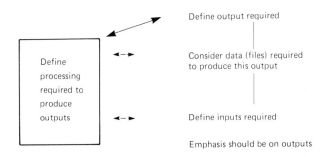

Figure 21 *Defining requirements*

system is not clogged up by historical data. This data should not, however, be lost, but should be accessible whenever need arises.
9 The design of the system should not hinder future developments.
10 A clear growth path should be outlined for any hardware proposal.

System description
This section describes the requirements in detail. It should be broken down into subsections corresponding to each of the major subsystem, for example

- personnel records
- establishment
- training
- pension fund
- recruitment.

Each subsection should describe the requirements in detail. In defining the requirements it is difficult to avoid having the outline of a basic system design in the background. This can be helpful in broadly testing the feasibility of providing certain requirements, but if any such design is hinted at it should be emphasized in the specification that it is used only for purposes of clarifying ideas and should not of itself impose any restrictions on the proposed design. In defining requirements the procedure should be as outlined in Figure 21.

To illustrate typical contents of this section three examples are used below.

1 Description of the training aids subsystem.
2 Definition of the type of screen display expected for the amendment of an individual training aid.
3 A sample report for listing training aids.

In defining screen displays and reports it is advisable to use a standard method of describing them (as shown in the examples), and to emphasize that the layout is not absolute. If a certain amount of flexibility is not allowed for in terms of layout and to a lesser degree in terms of contents then a number of package approaches will be automatically ruled out and a custom-built system or a substantially modified package are the only options left. It is good practice to include all sample screen and reports in appendices rather than clutter up the body of the specification with them.

Training aids
The training department may have a number of aids which are used on courses and are given on loan to employees for self-study or general training purposes. The requirement is for a mini-library or stock recording system which will keep track of training aids such as video cassettes, tape recorders, audio courses and textbooks, which have been issued to staff. The system should be capable of showing who has a particular aid at present and who its previous users were. The system is also required to provide on screen and in printed report format all training aids which are recorded as being currently issued to a particular employee.

Training aids data
It is envisaged that the following data will be held for each training aid

1 *Reference number* – a five-character unique reference number.
2 *Category* – a two-character code, the significance of which will be determined by the user. The interpretation of the code should be held in parameterized form in the system. The system should allow for up to 99 categories. Examples: 01 Video Cassettes; 02 Audio Cassettes; 11 Video Recorder; 12 Audio Recorder.
3 *Title* – a descriptive field of say twenty-five to thirty characters. This effectively interprets the reference number.
4 *Course* – number of course with which it is normally associated.
5 *Status* – in stock or issued at present.
6 *Comments* – free format field available for any note or comments.
7 *Date out* – if currently issued, this is the date issued in DDMMYY format.
8 *Date due back* – in DDMMYY format.
9 *Personnel number* – number of person to whom it is currently issued.
10 *Movement history* – employees to whom it has previously been issued.

Specification of proposed screen – No. S01
Screen title: Training aids file amendment
Access key: Reference number
Purpose: To allow for the amendment of any details held on a particular training aid including the recording of issues and returns.
Expected usage: 10 times per day.
Content: Self-explanatory. Movement equals the number of times the aid has been issued.

ABC Manufacturing Co.	*Training aids file amendment*
	(S01)
Reference no.:	0006
Category:	01 audio tapes
Title:	Teach yourself French – Pt 1
Course:	15 French for beginners
Status:	Out
Date out:	12.01.85
Due back:	12.02.85
Held by:	00051 John Douglas
Movement:	20
Previously issued to:	02361 John Davies
	Returned 11.01.85
	12469 George Watt
	Returned 03.12.84

Specification of proposed report – No. R01

Report title:	Training aids file listing
Purpose:	To provide a summary showing the status of all items on the training aids file or such extract of the file as may be requested. It should be possible to select for printing:

- a range of categories e.g. books only or books and video cassettes.
- only items which are on issue and which are overdue.

Sequence:	Reference number within category
Frequency:	On request – normally monthly for full listing and approx. three selective listings per month.
Period covered:	N/A
Volumes:	Full listing – 1500 lines
	Selective listing – 300 lines
Content:	Self-explanatory
	(*On due back field indicates item overdue)
Control totals:	Category and overall totals for all listed showing

- number of items
- number in stock
- number on loan
- number of items overdue

Other relevant information

This section describes sundry matters which are important but do not conveniently fit into any other section. For example, if a personnel number is already in existence for personnel and/or payroll purposes this numbering system should generally remain and accordingly should be described *viz.*

- the number of characters in it
- how it is allocated

ABC Manufacturing Co.   *Training aids file listing (R01)*   Date: 29/01/85 Page 1

Category	Reference	Title	Status	Course	Movement	Date out	Due back	Employee	Comments
01	1001	xxxxxxxxxxxxxx	In stock	95	00	–	–	–	
01	1002	xxxxxxxxxxxxxx	On loan	20	12	20.01.85	20.02.85	J. Bloggs	Hold for JNC
01	1003	xxxxxxxxxxxxxx	On loan	15	18	26.11.84	11.01.85*	T. Jones	
01	1004	xxxxxxxxxxxxxx	In stock	15	–	–	–	–	
01	–	Category totals	Total items	4	In stock 2	On loan 2	Overdue 1		

• the use of a particular form of check-digit, a description of the formula used and details of any exceptions.

Similarly the use cost centres should be discussed. The cost allocation and reporting system should be consistent with that used in the organization's financial systems. It is important that the personnel division does not introduce an independent cost coding structure. There may be occasions where there will be minor differences, but it should be possible to meet these needs without overturning the structure completely. This is not the forum for discussing the desiderata of a cost coding system and there is a variety of approaches, but it may be worthwhile to describe an approach which is flexible and convenient.

The organization is divided into a number of divisions (2-digit code). It is further divided into a number of cost centres (4-digit code). This is the basic cost unit against which personnel costs are allocated (within a costing system there would be a further breakdown over expense codes e.g. basic pay, overtime, shift pay). Cost centres are grouped by reporting purposes by means of a responsibility code (8-digit code). This code should be structured so as to be capable of indicating a number of levels of responsibility between cost centre and division (see Figure 22).

Any system must be capable to accurately reflecting any organizational changes. Responsibility for a cost centre may move from one department to another or indeed from one division to another. If a restructuring

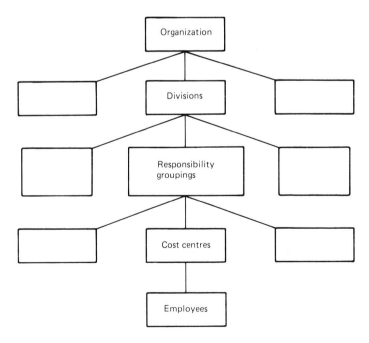

Figure 22   *Reporting levels*

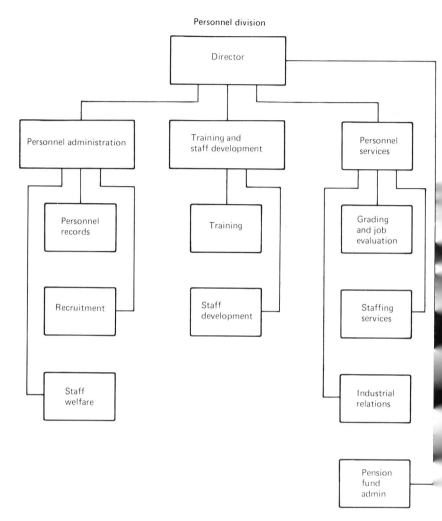

Figure 23   *Reporting structure in personnel division*

took place within the personnel division shown in Figure 23, which had the effect of moving staff welfare from the personnel administration department to the training and staff development department, this can be reflected within the system simply by changing the responsibility code for cost centre 4550 from 15020300 to 15030300 (see Figure 24). This has the effect of allowing the cost centre number for staff welfare to remain unchanged.

A number of systems would expect this change to be reflected by changing the staff welfare cost centre number and then amending this code on the records of all the employees attached to the staff welfare section. This is a very unsatisfactory arrangement.

Division/cost centre file

Division	Responsibility code	Cost centre	Name
15	15000000	0000	Personnel division
15	15010000	4510	Personnel directorate
15	15020000	4520	Personnel administration
15	15020100	4530	Personnel records
15	15020200	4540	Recruitment
15	15020300	4550	Staff welfare
15	15030000	4560	Training and staff development
15	15030100	4570	Training
15	15030200	4580	Staff development
15	15040000	4590	Industrial relations
15	15050000	4600	Personnel services
15	15050100	4610	Grading and job evaluation
15	15050200	4620	Staffing services
15	15060000	4630	Pension fund administration

Figure 24   *Cost coding for personnel division*

Spare attribute fields

In any system there should be a number of spare fields available. Suppliers of some packages tend to say this is no problem as they have left space for characters at the end of each record. Generally all this means is that if it is required to add some further fields the file structure will cope but modifications may still have to be made to the programs to cope with the extra fields. Having spare attribute fields means that there is a number of unnamed fields available within the system and the programs currently cater for updating and reporting upon them.

As an example take the situation where after the system has gone live there is a need to designate and list by cost centre all employees who are willing to work overseas. Since this requirement was not envisaged initially there will not be an 'overseas indicator' field on the employee record. However, if there is a single-character field AB on the record which it is possible to update via an existing screen, the classification can proceed immediately and listings can be produced of all employees who have a Y in this field.

Grade codes

If an existing grade coding system is in operation its structure and significance should be explained. For example, suppose a 3-digit grade code is in use and it has the following characteristics

1 The first digit indicates the grade family

e.g. 0 management
     1 services
     2 technical/operational
     3 secretarial/clerical/administrative.

2 The second and third digits do not have individual significance but in combination with the first digit make a unique number for each grade
e.g. 301 secretarial assistant
     302 senior secretarial assistant
     303 typist
     304 clerk/typist.

It is usual to have a coding system of this type in a payroll system. In a CPMIS the code may need to be more precise, for example where it is associated with conditions of service. In this case subgrades may arise where, although the same grade and salary scale is involved, there may be slight variations in conditions. For example, a grade C operator in assembly may have a different set of shift conditions to a grade C operator in dispatch.

Location codes

If recognized location codes are already in existence and used in applications such as payroll, asset register or telephone directory then there would have to be a very strong case made to justify the introduction of any new coding system.

Volumes

The ascertainment of reasonably accurate volumes of transactions and data is an essential part of the process of defining requirements. Documenting them in the specification of requirements enables proper sizings to be done by anyone who is invited to submit a proposal. At this stage factual data relating to the existing system and staffing levels and an indication of expected growth are required. This data can subsequently be related to a given systems proposal and it should be possible to obtain a reasonably reliable estimate of traffic on the system – usage of terminals, size of files and print volumes.

Table 1 shows typical entries in this section.

Table 1

		Expected to grow to
Number of employees (permanent)	3,500	4,300
Number of casual employees	50	100
(The number of individual casual employees employed in any one year is approx. 120 and it is usual to hold history of casual		

employment for a period of N years.)

Pensioners	1,000	1,500

(At current staffing levels the number of
pensioners will reach 1300 in five years
time.)

Number of recruitment competitions	200 (max.)	
Average number of applicants per competition	100	3,000 (max.)
Number of training aids used	1,000	1,500
Average number of issues of training aids per month	50	100
Number of training courses per annum	120	150
Average number of attendees per course	12	50 (max.)
Number of grade changes per annum	120	150
Number of wage/salary changes per annum	2,000	3,000
Number of grades	100	120
Number of salary scales	80	90
Number of allowance types	50	70

This section should also include a list of all standard forms in use with approximate usage figures per month – as the example in Table 2 shows.

Table 2

Form name	Volume per month
Probation report	20
Increment report	50
Staff appraisal form	35
Trainee assessment form	20
Annual leave card	120
Accident on duty report	15
Vacancy application form	180

File set-up

The file set-up process for any CPMIS can be a long arduous task and it is worth describing briefly how it can be approached (see Figure 25). If a computer-based personnel management system, however restricted in terms of facilities, already exists, or if there is some meaningful personnel data maintained in the payroll system this obviously will form the basis of setting up the files in the new system. The use of this data will probably necessitate the writing of a special conversion program or a number of programs. While it is not possible at this stage to define exactly what this program should do, it is at least possible to list all of the relevant transferable fields and their characteristics. Table 3 gives an example.

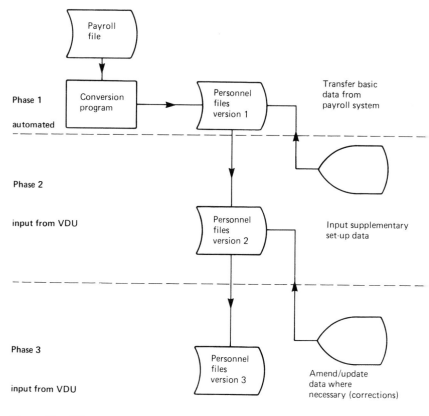

Figure 25   *File set-up process*

Table 3

Field name	Size	Format	Comments	Source
Personnel No.	5	99999	Modulus 11 Check digit	Payrol
First name	15	X(15)	No separate title field–generally ignored	Payroll
Surname	20	X(20)	Payroll	
Date of birth	6	DDMMYY	Payroll	

It may also be possible to derive other data automatically from a combination of fields e.g. grade, date of appointment to grade, and location, may be used to help determine conditions of service. This can be achieved by programming the relevant rules to cater for the majority of cases and then altering the result in exceptional cases.

Part 2

This part of the specification of requirements meets two needs

1 It describes features and facilities which, while not an essential part of the system (especially if it is acknowledged that insistence on some of them may seriously restrict the number of possible solutions available), are desirable or will have to be catered for outside the system.
2 It documents requirements which, however trivial, are then available for consideration in perhaps some other context. For example, a need to provide a computerized booking system for a few training classrooms is hardly worth considering in the context of a CPMIS but there may be a simple resource booking package available on whatever computer is eventually chosen or there may be a need to develop a corresponding system for some other part of the organization.

Items covered in this part are generally those described in Chapter 18. The areas covered may include

• manpower planning
• treatment of conditions of service
• facilities for keeping comparative statistics on other comparable organizations e.g. wage rates or generally available intercompany comparisons
• standard trade union agreements
• industrial relations information
• dispute information
• accidents on duty
• facilities booking e.g. training facilities and conference rooms
• word processing
• graphics.

Appendices

All examples of screen and report layouts required should be included in the appendices if they are to be included at all. The appendices should also include details of fields which should be held on the system, tables to be used etc. Examples of typical appendices are

• basic fields
• absenteeism types
• illness types
• recruitment – competition status codes
• recruitment – application status codes
• occupation classification codes
• experience classification codes
• languages
• language proficiency codes
• academic achievement codes
• professional qualification codes

- training aids categories
- reasons for leaving
- employee categories
- conditions of employment codes
- format in which salary scales should be held
- details to be held on each type of allowance.

While it is not essential at this stage to have decided on the detail of a number of these coding systems, the discipline of having to define them is a useful exercise and tends to increase the awareness of the amount of data which will have to go into the system and lead to consideration of how that data can be ascertained initially and subsequently kept up to date.

9 General requirements

Introduction

Regardless of the scope of the system required there are various features which every good personnel system should have. These are mainly concerned with the viability of the system, restrictions on access, flexibility, 'user-friendliness', and the support that is available for the system. These are considerations which apply in the case of virtually any computer-based system. Because data processing staff will tend to regard a CPMIS as being less crucial than some other real-time systems which have a greater impact on the day-to-day running of the business, some of these matters may be somewhat neglected. At the planning stage a hardware maintenance arrangement which is based on up to twenty-four hour response to call may appear adequate, but when the system is operational and there is a hardware fault, frustration will develop unless an engineer is on site within a very short period. This chapter describes a number of the general requirements which any good CPMIS should meet.

Security

The data held on the system should only be accessible to those who have authority to access it. There are two aspects to this

1 The possibility of non-personnel staff gaining access to the files.
2 The danger of personnel staff either viewing or updating records when they are not entitled to.

In the case of the former the situation is very much influenced by whether the system is dedicated to personnel or shares the corporate computer with a variety of other applications. Where the corporate computer is used, it is likely that comprehensive security operations will already be in existence and there is rarely any justification for the personnel function to be unduly concerned. It is likely that a major application on the main-frame will be the organization's financial systems. These systems demand very rigorous computer control procedures which will have been vetted by the finance division, internal audit department and the external auditors. In this case what is required is a critical study of the procedures in operation and the verification with existing users of the adequacy of the controls and procedures.

One possible area in which confidentiality may be accidentally breached is in the despatch of computer-produced reports. The data control section attached to any large computer installation will be handling a lot of output for a variety of users and it is conceivable that a relatively small volume personnel printout could be despatched to another user department by mistake. Where the system is run on a dedicated personnel computer the possibility of illegal access is probably reduced and the possibility of printed reports going outside the personnel division is unlikely to arise. On the other hand, there may be a tendency to adopt a less formal approach to operational security, because the computer is located locally, and this in itself could lead to breaches of security.

Access to the system within the personnel division and the ability to impose restrictions on who can use the facilities is largely determined by the CPMIS software itself. Access is generally restricted in three ways

1 Physical restrictions on particular computer terminals.
2 Use of authorized 'users' combined with passwords.
3 Use of passwords only.

Terminal restriction
Some systems do not support or have a very limited password facility, in which case terminal restriction may be useful. Each terminal has an 'address' and the computer can limit the information going to that terminal, or the functions accessible to it. For example, a terminal may only be allowed access to the training subsystem. In a dedicated personnel computer this method may have limited usefulness.

Users/passwords
This system is based on a hierarchy of users which has the system manager at the top and users with very restricted access at the base. The system manager has access to all functions and the level at which other users are at in the hierarchy determines which functions they can use. When they log on to the system the users input both the user number and password, which determine their status and restrict their access.

With passwords a user is given a limited number of attempts to input the correct password and if unsuccessful the terminal will normally be disconnected from the system and the unsuccessful attempts will be logged and reported on. This report normally goes to the system manager.

```
┌─────────────────────────────────────────────────────────────────┐
│  ABC Manufacturing Company              Log on screen             │
│                                         20/10/85  09–15           │
│          Personnel management information system                  │
│  Please enter  User number [      ]  Password [      ]            │
└─────────────────────────────────────────────────────────────────┘
```

Passwords only
With this system user numbers are not required and access to particular functions is dependent upon knowing the password for that function. It is a more straightforward approach from a system development point of view and generally works well. It does however, require the user to remember a number of passwords instead of one. This can be overcome by assigning a common password to a number of similar functions. However, in order to be effective, passwords must be changed frequently.

Passwords must be allocated by the system manager, unlike the previous method where the user has control over his/her own password and can change it at will. Under this system the user initially logs into the system using the system password and then is presented with the next screen which requires a function password for further access.

```
┌─────────────────────────────────────────────────────────────────┐
│  ABC Manufacturing Company              Log on screen             │
│                                         20/10/85  09–15           │
│         Personnel management information system                   │
│  Please enter system password [      ]                            │
└─────────────────────────────────────────────────────────────────┘
```

```
┌─────────────────────────────────────────────────────────────────┐
│  ABC Manufacturing Company            20/10/85  09–20             │
│          Personnel management information system                  │
│                      MAIN MENU                                    │
│  Function                                                         │
│    01      Parameter file maintenance                             │
│    02      Descriptor file maintenance                            │
│    03      Grades file maintenance                                │
│            etc.                                                    │
│    10      Add new employee                                       │
│    11      Amend existing employee record                         │
│    12      Input absence data                                     │
│            etc.                                                    │
│    20      Employee enquiry                                       │
│  Please enter function required [      ] and password [      ]     │
└─────────────────────────────────────────────────────────────────┘
```

In this approach there may also be a further password required at submenu level.

Resilience

Both hardware and software must be resilient. Hardware resilience is indicated by the up-time of the processor and its peripherals including VDUs. Software resilience is concerned mainly with the application software but to a lesser extent with system software. This should be verified as thoroughly as possible when proposals are being evaluated but a custom-built system or a substantially modified package may not be verifiable completely until it is operating in its normal environment.

What can be evaluated at proposal stage are the facilities which the system has to enable it to recover from a 'crash'. From both a hardware and a software position a crash should result in only a minimum amount of data being lost. The most usual problem in this area is the corruption of files on disk, either through a program bug or a hardware problem such as a head-crash. In this situation it is essential to be able to restore the file to the position it was in immediately prior to the problem.

The three principal ways of doing this are

1 Have all files duplexed. This means that every transaction which is processed updates two sets of files on different devices e.g. on different disk drives. In some critical systems there may also be a duplicate processor involved. In the case of personnel systems, especially non-main-frame systems, this option is not usually available.
2 Logging all updating transactions processed on a log file and reprocessing these transactions against the last copy of the file concerned. This emphasizes the need for regular security dumping of files and ensuring that the logging process and clearing out of the log file is consistent with the security dumping procedures.
3 Keeping a record outside the system of all updating transactions and reprocessing them by manually re-entering them into the system.

When using a micro or mini-computer the options available for placing files on different devices may be restricted. There should be more scope for spreading files over a number of disk drives on a main-frame. In using established transaction processing procedures on a main-frame, resilience may be virtually guaranteed, especially where a reputable DBMS (database management system) is used.

Query language and report generator

An essential element of any respectable CPMIS is the availability of a good query language and report generator. It is generally the presence of this feature which allows the system to respond to the *ad hoc* queries such as 'How many engineers do we have on the staff who can speak French fluently and who might be available to spend two years in Canada?'

The application system as developed does the housekeeping work. It provides a means of setting up and maintaining the basic data within the system. It also allows for the retrieval of information by means of enquiry on screen and by the production of standard reports which generally allow for limited options as to sequence, content and format. However, these methods of retrieval are designed to meet the main needs as perceived when the system or package was being designed. If a special report is required, the approach might be to specify and write a special program to produce the necessary information. There are various drawbacks attached to this approach

1 A programmer from the DP department has to be assigned to write the program.
2 The program must be specified clearly and there must be common understanding between the user who has the requirement and the programmer who has to produce the output. This will be easier when the programmer is familiar with the system. During the early life of the system, programmers who know the system well will be involved in writing these special programs but eventually programmers will be assigned to the task who have to come to terms with the system and its file structure before they can write the required programs.
3 The writing of a new program involves a certain amount of testing and debugging which introduces a delay.
4 Because of the inherent delays and perhaps difficulty in having a programmer assigned at all there will be a temptation to supress the need or to try and cope in a less efficient and less accurate way. This can be disastrous. It results in what should be one of the main advantages of having CPMIS – the ability to respond to *ad hoc* queries – being discarded because of the difficulties involved in retrieving information.

Of course if the basic data is not present it will never be possible to derive information, but once the data is present the system must allow for convenient and speedy retrieval.

A query language or report generator is designed to address this need. Report generators have been around for some time but have largely been used by specialists e.g. programmers, computer auditors or a data processing specialist within a user department. In recent years query languages have become available which are relatively easy for non-specialists to use. They are designed to be VDU-oriented but can also fulfil many of the needs previously met by report generators.

The need for such a product to be available alongside a CPMIS is very important and the subject is accordingly dealt with in more detail in Chapter 17.

Flexibility

A major problem with badly designed computer systems is inflexibility. This manifests itself in inability to

- add additional data fields
- add new functions or modify existing functions
- add or change standard values or descriptions
- move the software from one computer model to another.

There are various causes for all of these manifestations of inflexibility. They can all be remedied or alleviated to some degree but absolute flexibility is difficult to achieve. A balance has to be struck, otherwise at some point the user will suffer in terms of system complexity in the search for complete flexibility.

It is not intended to examine in detail here the tenets of good system design but to highlight the type of problems which inflexibility can give rise to and to indicate some points to look out for.

Parameterization

The use of a parameter file or files greatly enhances the flexibility of any system. It is not a question of whether or not a CPMIS should have one but rather the extent and quality of it.

To explain the concept of system/program parameters the following examples may help.

1 A CPMIS will generally need to display the organization name on screens or on printout. This can be done by coding into the program, as a constant, the organization's name, **ABC Manufacturing Co**. This would have to be coded into each program which displayed the name – perhaps twenty or thirty programs – as

    MOVE 'ABC MANUFACTURING CO.' TO PRINT-AREA-1

If the company changed its name to **XYZ Manufacturing Co**. this would have to replace the old name in each of the programs involved.

If, on the other hand the design of the system had allowed for holding a separate file with just the company name held in it, the process, while initially slightly more complex, would now be a lot simpler.

> COMPANY NAME FILE
> FIELD NAME: CO-NAME
> CONTENTS: 'ABC MANUFACTURING CO'

The company name file would be accessed by every program which needed to display or print the company name and the instruction in each program would be something like

    MOVE CO-NAME TO PRINT-AREA-1

This has the effect of moving the *contents* of the field called co-name. Accordingly by changing the contents of that field to **XYZ Manufactur-**

ing Co. there is no need to interfere with any of the 20 or 30 programs which may use the name.

2 If income tax and social insurance rates and conditions are hard coded as part of a payroll program which calculates net pay then the program will have to be changed and retested whenever any changes to rates, tax bands etc. have to be applied. If these rates and conditions are held as part of a parameter file then the only change required is the values in this file, and since no program change is involved program testing/verification is not involved.

3 A program is available to list all employees with salaries between £10,000 and £15,000. The selection criteria are coded as instructions within the program as follows

IF SALARY > £10,000 AND SALARY < £15,000

If the personnel director seeks a listing of all employees with salaries within the range of £13,000–£17,000 a programmer must be found who will either write a new program or change the instruction shown above to comply with the new requirement. This involves delay and inefficiency which could be obviated if the values had been parameterized. This request could then be met by running the program with these values e.g.

```
RUN PROGRAM PRO1
VALUE-1 = 13,000
VALUE-2 = 17,000
```

Instead of the instruction shown earlier the instruction within program PRO1 would read

IF SALARY > VALUE-1 AND SALARY < VALUE-2

In this case the values are generally known 'run-time parameters'

4 A validation program for checking input to a payroll system prints a warning message whenever an annual salary greater than £20,000 is input. This checking was coded into the program when it was written a number of years ago but now as with other similar messages it gives rise to a voluminous error listing.

This listing is now largely meaningless but in order to make it more meaningful sections of the program will have to be rewritten. This type of validation checking can be done much more flexibly from rules held in a parameter file. The following is an example of how such rules might be held

```
FIELD   1 SALARY VALUE e.g. £20,000
FIELD   2 GRADE CODE    e.g. 300
FIELD   3 GRADE CODE    e.g. 201
FIELD   4 GRADE CODE    e.g. 235
FIELD   5 GRADE CODE    e.g. 275
FIELD   6 MESSAGE       e.g. 'CHECK ANNUAL SALARY
                             INPUT'
```

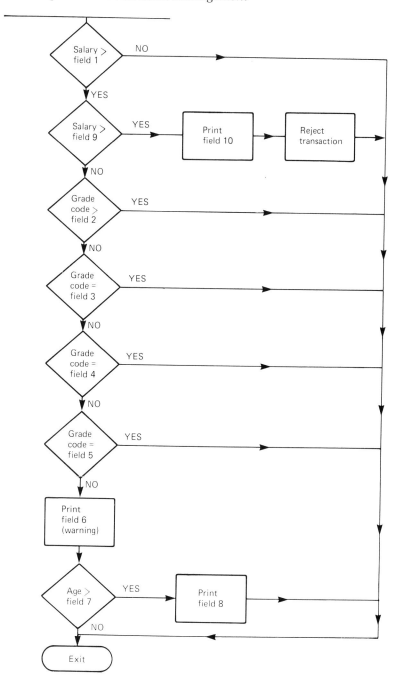

Figure 26   *Flow chart salary validation routine*

FIELD 7 AGE   e.g. 55
FIELD 8 MESSAGE   e.g. 'CHECK SERVICE PAY
                                 ENTITLEMENT'
FIELD 9 SALARY VALUE e.g. £40,000
FIELD 10 MESSAGE   e.g. 'INVALID SALARY VALUE'

This data could be used within the program as demonstrated by Figure 26.

In terms of the sample values this process

- accepts any salary of £20,000 or less
- rejects any salary of over £40,000
- accepts any salary within the £20,000 to £40,000 range provided the employee's grade code is greater than 300 or is equal to 201, 235 or 275.
- prints a warning message where an employee is in this salary range but is not in one of the accepted grades for that salary level
- checks the employee's age after the warning message has been printed and if over 55 suggests that service pay entitlements may have brought the salary over £20,000.

Within a CPMIS every value which may be varied from time to time and which is used to control a process within a program should be parameterized. These parameterized values can take the form of a parameter file or run-time parameters. Run-time parameters are generally not set up as a distinct file but are input on screen before the program is run e.g. 'list all cost centres from VALUE 1 to VALUE 2'. Values in the parameter file tend to have a longer life. A system can have a single large parameter file or a number of smaller parameter files. A common design is to have a relatively small parameter file which controls the system and a more extensive descriptor file or a series of descriptor files which contain largely valid codes and their interpretation. Typical contents of a parameter file are shown in Table 4.

Descriptor file

Data within the file can be held as a number of different tables. A typical manner of holding the data is

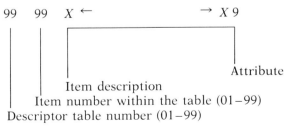

99   99 X ←   → X 9

                                    Attribute
            Item description
        Item number within the table (01–99)
    Descriptor table number (01–99)

In this format up to ninety-nine tables can be held and up to ninety-nine items can exist within each table. Each item has a description associated with it which is displayed on all relevant reports and screens. In setting

Table 4   Parameter file

Field	Sample contents
Organization name	**ABC Manufacturing Co.**
Retirement age – male	65
Retirement age – female	63
Sick leave limits	Number of uncertified sick days permitted per year
	Number of sick absence days permitted in year before reduced pay level applies
	(Corresponding time periods for other rules)
Contribution rates to pension scheme	Under 50 6.0 per cent
	Over 50 7.25 per cent
Annual leave year end	DDMM
Annual leave entitlement	If there are twenty different types of entitlement (days' leave per year) these can be set up and related to a code which is then attached to conditions of service for each grade. Thus when entitlements are revised the system can reflect this simply by changing the parameters.

up a descriptor file there will be a tendency to assign standard values to some codes so that the system can treat them in a certain way e.g. as sick leave or leave without pay. To introduce preassigned values for any given code, even in this way, leads to inflexibility and should be avoided. Flexibility is achieved by assigning an attribute from a range of attribute codes which themselves are of significance within the system.

If two of these codes are 1 – Treat as unpaid leave – and 2 – Treat as paid leave, it is possible to demonstrate their impact on flexibility. One of the tables holds all of the leave types as shown in Table 5.

Table 5

Code	Description	Attribute
01	Unpaid leave of absence	1
02	Sick leave	2
03	Maternity leave	2
04	Compassionate leave	2
05	Marriage leave	2
06	Study leave	2
07	Examination leave	2
08	Military service leave	2
09	Annual leave	2
10	Special maternity leave	1

The use of the attribute determines the significance of each type of leave and it's impact on post or establishment reporting. If it is decided that study leave should be treated as unpaid leave, then a simple change of attribute from 2 to 1 will implement the decision within the system. Examples of the type of data set up in the descriptor file are

- absenteeism types
- conditions of employment
- recruitment-competition status
- recruitment-application status
- illness types
- post types
- employee categories
- nationalities

Response time

Response time is defined as elapsed time in seconds between the initiation of an on-line enquiry and the return of the result to the screen. In any on-line system users will soon become frustrated if the system is slow to respond. A number of factors affect response time

1 *Hardware* – the speed of the processor, how much memory is available to the system and the type of backing store used.
2 *Software* – both the system software and the application software. The operating system can have an impact as can the way in which the system handles terminals. In some systems a certain amount of processing is carried out at the terminal or terminal controller, while in other systems the central processor does all the work. The efficiency of the application programs is also a key factor.
3 *Demands on the system* If the personnel system shares a computer with other applications, response times may be subject to variation depending upon the use of the computer by others. In designing any computer system estimates have to be made of the expected demands which will be put on it. This is sometimes not easy, especially as the introduction of a new system sometimes completely changes the way in which a business function is carried out. In almost all systems there will be peak demand well in excess of the average and this is what the system must cope with. Within the personnel management system response time will also be affected by the number of users and the demand which they place upon the system.
4 *Location* If users are located away from the computer access may be by communications lines which in themselves may affect response time.

In comparison with other business systems a personnel management system does not process many transactions so response time may not be a major factor. A number of the commands and transaction types will be low volume, for which efficiency is not as crucial as with other types which are used more frequently. An acceptable response time can vary so much, it is difficult to state what the norm should be. Typically response time is quoted by the package supplier as being less than 1 or 2 seconds. This in itself cannot be taken at face value and must be qualified. Throughout the working day an average of about 3–4 seconds is generally satisfactory. If response time on high-volume transactions goes above about 6–7 seconds operators will start to become impatient.

User-friendliness

'User-friendly' has become one of the great buzzwords of the computer age. It has become easy to regard it as a piece of sales jargon but it is vitally important. Some systems can afford to be less accessible to the user. These are generally systems with a limited number of specialist users. A personnel system will be used by a number of people within the division, most of whom will not have the time or inclination to come to terms with complex computer procedures, so if it is not easy to use they will simply refrain from using it.

The only way to become really convinced of the ease-of-use of a system is to sit down and use it. This can be done to some extent prior to deciding upon a particular system or approach. If an existing package or system is being considered it can be examined working with test data and ideally should also be seen working in a live environment. In the case of a package a visit to an existing live site is a must. Discussions with staff who use the system as part of their everyday work will quickly reveal their attitude to it. Seeing a package in this environment is also often the best way to get a feel for response time, although allowances must be made for factors such as the type of computer in use or the extent to which the system is sharing the computer.

Where a custom-built system is being considered it should be possible to build a prototype or model which will have screen layouts available for use on a VDU. This should be an integral part of any system proposal and is a very good means of explaining to potential users how the system will work. Seeing a screen layout on a VDU is infinitely more meaningful than looking at a printed screen layout chart. User-friendliness is made up of a number of things including the design approach, the layout of screen displays and reports, how easily keyboard functions relate to the system and the use of features such as reverse video, split screens and transaction scrolling within screens. Two factors to be considered in evaluating a system are whether it is menu-driven or command-driven, and the help facilities available.

Menu- or command-driven

In a menu-driven system the VDU screen shows the list of facilities which are available at that point to the user. The user makes a selection from these facilities – hence the term 'menu'. The selection of an option can lead to a further menu or sub-menu and this process can continue until the user has arrived at the required level.

In the example shown in Figures 27 to 30 three options are chosen from

---

ABC Manufacturing Co.

Personnel management information system

Subsystems available
  1 Personnel records
  2 Recruitment
  3 Training
  4 Pension scheme
  5 Establishment
  6 Query language
  7 Word processing

Please select option required [1] and press return

Figure 27   *Top level menu*

ABC Manufacturing Co.

Personnel records subsystem

  1 Employee record maintenance
  2 Salary change
  3 Absence input
  4 Grades file maintenance
  5 Cost centre maintenance
  6 Post file maintenance
  7 Salary scales file maintenance
  8 Allowances file maintenance
  9 Employee enquiry

Please select option required [1] and press return

Figure 28   *Personnel records menu*

ABC Manufacturing Co.

Employee record maintenance

  1 Set up new employee
  2 Amend existing employee
  3 Delete employee record

Please select option required [1] and press return

Figure 29   *Employee record menu*

ABC Manufacturing Co.

Set up new employee

Personnel no. [   ]   First name [   ]   Surname [   ]
Date of birth [   ]   Start date [   ]   Sex [   ]
Category [   ]   Grade [   ]   Salary scale [   ]
Point on scale [   ]   Cost centre [   ]   Post [   ]
In pension scheme (Y/N) [   ]

Figure 30   *New employee screen*

screens before the screen which allows for the input of the new employee details is available. While the menu approach is easy to use and guides the user along it can prove to be cumbersome.

Once details of one or a number of new employees are set up on the system and the user wants to get back to the main menu (subsystems available) the normal method is to retrace the steps. This is normally done by depressing one of the function keys as often as required which brings the user back as follows.

↓
Employee record maintenance (Figure 29)
↓
Personnel records subsystem (Figure 28)
↓
Subsystems available (Figure 27)

In a command-driven system the user is not guided to the same extent but it can be more convenient once he/she becomes familiar with the system. Instead of selecting an option or facility from a menu, an instruction is input which takes the user directly to the facility required. This instruction is known as a command and in order to facilitate access each command can be supplemented by one or more qualifiers or parameters. The ease of use of a command-based system is to a large extent influenced by the way in which the command codes are constructed. This is best explained by means of examples.

In the example a command comprises of three parts

1 The action required.
2 The entity (which is the subject of the action).
3 A qualifier (which may only apply in certain instances).

Action codes
A : Add
C : Cancel or delete
D : Display
H : Help
L : List

M : Modify or amend
P : Print
T : Transfer

Entity codes
AL : Annual allowances
AP : Application (recruitment)
CC : Cost centre
CO : Competition (recruitment)
DI : Division
EM : Employee
PO : Post
SA : Salary scale
TA : Training aid
TC : Training course

Some of the commands derived from action codes and entity codes are

AEM : Add a new employee
MEM : Modify or amend details about an employee
LCC : List cost centre
DEM : Display employee
DCO : Display competition.

Examples of the qualifiers used in the third part of the command are

CS : Conditions of service
EA : Earnings information
EX : External applicants
PE : Pension information
SH : Salary history
TR : Training information.

These could give rise to extended commands such as

DEMSH : Display employee salary history information only
DEMTR : Display employee training information only
DCOEX : Display external applicants for competition.

There can be various parameters associated with each command and the system recognizes their significance, for example

DEMSH 34127 300180 : Display salary history information for employee 34127 from 30.1.80 onwards.

ABC Manufacturing Co.

Personnel management information system

Command [AEM]   ID [   ]   [   ]

If AEM is inserted in the command box, the system will bring up a screen

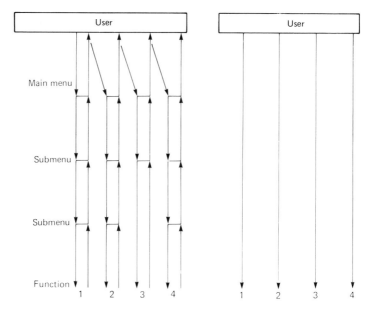

Figure 31   *Comparison of access routes – menu and command*

similar to that shown in Figure 30. A system will normally assume that
this screen is the one required until a new command is input.

Figure 31 shows how long-winded the access can be in a menu-driven
system in comparison with a command-driven one. Some systems would
be quite inefficient using a menu. However if proper attention is devoted
to screen content a lot of the problems in, this area can be alleviated.
Some menu-driven systems allow for short-circuiting the menu and
going direct to the system facility required thus combining the best of
both worlds. In the case of a CPMIS the advantages of the menu system
probably outweigh the disadvantages.

Help facilities
Every CPMIS must be capable of responding to the cry for help. This can
be done by means of documentation on the system – user manuals and
help cards – or by providing an on-line help facility. The extent of the
on-line facility will vary from system to system. A menu-driven system of
itself guides the user through the system, so it requires fewer help
facilities than a command-driven system.

On-line assistance should be easy to summon. Once available it should
be easy to traverse and once answers have been obtained it should be
easy to revert to where the user was in the system before help was sought.
There are various formats for providing on-line help. Figures 32 to 36
illustrate a menu-based system and one which is primarily geared to
respond to calls for assistance in respect of specific commands.

ABC Manufacturing Co.

Personnel manangement information system

Subsystems available
   1 Personnel records
   2 Recruitment
   3 Training
   4 Pension scheme
   5 Establishment
   6 Query language
   7 Word processing
   H Help facility

Please select option required [H] and press return

Figure 32   *Top level menu with 'help'*

ABC Manufacturing Co.

Personnel management information system

Help facility
   The system has a comprehensive help facility, which is subdivided
   under the following headings:
     A General description of the system
     B Use of the keyboard
     Subsystems
       1 Personnel records
      .2 Recruitment
       3 Training
       4 Pension scheme
       5 Establishment
       6 Query language
       7 Word Processing
     G Generating reports from the system

At any stage if you wish to go back to where you were before you sought
help please press key F6.

Please select option required [1] and press return

Figure 33   *Help screen – menu-based*

ABC Manufacturing Co.

Personnel management information system

Command [HELP] ID [AEM]

Figure 34   *Help request – command-based*

ABC Manufacturing Co.

HELP: AEM
This command is used to add a new employee to the personnel file.
It requires that a valid personnel number be entered in the ID field.
A valid number must have 5-digits including the check digit and the
number must not already exist on the file.
Once the ID is accepted the system displays a screen which invites you
to input the following fields

First name:	Mandatory	Up to 15 characters
Surname:	Mandatory	Up to 20 characters
Date of birth:	Mandatory	Format: DDMMYY
Start date:	Mandatory	Format: DDMMYY
Sex:	Mandatory	M or F

For further information press F1

Command [   ]   ID [   ]

Figure 35   *Help screen – command-based*

ABC Manufacturing Co.

Help: AEM (continuation screen)

Category:	Mandatory	Acceptable values are 1 Permanent and pensionable 2 Temporary 3 Casual 4 Contract
Grade	Mandatory	Valid grade code required. Must be in range 001 599 and must match a grade as set up on the grades file.
Salary scale	Mandatory	Must match a valid salary
Point on scale	Mandatory	Scale and scale point as set up on the system.
Cost centre	Mandatory	Should be a valid cost centre.
Post	Mandatory	Must match a valid and vacant post on the system.
In pension scheme	Optional	Can by Y (yes) or N (no). If left blank system will default to Y.

Command [   ]   ID [   ]

Figure 36   *Help screen – command-based (continuation screen)*

Support

The personnel division will require various types of support facility during the development, implementation and operational running of a CPMIS. The scope of the support will be dependent upon a number of things including whether the system is a package or is custom-built and whether it runs on the corporate main-frame or on a stand-alone computer within the personnel division. At this point support for hardware, system software (e.g. the operating system) and communications is ignored and support for the application system is considered. It is essential that the supplier of the CPMIS, whether from inside or outside the organization, should have the resources to provide the type of support required. Application system support is required at each of the three phases of the system

- development
- implementation
- operational.

Development

Once a decision has been made to develop a new system or modify an existing package the necessary manpower resources should be allocated. The personnel function will not have much say in deciding whether the resources allocated are going to be sufficient and the only way to establish this is to insist on a detailed development schedule listing all of the various tasks which have to be done, e.g. completion of programs or program modules, with a firm completion date logged against each test. If meetings are held regularly to monitor progress against these targets then slippage will indicate the allocation of inadequate resources and action should be sought to remedy the situation. It can sometimes happen that up to this stage personnel staff will have been dealing with salespeople who are anxious to get the business and may have quoted unreasonable timescales and deliberately underestimated the amount of effort required. When the salespeople withdraw to the background and the people who have to deliver the goods take over they may start to make noises about what they are expected to deliver and when. At this stage the customer should recognize the position for what it is. Since the financial arrangements will already have been agreed the customer should heed what the production staff have to say about timescale and revise implementation expectations accordingly or insist that additional resources be allocated to the project. Once the project commences the customer will want to have the best possible people working on the system but this may not always be achieved. Before the decision to go ahead is taken some form of commitment should be given as to who will be assigned to the system. The track record of those nominated can be checked out but there can never by any guarantee that they can remain with the system. The analyst or programmer who made such a good impression during the system investigation phase or the proposal stage, and whose work may indeed have influenced the final decision may have left the organization before the project gets under way.

In summary the steps which should be taken to try to ensure support during this phase are

- obtain commitments with regard to who will work on the project
- check out previous work done by these people
- agree a detailed development schedule
- meet regularly to review progress.

Implementation

In addition to the development staff who will have been working on the system there is need for other manpower resources to be available during this phase. These are

1 Programmers who may have to write special programs to assist with the file set-up. These may be conversion programs which will take data from existing computer-based systems such as the payroll. It may also be useful to have programs written which will allow for the take on of data in batch mode. Certain types of input e.g. absence history, may lend itself to transcription on to input forms and, since this data is not volatile, this can be done prior to the system being ready. Once on forms the data can be transfered to a magnetic medium. It can be verified and processed against the basic personnel file as soon as this has been set up.

2 Supervisory staff in each area who will become involved in implementation in the design of procedures, and introducing the staff who will use the system.

3 Temporary staff who will become involved in the basic slog of preparing the input and setting up the files. This may include data preparation staff who are experienced keyboard operators and who will input the data quickly.

Operational

Once the system has gone live there will still be a need to have access to the systems development staff who understand the system or package. They will be in a position to answer queries, to demonstrate how certain things can be done, and to verify that other things are being done properly.

Where a query language is being used an experienced programmer will be able to use it more efficiently than an inexperienced user and can be of great help in setting up re-runnable jobs or procedures for commonly required queries or reports.

Despite the most thorough system testing some bugs may still get through and it is only the process of live running which will unearth them. When these occur they should be investigated and cleared as soon as possible. As the system is being used there will be requests for changes and enhancements. These requests must be controlled, evaluated and, if appropriate, implemented in an orderly fashion. Once it is decided to implement these changes they should be done quickly and preferably by the programmers who know the system intimately.

10 Specific requirements

Introduction

It is not possible to define requirements which will meet every organization's specific needs. What is possible is to describe a comprehensive set of requirements which can then be related to an organization and, by acting as a type of checklist, will assist in clarifying what a system should do. One problem in defining requirements is that by breaking the requirements down into units, which correspond to subsystems, and in describing them as such they may appear as a number of discrete systems. This is not the case, all of the systems are interrelated and together they make up the total CPMIS.

The units described separately here and in following chapters are

- personnel records
- salary records
- absence recording and reporting
- pension records
- staff recruitment
- establishment reporting
- staff training and development
- word processing/letter production.

Personnel records

This is the heart of the system and all other aspects of the system revolve around it. The amount of information to be held may depend on the category of employee involved – permanent, casual or temporary, contract or pensioner.

The following information might be held for a permanent or regular employee

124

Personnel number
First name(s)
Surname
Title
Previous names
Category (e.g. permanent, casual, contract)
Date of birth
Sex (M or F)
Marital status (M – married, S – single, W – widowed,
    S – separated, D – divorced)
Home address
Home telephone number
Company (internal) telephone number
Grade
Post
Cost centre (e.g. personnel administration –   These three
    area office; region west)   fields may be
Division/department (e.g. finance, personnel,   interrelated.
    production, sales marketing)
Location (this is where an employee is based as distinct from the cost
    centre or budget centre)
Pay centre (where pay advice/cheque should be sent if different to
    location)
Salary scale
Salary point
Increment date (date on which the employee would normally move to the
    next point on an incremental scale)
Annual allowance (the allowance code and amount for each annual
    allowance to which the employee is entitled)
Automatic progression date
Employment status (e.g. full pay, half pay etc.)
Employment classification (e.g. managerial, clerical/admin., technical/
    operational)
Commencement date
Nationality
Ethnic group
Termination date
Reason for leaving (e.g. retirement, new job, death, dismissed)
Exit interview reason (reason for leaving organization as given at an exit
    interview e.g. better prospects, unhappy with boss, unhappy with
    company policy)
Expected retirement date
National insurance number
Private-health insurance number
Membership of company-promoted schemes (e.g. group life assurance,
    income protection scheme, benevolent society, credit union, savings
    club)
Details of authorized company loans to employee

Reference to sick leave file
Reference to disciplinary file (it is generally advisable to avoid all reference to disciplinary or similar records)
Trade union membership
Details of next-of-kin

In the case of casual or temporary employees it may only be necessary to hold a limited amount of information. If casual staff represent a significant proportion of the workforce it will be important to highlight this fact since it may impinge on system design and backing store requirements.

The type of information required for casual employees might comprise

Personnel number
Name
Home address
Telephone number
Date of birth
Sex
Commencement date
Expected date of termination of employment
Actual date of termination of employment
National insurance details
Grade
Post
Cost centre
Division/department
Location
Salary scale
Salary scale point
Pay centre
Reason for employment (e.g. replacement of employee on sick leave or maternity leave, or to cope with seasonal peak)

Salary records

Salary records deal with

- salary scales and their history
- annual allowances and their history
- employee current salary and allowances and the history of salary and allowance movement for each employee
- the implementation of general salary increases.

Salary scales

The salary of every employee should be derived from a salary scale held on the system. To achieve this, every salary scale in the organization must be set up on the system. This may sound straightforward but virtually every organization has its quirks. There will inevitably be overscale payments and personal salaries. Special scales may have to be set up to accommodate these exceptions and this should be considered early on in the course of system implementation.

The following information should be held for each scale

Scale number (e.g. 006)
Scale name (e.g. supervisor grade 5)
Effective date (date from which the scale applies)
Scale points (the system will have to cope with the number of points on the longest scale which exists or is likely to exist within the organization)
Reason for scale adjustment (e.g. sectional productivity agreement, or cost of living increase)

The system would be expected to hold a history of the changes to each scale. How far back this history should go is a subject for debate. If the organization has a large number of scales, history which goes back over many years will require a lot of file space and this may be a limiting factor. If history over, say, three years old would seldom be accessed on-line, instead of cluttering up the system it may be better available in paper form. It is probable that a salary book or salary card will have to be produced anyway and that old versions of this will provide the necessary history.

It is important, however, that the salary history is held on each employee indefinitely. This should be achieved by holding the scale, point on scale and actual salary at each change date on the employee record. In this way it is possible to dispense with older scales. An example of a screen layout for a single salary scale is shown in Figure 37.

A factor which may influence the extent to which scale history is held is the number of versions which can be conveniently printed or displayed on screen. If a large number of scales is involved, it may not be acceptable to print more than a single page per scale.

Annual allowances
The system will have to record details of all annual allowances which are in use and the individual employees who are entitled to be paid these allowances. The generic title for these allowances varies from organization to organization and it is important to understand just what is meant.

Basically they are allowances which tend to be expressed as an annual figure, are paid more or less automatically in the same way as basic wage or salary. They are generally paid for a reasonably long time period and an employee's record will note the entitlement to be paid the allowance. They are sometimes referred to as fixed annual allowances to distinguish them from temporary allowances, which are paid on a week-to-week or month-to-month basis. The entitlement to these temporary allowances is generally associated with the conditions of employment attached to a

ABC Manufacturing Co.

Salary scales enquiry

Scale No: 006   Supervisor Grade 5

Point on scale	Current 20/10/85	------------ *Previous values* ------------		
		16/03/85	31/12/84	16/03/84
01	8,608	8,341	8,098	7,900
02	8,934	8,657	8,405	8,200
03	9,261	8,974	8,713	8,500
04	9,587	9,290	9,020	8,800
05	9,915	9,608	9,328	9,100
06	10,242	9,924	9,635	9,400
07	10,569	10,241	9,943	9,700
08	10,896	10,558	10,250	10,000
09	11,223	10,875	10,558	10,300
10	11,549	11,191	10,865	10,600
11	11,876	11,508	11,173	10,900
12	12,094	11,719	11,378	11,100
13	12,312	11,930	11,583	11,300
14	12,531	12,142	11,778	11,500
15	12,758	12,353	11,993	11,700
	Cost of living 3.2%	Supervisors' agreement phase 2–3%	Cost of living 2.5%	Supervisors' agreement phase 1–5%

Figure 37   *Display of salary scales*

grade. Within the system they are held by grade and their value can be a parameterized value associated with grade. These allowances tend to be returned on a regular timesheet or attendance return.

Examples of each type of allowance are:

Annual
Motor car
Clothing
Overseas
Substitution (long term)
On-call
Temporary
Shift allowance
Meal allowance
Encroachment
Substitution (short term or *ad hoc* in nature)

The following information would be held for each annual allowance

Allowance code
Allowance name

ABC Manufacturing Co.

Annual allowances enquiry

Allowance No: 031   Overseas – Brussels

Value	Date of adjustment	Reason
Current – £1900	20/10/85	Cost of living 3.2%
1841	03/05/85	Review 10%
1673	31/12/84	Cost of living 2.5%
1632	30/09/84	Productivity agreement

Figure 38   *Display of annual allowances*

ABC Manufacturing Co.

Employee current salary and allowances enquiry

Personnel No. 43267   Whiteside John David

Salary scale: 006 (7,036–10,987)
Point: 08 (9,037)
Date: 15/10/85
Reason: Increment
Annual increment date: Oct. 15
Automatic progression date: 15/10/89
Total annual allowances: 1,530

Code	Allowance	Pensionable	Personal	Amount	Date
003	Overseas – Paris	No	No	1,100	20/03/85
004	Motor car	No	No	430	12/04/85

Figure 39   *Display of current salary and allowances for an employee*

Personal (generally this is a yes/no field: yes to indicate that the allowance is related to the individual rather than to the post which he holds)

Classification (e.g. pensionable or non-pensionable: this determines whether it should be treated in the same manner as salary or basic pay for pension purposes)

Method of adjustment (by negotiation, salary related or fixed)

Annual value

Date of adjustment

Reason for adjustment (e.g. general salary increases)

As with salary scales, the system should maintain a history of the changes which have occurred. An example of a screen layout for a single annual allowance, showing the current value and previous values, is given in Figure 38.

ABC Manufacturing Co.

Employee salary history enquiry

Personnel No. 43267   Whiteside John David

Cost centre:	Drawing office
Division:	Engineering
Post:	Draughtsperson grade 2 E 30203
Current salary:	032/07 £12,068
Annual allowances:	£ 1,047

Date	Salary		Grade	Cost Centre	Reason
31/12/85	032/07	£12,068	Draughtsperson grade 2	Drawing office	Increment
20/05/85	032/06	11,493	Draughtsperson grade 2	Drawing office	Productivity award 5%
31/12/84	032/06	10,946	Draughtsperson grade 2	Drawing office	Increment
20/09/84	032/05	10,646	Draughtsperson grade 2	Drawing office	Promotion
30/04/84	035/04	8,426	Draughtsperson grade 3	Drawing office	Promotion
31/12/83	046/03	5,987	Technical assistant	Design	Commenced

Figure 40   *Employee salary history display*

Employee salary and allowances

The system will be required to hold details of an employee's current salary and allowances (see Figure 39). It is also essential that it retain a history of salary movements over a number of years (see Figure 40). How far back the system should go in terms of holding salary history is also a subject for debate. Three options are available

1 Hold all movements indefinitely.
2 Hold only movements within the past *n* years as accessible through the normal system. History prior to a certain date is extracted from the main system and is then accessible from an archive file when required.
3 Only hold movements within the past *n* years and use hard copy or microfilm for older movement.

The method chosen will depend on a number of factors but either of the first two options is preferable to the third. If it is decided to hold all history it is important to ensure that this does not make the system more cumbersome to use. The screens on the system which display salary

Table 6

Date	Scale	Point	Amount	Reason
30/10/85	030	12	11,511	Increment
15/06/85	030	11	11,186	Productivity 3.7%
12/02/85	030	11	10,786	1984 Review 4.5%
30/10/84	030	11	10,322	Increment
12/01/84	030	10	10,022	1983 Review 3%
30/10/83	030	10	9,730	Increment

history should show the latest (current) salary first and work backwards (see Table 6).

It should then be possible to exit from this screen at any point. Some systems show history in the reverse order – the oldest on file first. In this case it should be possible to input a starting date with the enquiry request so that all the dates after the starting date are shown. For example, if 01/10/84 is the starting date the following sequence would be given for the dates shown in Table 6

30/10/84
12/02/85
15/06/85
30/10/85.

As well as showing the actual salary value it is important to show the scale number and point. Within a few years salary values quickly lose significance for review purposes – this is particularly true since the mid-1970s. The use of the scale and point along with the reason for salary change provides a much more satisfactory picture.

Another point to remember is that it is possible to have a number of salary values with the same implementation date. In this case it is essential to show which ones have been superseded, otherwise a very confusing situation will arise. The problem arises from the retrospective application of wage awards and is best described by means of an example.

Suppose an employee has the recent salary history shown in Table 7.

Table 7

Date	Scale	Point	Amount	Reason
30/10/85	028	05	13,261	Increment
15/05/85	028	04	12,961	Promotion
30/10/84	024	08	12,230	Increment

In December 1985, following protracted negotiations, a sectional agreement is signed which grants an 8 per cent salary increase backdated to 13 November 1984. The impact of this is shown in Table 8.

Table 8

Date	Scale	Point	Amount	Reason
30/10/85	028	05	14,322	Sectional agreement
30/10/85	028	05	13,261*	Increment
15/05/85	028	04	13,739	Sectional agreement
15/05/85	028	04	12,961*	Increment
13/11/84	024	08	13,208	Sectional agreement
30/10/84	024	08	12,230	Increment

*Superseded

ABC Manufacturing Co.

Employee allowance history enquiry

Personnel No. 43267   Whiteside John David

Cost centre:	Drawing office,	
Division:	Engineering	
Post:	Draughtsperson grade 2	E 30203
Current salary:	032/07 £12,068	
Annual allowances:	£ 1,047	

Date	Allowance type	Amount	Reason
21/05/85	005 Motor car	£1,000	Review
12/01/85	031 Drawing materials	£47	New allowance
20/09/84	005 Motor car	£800	Promotion
20/09/84	026 Protective clothing	0	Cancelled on promotion
31/12/83	026 Protective clothing	£150	Commencement

Figure 41   *Employee allowance history display*

This gives rise to two salary figures on both 15/05/85 and 30/10/85 and the system must show which one takes preference at these dates.

Generally speaking there is not the same requirement to hold a comprehensive history of allowances. It is usually sufficient to know what allowances have been paid to an employee and for what period. The main questions to be answered relate to the number of allowances in operation, and how significant they are in terms of an employee's total remuneration package. If they are significant and the computer system does not keep an adequate record of them a manual system will have to back it up. One of the objectives of introducing a CPMIS is to replace in as far as possible existing manual records so this should also be taken into account in deciding how to deal with allowance history. Figure 41 shows how an employee's allowance history could be displayed on screen.

General salary increases

Facilities which allow for the implementation of general salary increases are a very important part of a CPMIS. The procedure must be flexible enough to cater for a wide variety of agreement types. Salary scales and then individual employee salary will have to be updated. Under a manual system this is a very laborious process and is generally done under considerable pressure with pay staff working overtime because as soon as agreement of the payment terms has been reached the new rates must be reflected in pay packets as quickly as possible.

One of the major difficulties is that the terms of such agreements are seldom agreed prior to the date from which the terms apply. Consequently they are processed retrospectively, and since individual employee pay rates may already have changed between the application date and the implementation date complications will arise. The facilities which are normally provided by packages in this area are

1 A modelling facility.
2 The facility to apply general salary increases.

The modelling facility is the ability to get answers to questions such as 'How much will it cost to implement a 3.5 per cent increase for all staff?'. This is the type of question from the personnel director that the computer salesperson is delighted to hear. It can be demonstrated quite easily by applying 3.5 per cent to the individual salaries of everyone on the file, but not updating any of the records. In this way it is possible to then look at the impact of an alternative 5.5 per cent or even to apply a second phase of 2.5 per cent.

This is fine but a computer is hardly necessary to provide such answers and in reality such modelling must take a number of other factors into account, for example

● restrictions to particular grades or categories of employee
● the impact on earnings other than basic pay – overtime, shift payments etc.
● the implementation of annual increments.

The usefulness of such a facility can be gauged to some extent by asking key questions such as 'How will the facility assist me in the preparation of annual payroll budgets?'. The implementation of a general pay increase is usually fairly similar to the modelling facility, the only difference being that the files are updated. The procedure is that the parameters governing the increase are input to the system and these parameters are used to update the salary scales. As soon as the scales have been updated the system is instructed to apply the new scales to the relevant employees. Similar procedures apply to the updating of annual allowances, if there is sufficient of them to justify such an approach.

The implementation of general pay increases after the date from which the new rates apply causes problems for many personnel systems. Some of them can only cope when aided by a substantial amount of manual intervention and a complicated series of updates of scales and of individual employees. To illustrate the problem the impact on a single employee of a retrospective pay award is demonstrated.

George Cole is a draughtsperson grade 1 on scale 030, (this is the scale which applies to his grade). His recent salary history and the history of scale 030 are both shown in Figure 42. This shows his normal annual increment plus some special increases – annual reviews and a 3.7 per cent increase resulting from a productivity agreement. For the past few years staff in the drawing office have been negotiating a relativity claim. They claim that their rates of pay have not kept pace with comparative grades both inside and outside the organization. The claim has been processed by the normal internal negotiating machinery and eventually was adjudicated on by an independent arbitrator. The arbitrator's award is a 2.5 per cent relativity increase backdated to 1 January 1984. Since

		George Cole – draughtsperson grade 1 salary history		
		Annual salary		
Date	*Scale*	*Point*	*Amount*	*Reason for change*
30/10/85	030	12	11,511	Increment
15/06/85	030	11	11,186	Productivity agreement 3.7%
12/02/85	030	11	10,786	1984 review 4.5%
30/10/84	030	11	10,322	Increment
12/01/84	030	10	10,022	1983 review 3%
30/10/83	030	10	9,730	Increment

	Scale history – scale 030 – draughtsperson grade 1			
Point	*15/01/83*	*12/01/84*	*12/02/85*	*15/06/85*
1				
2				
3				
4				
5				
6				
7				
8				
9				
10	9,730	10,022	10,473	10,860
11	10,021	10,322	10,786	11,186
12	10,313	10,622	11,100	11,511
13				
14				
15				
	1982 review 3.5%	1983 review 3%	1984 review 4.5%	Productivity agreement 3.7%

Figure 42   *Retrospective pay award – position prior to implementation*

this date everyone on the relevant scales have had three special pay increases in addition to annual increments.

Figure 43 shows the impact on Scale 030 and on George Cole's salary history. From examining the impact on just one employee's record it is possible to gain some appreciation of the amount of work which has to be done to implement the award. Having implemented the award, arrears of basic pay will then have to be calculated and paid. Usually this is the responsibility of the payroll department rather than the personnel department but there are substantial benefits to be obtained by being in a position to provide the following information to the payroll section

Employee number   48639
Name   George Cole

George Cole — draughtsperson grade 1

SALARY HISTORY

ANNUAL SALARY

Date	Scale	Point	Amount	Reason for change	
30/10/85	030	12	11,799	Relativity 2.5%	
30/10/85	030	12	11,511	Increment	Superseded
15/06/85	030	11	11,465	Relativity 2.5%	
15/06/85	030	11	11,186	Productivity 3.7%	Superseded
12/02/85	030	11	11,056	Relativity 2.5%	
12/02/85	030	11	10,786	1984 review 4.5%	Superseded
30/10/84	030	11	10,580	Relativity 2.5%	
30/10/84	030	11	10,322	Increment	Superseded
12/01/84	030	10	10,272	Relativity 2.5%	
12/01/84	030	10	10,022	1983 review 3%	Superseded
01/01/84	030	10	9,973	Relativity 2.5%	
30/10/83	030	10	9,730	Increment	

Scale history — scale 030 — draughtsperson grade 1

Point	15/01/83	01/01/84	12/01/84	12/01/84	12/02/85	12/02/85	15/06/85	15/06/85
10	9,730	9,973	10,022	10,272	10,473	10,735	10,860	11,132
11	10,021	10,272	10,322	10,580	10,786	11,056	11,186	11,465
12	10,313	10,571	10,622	10,888	11,100	11,378	11,511	11,799
1982 review 3.5%	Relativity 2.5%	1983 review 3% Superseded	Relativity 2.5%	1984 review 4.5% Superseded	Relativity 2.5%	Productivity 3.7% Superseded	Relativity 2.5%

Figure 43 *Retrospective pay award – position after implementation*

Grade	030 draughtsperson grade 1
Cost centre	4306 drawing office
Old salary	scale 030
	point 12
	amount £11,511
New salary	scale 030
	point 12
	amount £11,799
Comment	implementation of 2.5% relativity award from 1/1/84
Arrears for period from	01/01/84
to	01/01/86
	£526.19

The degree of effort required to calculate the arrears manually can be gauged from examining Figure 44. The process will also have to take account of such factors as

```
┌──────────────────────────────────────────────────────────────────────┐
│                                                                        │
│                  George Cole – draughtsperson grade 1                  │
│                                                                        │
│                  Calculation of arrears due on                         │
│                  implementation of 2.5% relativity award               │
│                  from 1/1/84 to payroll period starting                │
│                  1/1/86                                                 │
│                                                                        │
│                                                                        │
│   Dates            Days      New       Old      Annual     Arrears     │
│                    involved  salary    salary   increase               │
│                                                                        │
│                    £         £         £        £          £           │
│                                                                        │
│   01/01/84 - 12/01/84   11     9,973    9,730     243        7.32       │
│   12/01/84 - 30/10/84  250    10,272   10,022     294      201.37       │
│   30/10/84 - 12/02/85  106    10,580   10,322     258       74.93       │
│   12/02/85 - 15/06/85  122    11,056   10,786     270       90.25       │
│   15/06/85 - 30/10/85  136    11,465   11,186     279      103.96       │
│   30/10/85 - 01/01/86   62    11,799   11,511     288       48.92       │
│                                                                        │
│           ↑                      ↑                         £526.19      │
│      Payroll effective                                        ↑        │
│      date                                                              │
│                         Annual salary to be                            │
│                         used in payroll system                         │
│                         from 1/1/86            Arrears of basic         │
│                                                to be paid in            │
│                                                first payslip            │
│                                                in January 1986          │
│                                                                        │
└──────────────────────────────────────────────────────────────────────┘
```

Figure 44   *Retrospective pay award – calculations of arrears*

- employees who have joined the drawing office since the date from which the award applies
- relevant employees who are no longer on the appropriate scales but who have been on them at some time during the period
- pensioners whose pension may be related to the current rates applicable to their grade at the date of retirement.

Figure 45 shows the processing sequence involved in implementing a general pay increase. A typical screen layout for inputting the parameters to the processing screen is shown in Figure 46.

Absence

A well-developed absence subsystem is an essential part of any CPMIS. It is, however, an aspect which can cause problems at the implementation stage and if this leads to inaccurate or incomplete absence reporting the whole system may become suspect and other reports emanating from the system may not be treated seriously. The problem can arise where proper

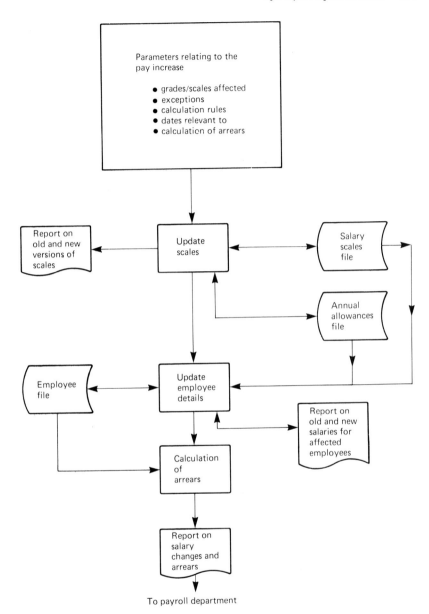

Figure 45 *General pay increase process*

ABC Manufacturing Co.

*Implementation of general pay increases
adjustment of salary scale*

Salary scales to which increase should be applied – all scales [   ] (*Y* or *N*)

Scale ranges	[	] to [	], [	] to [	]		
	[	] to [	], [	] to [	]		
Individual scales	[	], [	], [	], [	]		
	[	], [	], [	], [	]		
	[	], [	], [	], [	]		

Specification of increase:
Percentage of basic salary   [   ] (Format 99.99)
Plus annual value   [   ]
Minimum increase p.a.   [   ]
Maximum increase p.a.   [   ]

Application date   [   ]
Description of increase   [   ]

Update files [   ] (*Y* or *N*)

Figure 46   *Parameters for implementing a general pay increase – salary scales*

procedures for returning details of all absence throughout the organization either do not exist or where they do exist they are not being enforced. There is no point saying 'We now have a computer system and we must get the returns in'. This is too late. A much better approach is to say 'We are starting to look at computerization now. We will have a system operational in about twelve months' time and within the next six months we must ensure that every section is submitting its returns accurately and properly every week'. Unless this happens the GIGO (garbage in garbage out) syndrome will rule. Absence recording and reporting should as a general rule cover all types of absence, but annual leave may be the exception to the rule. The various absence types should be set up as parameters in the descriptor file. This should allow for growth in the number of types of leave and should also determine how the various types should be treated for establishment reporting purposes. The following rules might apply

- long-term leave without pay will give rise to a vacancy of a certain type
- short-term leave without pay will give rise to a short-term vacancy
- maternity leave may also give rise to a short-term vacancy
- sick leave and annual leave will not impact on establishment at all.

The two types of leave which deserve most consideration are annual leave and sick leave.

Annual leave

Usually it is only appropriate to hold details of annual leave taken within a CPMIS if this is currently the practice under the existing system. If a regular weekly absence return, which includes annual leave taken, is received by the personnel division from all departments in the organization then it is sensible to input this data into the system. If, on the other hand, control of annual leave is decentralized, there is very little point in trying to change the system. In this case record-keeping is the responsibility of department managers and the role of the personnel management division is to ensure that each employee is given the statutory amount of leave within the specified period and that the organization's own rules governing when leave should be taken and how much leave, if any, can be carried forward into the following leave year are observed.

This can also be achieved by getting an annual return from each department manager but there is very little benefit to be derived from inputting this data. Where weekly or other regular reports are received the computer can provide some benefits. An employee's annual leave entitlement can be determined by the system by examining the conditions of employment which are attached to the employee's grade. Thus it is possible to keep a complete annual leave record for an employee. The system can then produce reports on the pattern of annual leave in all departments and can highlight areas where there is still a lot of annual leave to be taken before the end of the leave year. Figure 47 is an example of an enquiry screen showing an employee's annual leave record.

If an organization's annual leave year runs from January to December a report could be produced around the beginning of October highlighting areas where there is still a lot of leave to be taken before the end of the year (see Figure 48). After the departments involved have been informed, this report could be produced a number of times between then and the end of December to see the impact of the exhortation.

ABC Manufacturing Co.

Employee annual leave enquiry

Personnel No. 43267   Whiteside John David
Grade 023   Supervisor grade 5   A/L Entitlement 21 days

Start	Finish	Days	Balance
01/01/85	–	3.0 c/f from 1984	3.0
01/01/85	–	21.0 1985 entitlement	24.0
13/03/85	13/03/85	0.5	23.5
03/06/85	12/06/85	10.0	13.5
22/07/85	26/07/85	5.0	8.5
29/08/85	30/08/85	2.0	6.5

Figure 47 *Employee annual leave enquiry*

ABC Manufacturing Co.

Annual leave review report 1/10/85

To: Director of Finance

The following is a list of employees in your division who still have more than three days annual leave to be taken between now and the end of December.

Director of Personnel

Department	Employee	Balance Jan. 1	Entitlement	Taken	Balance
Management	Brown J.R.	3.0	20.0	15.0	8.0
accounts	Davies T.K.	0.0	20.0	10.0	10.0
	Fitzroy Bob	0.0	23.0	15.0	8.0
Cashier	Blake Miss R.	1.0	18.0	2.5	16.5
	Stuart M.	3.0	18.0	15.0	6.0
Payroll	Hill Alan	0.0	20.0	13.0	7.0
	Rankin Norman	0.0	21.0	15.0	6.0
	Templeton W.A.	5.5	18.0	5.0	18.5
Receivables	Dillon P.	0.0	21.0	15.0	6.0
	Elgar Thos.	2.5	20.0	18.0	4.5

Figure 48   *Report on annual leave outstanding*

Sick leave

Treatment of sick leave input should be related to the organization's sick leave rules and regulations. These rules are generally specified in the parameter file and deal with such items as

- the number of days sick absence in a given period which are allowed without a doctor's certificate
- the number of days sick absence in a year which triggers off a review of pay
- the number of days sick leave in a period of four years allowed before pay is automatically reduced.

These rules determine how long sick leave history must be held in the system e.g. a rolling four years to meet the requirements set out above.

Data input from the sick leave return might consist of

Personnel number
Illness start date
Illness finish date
Number of days
Certified or uncertified
Illness type
Payment code

A number of points must be made concerning some of these data items.

1 *Start and finish date* Provision must be made for continuing illness and for certification to a date after the end of the period covered by the return.
2 *Number of days* The system can calculate the elapsed days based on the start and finish dates and it can be programmed to either count or ignore certain days e.g. Saturday and Sunday. It will be necessary to override this calculation to cater for half days and in certain cases of unusual rostering arrangements it may also be necessary to amend the system calculation.
3 *Certification* Provision should be made to allow for the subsequent certification of illness for which an appropriate certificate was not available at the date of the return. The possibility of getting a certificate prior to sick leave must also be provided for e.g. a planned period of hospitalization.
4 *Illness type* Illness types are again parameter values as held in the descriptor file. Where it is appropriate to input this data provision must be made to allow for changing it subsequently if necessary.
5 *Payment code* If, for example, the sick leave rules state that the employee remains on full pay for a certain period and then moves on to a phased pay reduction this facility would allow for conveniently overriding these rules in certain circumstances.

In some systems it is not possible to amend or delete sick leave data once it is input or to cope conveniently with continuing sick leave. It should be possible to cope with these situations because

- all data will not always be available at the date when the return is due to be made
- mistakes will invariably be made which will have to be corrected.

Outputs which this subsystem should produce are

1 *Illness statistics*
   - number of days lost by each department or division (Figure 49)
   - analysis of days lost by calendar month or budget period
   - analysis of days lost by day of week
   - number of days attributable to each illness type
   - number of days lost analysed by grade, employee age, occupation, region, staff category (permanent, contract etc.).
2 Report on staff approaching or who have exceeded certain limits. (e.g. seven uncertified days in one year).
3 Report on employees with high number of absences recorded.
4 Report highlighting employees with a number of one-day or half-day absences occurring on Fridays or Mondays. Such a report may be of value in the case of staff who work a Monday to Friday week. Where other working patterns are in operation the key days to examine are the ones at either end of the work period.
5 Lists of departments which have not been submitting sick leave returns. (A return should be made for every period – if there are no absences a 'nil return' should be submitted.)

ABC Manufacturing Co.   29/10/85

Sick leave report for: personnel division

Cost centre: Personnel administration: 4 weeks ended 27/10/85

Name	No.	Start	Finish	Days	Cert.	Uncert.
J. Roberts	10347	07/10/85	13/10/85	7.0	7.0	–
N. Jenkins	12468	09/10/85	09/10/85	0.5	–	0.5
J. Carter	12793	22/10/85	28/10/85	7.0	7.0	–
I. Cooper	20497	21/10/85	22/10/85	2.0	–	2.0
Cost centre total				16.5	14.0	2.5
Cost Centre: Industrial Relations						
R. Binns	09786	08/10/85	09/10/85	2.0	–	2.0
O. Clegg	12539	14/10/85	14/10/85	1.0	–	1.0
R. Anderson	17864	21/10/85	21/10/85	1.0	–	1.0
Cost centre total				4.0	0.0	4.0
Cost Centre: Staff welfare						
G. Stewart	11213	07/10/85	27/10/85	21.0	21.0	–
H. Wilson	17216	07/10/85	13/10/85	7.0	7.0	–
K. Burgess	21314	14/10/85	14/10/85	1.0	–	1.0
Cost centre total				29.0	28.0	1.0
Cost Centre: Training						
B. Cole	10369	14/10/85	20/10/85	7.0	7.0	–
H. Kemp	21385	14/10/85	15/10/85	1.5	–	1.5
M. Howarth	21511	24/10/85	25/10/85	1.5	–	1.5
Cost centre total				10.0	7.0	3.0
Total for division				59.5	49.0	10.5

Figure 49   *Divisional sick leave return*

6 Standard letters to employees whose sickness record takes them over any of the boundaries specified in the regulations.

7 Lists of employees on reduced pay because of sickness.

The enquiry screens showing details of an employee's sickness record should show

• a summary of the sick absences designed to coincide with the organization's rules and regulations.

• details of all individual periods of sick absence.

Figure 50 provides an example of an enquiry screen showing an employee's record.

The use of illness types within the system must be very carefully considered. In some organizations this information concerning indi-

---

ABC Manufacturing Co.

Employee sick leave enquiry

Personnel No. 43267   Whiteside John David

	Last 12 months		*Last 4 years*	
Sick file ref. W426	Days certified	12.0	Days certified	105.0
	Days uncertified	3.0	Days uncertified	20.0
			Full pay	110.0
			Half Pay	15.0
			Days unpaid	0.0

Start	*Finish*	*Days*	*Certified*	
12/11/85	15/11/85	4.0	Y	Number of separate
18/10/85	18/10/85	0.5	N	Mondays
11/10/85	11/10/85	0.5	N	In 12 months – 1
18/09/85	20/09/85	3.0	Y	In 4 years – 3
17/06/85	18/06/85	2.0	N	Number of separate Fridays
12/01/85	16/01/85	5.0	Y	In 12 months – 0
03/02/84	15/02/84	13.0	Y	In 4 years – 1

Figure 50   *Employee sick leave enquiry*

vidual employees is held within the medical department and does not form part of the personnel records system. Where it is input to a CPMIS it must be recognized that this is probably the most sensitive piece of information held in the system so confidentiality should be assured. In general employee enquiry screens should not include any reference to illness type and the data should only be used for overall analysis purposes.

11 Pension records

Whether pension scheme records form part of a single CPMIS or are maintained in a separate system depends on a number of factors including

1 The organization structure – where responsibility for pension scheme administration rests within it.
2 The size of the organization – a larger organization will be more likely to have a separate pension department which is seen as having a certain amount of independence from other functional areas.
3 The age of the organization – the ratio of pensioners to serving staff will generally be higher in older organizations.

Pension records in the context of a CPMIS are concerned with

* keeping records of each employee's pensionable service and any contributions made to the pension fund
* providing the data required for actuarial analysis
* paying the pensioners.

Since payment of pensions is a payroll-type operation it is usually handled by a separate payroll system. It is often the case that the payment system has been computerized for some time before computerization of the records and administrative aspects is considered.

A number of specialist pension administration packages are available and their general features are described below. The pension fund requirements of a CPMIS as outlined are geared towards making the best use of the data that is already held on the personnel database with a limited number of items being added specifically for pension fund purposes. Some of the requirements of pension fund administration can be quite complex and this can give rise to two potential problems

1 A great deal of effort can be devoted to catering for situations which

ABC Manufacturing Co.

Employee pension scheme data

Personnel No. 43267   Whiteside John David
Cost centre: Drawing office
Division: Engineering
Post: Draughtsperson grade 2   E30203
Salary scale: 412 (8657–12,482) since 20/09/85: £11,297 increment

Pensionable service with ABC
Normal service   15.0216 years
Recovered service   0.0201 years
Extra service purchased   <u>2.5000</u> years
          Total   17.5417

Pensionable service in other organizations

	From	To	
ABC Overseas Ltd	01/01/68	31/12/68	1.0000 years
Design Services Ltd	01/07/64	31/12/67	3.5000 years

Contributions to fund to date

	Normal	£8,326.50
	Additional	£1,036.00

Figure 51   *Display of pension scheme data for employee*

might arise but do so infrequently. In order to service these requirements the systems development effort required, the increased complexity of the system, and the additional data which it is necessary to
input may be out of proportion to the potential benefits which are
likely to accrue.
2 The requirements of pension administration could take over the
system. This can result in the pension tail wagging the personnel dog
and the main purpose of the system may tend to be lost sight of.

In the case of serving employees the following data may be relevant (see
Figure 51).

Personnel number. (Again it should be stressed that the same number
should apply through the employee's life or association with the
organization.)
Name
Home address
Marital status
Name of spouse
Date of birth of spouse
Next-of-kin details
Sex
Children (Details of children may be held on a separate children's file.

This data can be difficult to maintain. If the only reason for holding the data is to provide for actuarial valuation of the scheme it may be worth trying to have the actuary accept national or other norms rather than devote a lot of effort to trying to maintain the accuracy of this data. On the other hand if the organization is involved in paying some form of child allowances this data may have to be maintained anyway.)

Salary details

Grade

Date of entry to scheme (the system should allow for exit and re-entry dates)

Contribution rate

Pension contributions to date (this should cater for special contributions such as are involved in buying extra service)

Pensionable service (The system should allow for any facility to buy extra service through special contributions, and buying back periods of non-pensionable service e.g. temporary employment or strike periods.)

Transferred service (The system should cater for any arrangements which allow an employee who joins the organization to bring with him/her pensionable service accumulated in previous employments. This involves holding perhaps a number of entries for an employee and maintaining a file containing the code and the names of each company involved. This approach will enable the organization to list all previous service credited by reference to previous employers. This can be useful for negotiating service transfer agreements e.g. between companies in the group.)

Preserved pension (details of former employees who, having left the organization, still retain rights to a pension at some future stage)

In order to keep contributions efficiently up to date there should be a link between the organization's payroll system and the CPMIS. In this way the process can be automated completely.

For pensions the following additional data may be required

Status (e.g. pensioner, spouse, ex-gratia pension)

Lump sum paid on retirement

Date of resignation from scheme

Normal retirement date

Last day of service

Period on which pensionable service is based

Remuneration on which pension is based (salary scale, point on scale, pensionable allowances). This data will be relevant if there is an arrangement whereby the pension paid is adjusted in line with general pay increases.

If the database is to serve for payment purposes it will have to hold further data such as tax and bank account details if credit transfers are involved. The following reports produced by the CPMIS will be useful in the administration of the pension scheme (see Figures 52 and 53)

Pension scheme membership listing 20/11/85

Personnel No.	Name	Cost centre	Sex	Marital status	Eligible children	Date of birth	Age	Date joined scheme	Date left scheme	Service to date (yrs)	Pensionable salary	Contributions to date
12468	J. Hatch	4306	M	M	3	200345	40	120165	–	20.8241	£17,401	£8,432
13469	T. Browne	2046	M	S	–	230565	20	180683	–	2.5736	£ 9,210	£1,031
15468	M. Rankin	3047	F	S	–	180360	25	240580	–	5.5321	£12,040	£2,976

Figure 52   *Sample report – pension scheme membership listing*

ABC Manufacturing Co.   20/11/85

Analysis of active members of pension scheme

Age	Total	Under 20	20–30	31–40	41–50	51–60	61–65	Over 65
Male	1977	402	306	509	312	208	210	30
Female	1103	387	286	147	103	97	80	3
Total	3080	789	592	656	415	305	290	33

Salary	Total	Under £8000	£8000–9000	£9001–10,000	£10,001–12,000	£12,001–14,000	£14,001–16,000	Over £16,000
Male	1977	302	288	148	217	306	407	309
Female	1103	280	317	120	80	105	98	103
Total	3080	582	605	268	297	411	505	412

Pensionable service	Total	Under 5	5–10	11–20	21–30	31–40	41–43	Over 43
Male	1977	530	350	308	379	209	103	98
Female	1103	425	310	192	61	52	40	23
Total	3080	955	660	500	440	261	143	121

Figure 53   *Sample report – age, salary and pensionable service analysis*

ABC Pension scheme

Benefit statement at: 25/11/86

No.:   38487
Name: J.D. Conway
Date of birth: 20/10/1943
Cost centre: Central stores
Marital status: Married
Date joined scheme: 12/01/63   Retirement date: 20/10/2008
Normal service: 23.8326   Grade: STORES MANAGER
(years)   Annual pensionable
Purchased service: –   allowances: £1577
(years)   Children under 18 years: 3
Transferred service: –
(years)
Total pensionable
service: 23.8326
Contributions
to-date (normal):   £23,068.78
Contributions
to-date (extra):   –

On the basis of present salary and allowances you would be entitled to a pension of £13,650 p.a. and a lump sum of £20,360.

If you retire now on grounds of ill-health your annual pension will be £8900.

If you leave before reaching 65 you would at present have an entitlement to a deferred pension of £7890 p.a.

If you resign from the scheme now your contributions refund net of income tax will be £20,368.24.

In the event of death in service your dependants would currently receive a lump sum of £59,300 and your widow would receive an annual pension of £6300 p.a.

If you have any queries please contact the pensions scheme office at extension number 2017.

J.M. Davis
Manager Pension Scheme

Figure 54   *Benefit statement*

1 Age profile of members.
2 List of dependants.
3 Benefit statements for all members.
4 Actuarial analysis of membership – profiles by sex, age, service, salary
5 Diary reports
  • impending retirements
  • children reaching a certain age

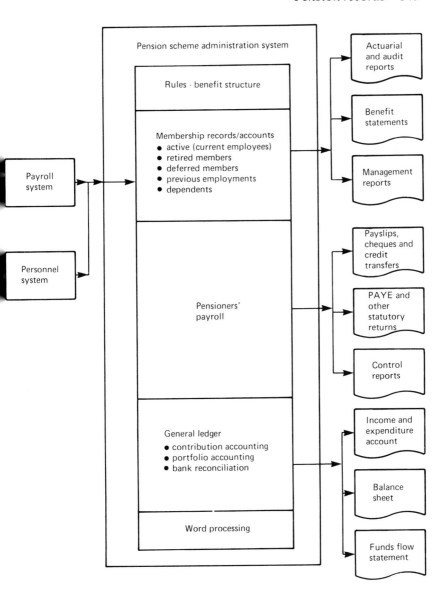

Figure 55 *Pension scheme administration system*

- long-service achievement dates
- impending pensioner verifications (confirmation that the pensioner is still living).

6 Lists of employees over normal retirement age but still working.

A dedicated pension administration system embraces every aspect of the business not just a record of members and their rights (see Figure 55). It would include a full payroll system for pensioners and a general ledger system to handle all of the accounting records of the scheme including records of its investment portfolio.

Actuarial requirements

The pension scheme actuary requires detailed information concerning the membership of the scheme in order to arrive at an assessment of the viability of the scheme. Obtaining and classifying data from manual records is very time-consuming, so having access to the data held in a computer-based system is of great benefit to the actuary.

The system should be capable of providing reports which will provide the data in a meaningful manner. If the data can be transferred, e.g. via magnetic tape, to the actuary's computer this may assist even further.

The following reports are typical of those required for actuarial purposes

1 A list of all members of the scheme as at valuation date and in date of birth sequence showing
   • date of birth
   • sex
   • marital status
   • date of commencement of pensionable service
   • period of pensionable service recovered
   • additional pensionable service purchased
   • pensionable service transferred from other organizations.
   • total normal contributions to scheme (total to date)
   • total additional voluntary contributions to the scheme
   • pensionable salary and allowances as at valuation date
   • pensionable salary and allowances as at previous valuation date.
2 A list of all members in receipt of a pension as at valuation date in date of birth sequence including
   • date of birth
   • sex
   • marital status
   • date of birth of spouse
   • date of commencement of pension
   • annual amount of pension as at valuation date
   • annual amount of pension as at previous valuation date.
3 A list of all members who are entitled to a deferred pension as at the validation date. Again this report would be in date of birth sequence and would contain
   • date of birth
   • sex
   • marital status
   • date of birth of spouse
   • date pension due to commence

- annual amount of pension.

4　A list of all members who are not currently in the scheme but who have been members of the scheme since the date of the last actuarial valuation. This list would show

- date of birth
- sex
- marital status
- date of birth of spouse
- date of entry to scheme
- date of exit from scheme
- nature of exit (e.g. retirement, death, withdrawal from scheme).

5　A list of each person who was in receipt of a pension at any time since the last actuarial valuation but who is not currently in receipt of a pension. This list should contain

- date of birth
- sex
- marital status
- date of retirement
- date of cessation of pension (death).

6　A similar list showing each person who was entitled to a deferred pension at any time since the last evaluation and who does not feature on the list described at (3) above. This list should contain

- date of birth
- sex
- marital status
- date of death/retirement.

It is clear from these requirements that the system should retain the date of the last actuarial evaluation and should also retain the records of all relevant movement since the date of the last evaluation.

12 Recruitment

The recruitment subsystem is an important element of any CPMIS. Its degree of importance is obviously related to the level of recruitment, the response to recruitment drives in terms of the number of applicants, and the level of internal staff movement. It may well be that this area offers the greatest scope for streamlining administrative procedures and for realizing real gains in terms of manpower savings. The extent of these savings will to some extent depend on the efficiency of the recruitmen administration system prior to computerization. If a good word processing system is in use, savings may already have been achieved.

By its nature recruitment activity tends to come in waves and very few organizations can manage to spread the activity evenly throughout the year. The activity may coincide with seasonal peak activity, with the fluctuations of contract work or with the publication of examination results. Once a recruitment campaign gets under way there will be peaks of activity within the campaign – in this context campaign is taken to mean any competiton or series of competitions which attracts a large number of applicants. In the current employment climate an advertisment placed by a well-established organization seeking secretarial or clerical staff may attract several thousand applications.

As soon as the applications start to arrive they have to be acknowledged and then letters have to be sent out either inviting applicants for interview or informing them that they have not been successful in reaching the interview stage. All of this must be done quickly and efficiently and then the activity on the administrative front will be reduced as the interview phase commences.

Recruitment should be an obvious integral part of any CPMIS but many systems ignore it completely. In some cases this may not cause problems and it can be dealt with by a stand-alone word processing based system. However, if a primary objective of the CPMIS is to attempt to integrate personnel information, the links between al

152

aspects of the system must be close. The recruitment process is activated by the creation of a vacancy within the organization. The administrative procedures involved in authorizing a vacancy or the filling of vacant post must ensure that the decisions are reflected within the establishment subsystem, otherwise there will no proper control over staff numbers. Establishment reporting must take account of the status of competitions to fill authorized vacancies and as soon as offers have been made this fact should be reflected in reports.

Many vacancies will be filled by internal competition only and there will also be applications from existing staff members for positions which are open to external applicants. In these cases data from the personnel records sub-system should be used, to avoid duplicating the input of data which is already held within the system. The system should also be in a position to maintain a record of all positions which an employee applied for, the date of the competition and an indication of the result for the employee. In the case of external applicants when the person eventually becomes an employee a certain amount of data will already have been generated, including the remuneration and conditions of employment, and this should form the basis of the new employee's record in the system. The interrelationship between the recruitment subsystem and the rest of the CPMIS is shown in Figure 56.

When an offer of employment is eventually made to a candidate the letter produced by the system should include the conditions of employment relevant to the post. This is obtained by reference initially to the abbreviated conditions which the system should hold for display on enquiries relating to existing employees. These summary conditions should point to a file or an area on the database which contains a detailed description of conditions.

Competitions

The following data would typically be held for each competition set up on the system.

1 *Competition number* This is a unique number attached to each competition. It could be a simple four or five digit number with the numbers allocated consecutively as competitions are set up. While there should not be tendency slavishly to follow procedures and methods used under an existing manual system, if an established competition numbering system is in operation it may be appropriate to use it. An example from such a numbering system is 85/027 which indicates the year of the competition and the number of the competition within that year. This is a worthwhile idea but generally a number which includes a department code should be avoided. This could give rise to confusion and it is better that the department be held as an attribute of the competition, i.e. as a separate field on the competition record.

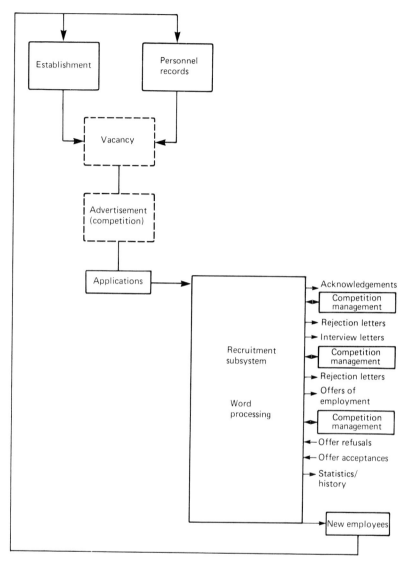

Figure 56   *Recruitment cycle*

2 *Competition name*   e.g. deputy director of personnel.
3 Internal or external.
4 *Competition status*   This indicates one of the various stages which a competition goes through. These stages are held as status codes and their interpretation should be held in the system's descriptor file.

These codes should cater for all possible stages although for practical reasons it may be sensible to group these stages into blocks. Typical stages are

- open
- closed (after closing date)
- first interview in progress
- second interviews in progress
- short list
- offers sent out
- closed – competition over.

5 Closing date for receipt of applications.

6 *Interview dates* from — to — These dates can be related to the status of the competition e.g. first or second interviews.

7 *Interview location* See the corresponding field in the next section relating to information held about applicants.

8 Number of vacancies.

9 *Recruiter* The code or name of the recruiter responsible for the competition.

10 *Note* This is a free-format comments field, for example 'A panel will be created as a result of this competition'.

It may be appropriate to hold summary details relating to the competition on this file e.g. number of applicants, number called for first interview, number called for second interview etc.

Job applicants

The following is the type of data which should be held for each candidate

1 *Application number* This is a number which must be unique within a competition but otherwise should have no real significance.

2 *Competition number* The number of the competition to which the application refers.

3 *Internal/external applicant* This field holds either 'yes' or 'no'. If the answer is 'yes' the system should expect the employee's personnel number to be input and it will then retrieve the name, cost centre/ location, grade, sex, date of birth, and any other data which is necessary. Otherwise the system should expect the remaining data to be input.

4 Applicant's name.

5 Address of applicant.

6 Sex.

7 Phone number.

8 *Source code* This code relates to how the application arose e.g. advertisement in a particular newspaper or journal.

9 Date of acknowledgement of application.

10 *Occupation code* This relates to one of the codes which would be set up on the descriptor file to classify all of the occupations relevant to the organization. This is used for analysis purposes and could be used for searching for people with particular occupation codes, e.g.

'How many chemical engineers do we have and how many are on recruitment panels following last season's interviews?'

11 *Application status*   This is similar to the competition status except that it relates to an individual applicant within a competition. Typical statuses are

- application form sent out
- application received
- application acknowledged
- letter of regret sent out
- called for interview
- interviewed – hold
- called for second interview
- letter of regret sent out
- placement on panel
- offer made
- offer accepted
- offer declined
- new offer made
- new offer accepted
- new offer declined
- awaiting medical report
- awaiting references
- all clear.

Once an offer is made it may be necessary to reflect this in establishment reports. Rather than assign fixed codes to this status and later statuses it is better to assign an attribute code to each status and this determines how it should be treated by the system.

12 *Interview date and time*   This relates to the next interview due as indicated by the application status code, e.g. second interview.

13 *Interview location*   This can be a free-form input field or can be a code related to an entry in the descriptor file (e.g. interview room 1 or Park Hotel). This data should perhaps be held at competition level but there should still be a facility to supersede the competition location for individual applicants.

14 *Note*   This is a free-format comment field available for entering any particular notes concerning an applicant e.g. 'Not available for interview during July'.

The system in operation

The design of the system should ideally allow for the replacement of all manual operations associated with recruitment by computer operations. The extent to which this can be achieved may relate to the total budget for the system (the availability of VDUs and high quality printers) and the significance of recruitment activity in the total personnel workload. The aim of the system should be to eliminate completely or reduce to an absolute minimum any other record-keeping or diarying. The design of the system should take account of this so that, for example, when the application status is being changed to 'called for inter-views' it will require that the date and time of interview be input. This is then used in providing letters for all applicants with the 'called for interview' status code.

Apart from the staff involved in recruitment administration, the re-cruiters or interviewers must also be involved in the design of the procedures around the system. The forms used in recording the decision of the interview board and in advising of the employment terms to be offered to successful applicants must be integrated into the overall personnel procedures.

Enquiries

The system must allow for easy access to any competition or applicant, but especially to the applications. The competition file itself will hold comparatively little data – mainly identification data and the overall status of the competition. The main need will be to access the applica-tion file and this must be possible in a number of ways. The questions which should be answered instantly by a VDU display include

- 'Who are applicants for the Welfare Officer job?'
- 'Has Joe Bloggs applied for production manager job?'

ABC Manufacturing Co.

Job applicant enquiry

Competition: 0142   Quality controller   External
Closing date: 15/08/86 Vacancies: 1
Status: First interviews in progress

Application No. 86/031   Status: Called for first interview

Joseph P. Bloggs   Interview date: 29/01/86 (Wed.)
25 Greenville Drive   time: 11.30
Birmingham B31 2RW   venue: Conf. room 3

Date application received: 08/01/86
Date application acknowledged: 15/01/86
Phone numbers – Home 082–486–3021   Business:

Sex: Male   Occupation: 20 Industrial chemist

Internal applicant – No.   Cost centre
                           Post

Note: Unsuccessful applicant for chief chemist post last August
       (competition 1047)

Figure 57   *Display of job applicant record*

ABC Manufacturing Co.   29/01/86

Interview schedule for competition
0152 – budget accountant

Recruiter: Martin Ryall
Closing date: 22/01/86   Vacancies: 1
Status: First interviews
Note: Chief accountant will be away for the month of March

Day	Date	Time	Venue	Application Number	Name	Internal
Wednesday	22/02/86	09.15	Interview room 1	017	John Warren	No
		10.15	Interview room 1	023	T.F. Gibson	No
		11.15	Interview room 1	047	P.R. Carson	Yes
		12.15	Interview room 1	031	A.R. Smith	No
		14.30	Conference room 3	009	T. Weatherall	No
		15.30	Conference room 3	013	Thos. Davies	No
		16.30	Conference room 3	014	M. Haydock	Yes
Thursday	23/02/86	09.00	Conference room 3	019	H. Collins	Yes
		10.00	Conference room 3	021	S. Whitehead	No
		11.30	Conference room 3	027	S. Philips	No
		12.30	Conference room 3	033	R.A. Richards	No
Friday	24/02/86	14.00	Conference room 3	038	B. Rees	No
		15.30	Conference room 3	041	W. Bates	No

Figure 58 *Competition interview schedule*

- 'What jobs has Joe Bloggs applied for recently – was he on the short list for the design job?'
- 'Which engineers have applied for jobs recently?'

All of these requests require that access to the application file be provided via a number of keys *viz.*

- application number
- competition number
- applicant name
- occupation code.

Figure 57 shows a typical screen display of a job applicant. This screen could be obtained by requesting it by application number. However, such numbers are unlikely to be known by anyone except those directly involved in the administration of the competition. Once a particular method of access is chosen it should be possible to move on to the rest of the records using this sequence simply by depressing a particular key e.g. RETURN or SEND. This shows one of the reasons why application numbers should be allocated in a logical fashion. The most usual methods of accessing this data is by applicant name or competiton number and any recruitment system should provide for them.

Reporting
Reporting from the recruitment system consists of three types

- letters to applicants
- administrative reports
- management reports.

Letters are produced by the letter production or word processing facilities of the system. It involves the merging of the data from the competitions file and applications file – determined by status codes – with standard letters held on the system. Procedures in this area should be very tight to ensure that everything happens in the correct sequence and that nothing can be overlooked. Once a status code on an application record is changed to indicate that the applicant is to be called for interview, the procedures should insist that the relevant letter is produced. These procedures can be completely automated or they can be a combination of computer and external control procedures.

Administrative reports should be produced by the system to enable the recruitment administration section to manage their work effectively. Such reports will include

1 List of applicants called for interview – showing the date and time (Figure 58) – by competiton.
2 List of applicants for a competition to be sent with the application forms to the recruiter and on which the decision to call for interview or reject can be entered.
3 List of applicants called for interview – by venue and date.

Such reports supplement the on-line system and provide a good service to the recruiters. Telephone enquiries from applicants, such as the following, will be answered by reference to a VDU

- 'I have not received any communication from you concerning my application for the researcher post. What is the situation?'
- 'Can I confirm the date and time of my interview for the budget accountant position?'
- 'I have Mr Brown at reception. He is a candidate for the stock controller job. Where are the interviews being held today?'

It is also good practice occasionally to print out full details of current

ABC Manufacturing Co.				29/01/86
Summary of Competitions 0149–0152				
Comp. No.	0149	0150	0151	0152
Comp. Name	Design asst.	Sales exec.	Stock controller	Budget accountant
Recruiter	Tom Davies	John Bates	R. Felton	Martin Ryall
Vacancies	3	2	1	1
Closing date	10/12/85	17/12/85	16/01/86	22/01/86
Status	Offer accepted	Offer made	Second interview	First interview
Date of status	27/01/86	21/01/86	23/01/86	27/01/86
No. of applicants	36	52	18	53
• First interview	20	22	12	13
• Second interview	8	6	4	–
• Offer made	3	1	–	–
• Offer accepted	3	–	–	–

Figure 59   *Summary of competitions*

competitions. This will then provide a measure of local back-up in the event of the computer not being available.

Management reporting is concerned with summaries of recruitment activity – a synopsis of the current competitions, analysis of competitions and applicants over a period by division, recruiter, source, sex, occupation etc. Figure 59 shows an example of a summary of recent competitions.

The question will arise as to how long recruitment data should be held on the computer after the competition has been completed. The system can be a devourer of disk space during periods of high recruitment activity, and there may be a tendency to hold on to recruitment data for longer than is necessary, for instance in order to provide statistics at the end of the year. Unless disk capacity is freely available the data should be deleted at regular intervals and either summary data only retained on the system or adequate statistics – which can be manually consolidated at the end of year – printed prior to deletion. In any event appropriate 'housekeeping' routines will have to be established and the main question then is determining the frequency with which these routines are applied to the database.

13 Budgets and establishment

One the main functions of a CPMIS is to provide information which helps to exercise tight control over the number of employees. This can be done in a number of ways and again the approach taken will be influenced by the size and nature of the organization. One approach is to rely on regular reports showing per department the numbers currently serving, movements in and out over a specific period and comparisons with previous periods. Figures 60 and 61 provide a simple example of such reports. Such reporting is quite useful and very often a computer-based system which produces such reports will save a considerable amount of time compared with a manual system.

The basic defect in this approach is that it is reporting history – it shows what has happened and as far as corporate management is concerned all that can be done is to close the stable door perhaps after the horse has bolted. Extra staff may already have been recruited and once this has happened it is not easy to revert to the earlier situation.

There are two methods of trying to avoid this situation – budget and establishment. A budget is a quantitative interpretation prior to a defined period of time, of a policy to be pursued for that period to attain a given objective. In the case of Figure 60 the budget could state that the total numbers during the year to 31 December 1985 should not exceed fifty-five permanent staff and twelve temporary staff at any point. In this case the report would also show the budget figures and the variations from it. This system has the benefit of reviewing the staffing levels and relating them to the expected level of activity during the budget period. It can be effective if it is taken seriously and if there is a strict procedure of reviewing actual performance against budgets. One disadvantage is that it can become a once-a-year exercise at budget setting time and that there may be a tendency to staff up for activity within the budgeted year and to emphasize that rather than the longer term plans. Generally the success of the system is linked to the effectiveness of the overall

161

ABC Manufacturing Co.
Personnel division – Manchester

Manpower summary report

Quarter ended 31/12/85

Personnel admin. and welfare department

	Movements during quarter				Number serving		
	In		*Out*			*Perm.*	*Temp.*
	Permanent	*Temp.*	*Permanent*	*Temp.*	Number serving at 31/12/85	57	12
Commencements	2	3			Number serving at 31/12/84	52	13
Retirements			1	3			
Resignations			1	—	Comparison with last year		
Long-term leave					Under	—	1
Dismissal			1	2	Over	5	—
Transfers							

Figure 60   *Simple manpower summary report*

ABC Manufacturing Co.

Analysis by grade

Quarter ended 31/12/85

	31/12/85		31/12/84		*Comparison*	
Grade	*Permanent*	*Temporary*	*Permanent*	*Temporary*	*Permanent*	*Temporary*
Manager grade 5	1	—	—	—	+1	—
Manager grade 4	2	—	3	—	−1	—
Manager grade 3	2	—	1	—	+1	—
Executive grade 3	4	—	3	—	+1	—
Executive grade 1	3	—	2	—	+1	—
Training executive	1	—	1	—	—	—
Welfare officer	1	—	1	—	—	—
Senior clerk	12	—	15	2	−3	−2
Clerical officer	27	6	23	6	+4	—
Secretary	4	6	3	5	+1	+1
Totals	57	12	52	13	+5	−1

budgetary control system within the organization.

The other method (establishment) is the approach which is described here in further detail. The establishment is the 'approved' staff numbers which an organization should have. It is a very effective way of controlling staff numbers as long as the establishment is constantly reviewed and adjusted to take into account changes in the way in which the organization operates. There can be a tendency not to adjust establishments and to continue to quote serving staff against out of date nominal establishment figures.

If a department within a personnel division has twenty staff serving against an establishment of twenty and it is envisaged that the computerization plan will reduce the staff by ten – in two equal phases in June and December – this can be reflected in one of two ways.

1 *Personnel administration – establishment twenty*
  Jan. 1985   Establishment twenty; serving twenty.
  June 1985   Establishment twenty; serving seventeen. Impact of first phase of computerization – three staff redeployed.
  Dec. 1985   Establishment twenty; serving twelve. Impact of second phase of computerization – two retirements and three cases of redeployment.
  June 1986   Establishment twenty; serving twelve.

This example shows staffing to be eight down on establishment, whereas in reality there should be an explanation of why two additional people are employed.

2 *Personnel Administration – Establishment twenty*
  Jan. 1985   Establishment twenty; serving twenty.
  June 1985   Establishment fifteen; serving seventeen. First phase of computerization completed. Three staff redeployed. Two staff still assisting with implementation of Phase 2.
  Dec. 1985   Establishment ten; serving twelve. Second phase of computerization completed. All staff saving realized but two still retained to input sick leave history.
  June 1986   Establishment ten; serving twelve. Two temporary staff taken on to deal with administration of supervisory training course.

An establishment system ensures that staffing levels are constantly kept under review and a computer helps to do this. Using a computer system will involve a certain amount of additional effort – especially at the initial file set-up stage – but generally the effort will be repaid in terms of the additional control which it offers.

Post file

The key to an establishment system is the setting up of a post file. A record must be set up for every post in the organization. If an organization employs 5000 people this means that 5000 posts will have to be set up on this file. This is where most of the additional set-up work is involved. It should not normally be possible to add a new employee to the system unless it is possible to associate the employee with an existing and vacant post. Each post record holds the post number, name, location and the nature of the post.

Typical of the contents of a post file record are –

1 *Division*   e.g. personnel.

2 *Cost centre*   e.g. personnel administration.

3 *Post code*   This must be a unique code within the cost centre which identifies the post. The way in which this number is assigned may be important. Its format must facilitate the generation of new ones and it may be used in generating or formating reports. One example of a format is C302 06. C indicates the level of seniority within the cost centre; 302 the grade code; and 06 the serial number to identify an individual post.

4 *Post name*   e.g. welfare officer.

5 *Post type*   This is a code which should relate back to the system parameter file or descriptor file e.g. 01 permanent, 02 temporary, 03 short term.

6 *Post review date*   The date on which the validity of this post should come up for review.

7 *Limited post*   If the post is established for a limited period only the start and end date of this period should be indicated to the system. If the post is not renewed or the dates are revised and the employee is still serving outside this period the system should draw attention to this fact.

8 *Personnel no.*   The employee occupying or about to occupy the post should be indicated.

9 *Occupancy type*   This again is a code which relates back to the descriptor file. Typical values are vacant or seasonal.

Cost centre: management accounts	
Post	*Post code*
Management accountant	A49301
Budget accountant	B49401
Cost accountant	C49501
Factory accountant – A	D49601
Factory accountant – B	D49602
Assistant cost accountant	E49801
Accounts clerks (7)	G50301–07
Trainee accountant	G38701
Secretaries (2)	K28701–02

Figure 62   *Coding of posts within a cost centre*

ABC Manufacturing Co.

Staff level enquiry 28/10/85

Division	Estab. posts	Total serving	Net offers	Permanent	Temporary	Contract	Other	LWP	ML
Personnel	100	95	2	82	6	2	5	1	2
Production									
Finance									
Sales									
Distribution									
Totals									

Note: LWP = Leave without pay
ML = Maternity leave

Figure 63 *Staff level enquiry – organization*

By using a post file in this way the structures of the organization is reflected almost completely. This arrangement does not provide the organization structure within a cost centre – see Figure 62 for an example of post coding within a cost centre. If it is required to indicate all reporting relationships this can be achieved by using the post code to indicate a hierarchical level and by denoting on each employee record the personnel number of the person to whom he or she reports. In this way it is possible to generate a report or chart showing all relationships within the organization.

System outputs

Output from this part of the system will be both on screen and on paper. On screen it should be possible to examine the up-to-date position on staffing vis-à-vis establishment as shown in Figure 63. It should then be possible to take this down to more detailed levels through division and cost centre as shown in Figures 64 and 65. The latter shows individual posts and employees. In practice it would be normal to provide summary data for each type of post. These reports should also be available in printed form. As a general rule as much output as possible should be available on screen – with a print option. Some outputs cannot be conveniently accommodated within the 80-column width of a VDU and a printed report must be used. Figure 66 which provides an analysis of staffing levels over a twelve-month period is one such report.

Management information

It is worth noting what sort of management information is required by a CPMIS.

1 Reports produced must serve a useful purpose. There is not much point in producing a report showing on a month-by-month basis the number of job applicants who have gone through the various recruitment phases if nobody wants this information. There is sometimes a tendency in computer-based systems to produce fancy reports just because the data is available.
2 Reports must be easily understood. Most reports and screens can be designed to be easily read and understood. In the occasional case where this is not possible a manager should have easy access to a description of the significance of the output. This can sometimes arise where a report contains a number of percentage fields and it is not possible to describe them meaningfully. In this case the significance and basis of calculating each percentage should be readily available.
3 Terms used in reports or on screen should be clearly defined. A typical example is non-workable time – what exactly does this include?
4 Reports must contain a level of detail appropriate to the target level of management. If they are designed to assist managers or supervisors effectively to control operations they should relate directly to the

Cost centre	Estab. posts	Total serving	Net offers	Permanent	Temporary	Contract	Other	LWP	ML
Personnel director	5	5	–	5	–	–	–	–	–
Personnel admin.	40	38	1	33	3	–	2	–	2
Industrial relations	21	18	1	16	2	–	–	–	–
Welfare	8	6	–	6	–	–	–	1	–
Training	16	20	–	15	–	2	3	–	–
Job evaluation	10	8	–	7	1	–	–	–	–
Totals	100	95	2	82	6	2	5	1	2

Figure 64   *Staff level enquiry – division*

ABC Manufacturing Co.   *Staff level enquiry*   28/10/85

WELFARE

Posts Name	No.	Name	Cat.	Grade	Age	Sex	Salary
Welfare officer	A20301	Jean Walkin	Perm.	203	35	F	18,302
Asst. welfare officer	B20401	John Rees	Perm.	204	33	M	16,207
Welfare education asst.	C21301	Elizabeth Hallowes	Perm.	213	28	F	13,200
Staff nurse	D21901	Janet Harris	Perm.	219	29	F	15,300
Staff nurse	D21902		Vacant since 12/07/85				
Research assistant	E23301	Harry Martin	LWP since 15/03/85				
Clerk-grade 1	F25701	Hilary Green	Perm.	257	21	F	10,203
Secretarial assistant	F25301	Shirley Black	Perm.	253	18	F	7,300

Established posts: 8   Serving: perm. 6, LWP 1, vacant 1

Figure 65   *Staff level enquiry – cost centre*

ABC Manufacturing Co.

Monthly staff levels

Staff serving at end of month from June 1985 to May 1986

	June	July	Aug.	Sept.	Oct.	Nov.	Dec.	Jan.	Feb.	Mar.	Apr.	May
Division: Production												
Permanent												
Temporary												
Contract												
Other												
Total												
Division: Sales												
Permanent												
Temporary												
Contract												
Other												
Total												
Totals for organization												
Permanent												
Temporary												
Contract												
Other												
Total												

Figure 66 *Twelve month staff level enquiry*

responsibilities of the recipient. They should also only include information which is relevant and padding with redundant information should be avoided.

5 Outputs from the system must be up-to-date and if it is not it is because procedures are not being adhered to. Reports such as those emanating from the establishment subsystem should be produced for a period or at the end of a period which is consistent with other output. If the organization operates a budgetary control system based on thirteen four-week periods, establishment reporting should normally coincide with this system instead of using calendar months.

6 Output from the system must be accurate or at least have an acceptable level of accuracy. In some systems absolute accuracy is not essential and indeed waiting for complete accuracy may mean that the information is out-of-date and useless by the time it arrives. In a personnel system there is little excuse for not being accurate but two examples will serve to illustrate the point

- To wait for the absence returns (apparently delayed in the postal system), from a small outlying department would delay the issue of the weekly absence report for the whole organization
- Departmental reports on total salaries and allowances by division and department may be more readable if they are shown in thousands of pounds rather then pounds.

7 Exception reporting should be a normal feature. It is much more meaningful to have a report identifying only those employees who have more than twenty days sick leave in the past year than to have a complete list of everybody with sick leave and then pick out the bad cases.

14 Training

The requirements of the training department can generally be analysed under three headings.

1 Qualifications/academic achievement.
2 Courses.
3 Training aids.

This classfication may not always be relevant and in some cases the training department may not even be part of the personnel division. This may be further evidence of the need to take a broad view of the personnel management system. The training department, like personnel, is primarily concerned with the people resource and its development. If an independent training system is developed there may be some duplication of data between the two systems, neither system will have the complete picture, there may be conflict as to which system should hold what data and there may even be constant argument and competition as to which data is correct.

Some training departments may have further needs that those described here. These may include

- the need to be able to schedule and book training facilities
- the facility to hold detailed information concerning the progress of apprentices
- a costing/charging system for the department so that both direct and indirect training costs can be charged out to user departments.

Professional qualifications
It is generally sufficient to allow for up to four qualifications per employee. Where more than four qualifications are involved the four senior qualifications should be input. Where an employee acquires a

more senior qualification, e.g. moving from associated membership to fellowship, the latter should replace the previous entry unless it is significant to know when each grade of membership was attained. Generally a two-digit code will be required to indicate the various qualifications and a single-digit code to indicate the level attained. The valid codes and their associated descriptions should be set up in the descriptor file and since a two-digit code is required the system should allow for up to ninety-nine types of qualification. The same applies in the case of other classifications such as academic achievements, languages and occupations.

To indicate the qualification level the following codes should suffice

Code	*Level*
01	Student
02	Licentiate
03	Associate
04	Member
05	Fellow

The following is an extract from a typical list of qualifications

Code	*Description*
01	Chartered Institute of Finance and Accountancy
05	Chartered Institute of Actuaries
10	Chartered Institute of Bankers
20	British Computer Society
22	Irish Computer Society
25	British Institute of Management
30	Institute of Data Processing Management
35	Institute of Cost and Management Accountants
40	Institute of Administrative Accountants
45	Institute of Management Services
50	Associate of Certified Accountants
55	Institute of Chartered Secretaries and Administrators
60	Institute of Chartered Accountants
65	Association of Accounting Technicians
70	Incorporated Institute of Clerks of Work of Great Britain
75	Incorporated Association of Architects and Surveyors
77	Institute of Materials Handling
79	Institute of Marketing
81	Institution of Mechanical Engineers
83	Institution of Electronic Engineers
85	Institution of Civil Engineers
87	Royal Institute of British Architects
89	Royal Institute of Chartered Surveyors
91	Institute of Taxation
93	Institute of Personnel Management
95	Institute of Production Control
97	Institution of Works Managers

This list is not in any particular order. In practice they should be grouped in some logical blocks or in alphabetic sequence with adequate gaps for new entries. Some organizations may want to record progress achieved towards obtaining a professional qualification. In this case it will be necessary to record details of examinations passed and the examination date.

Academic achievements

The purpose here is to indicate the education level of an employee. One way of looking at this is just to hold one item per employee – the highest achievement. Alternatively the same approach may be taken as has been described for professional qualifications, by allowing for a number of entries per employee and showing the level attained and the date achieved against each entry.

For example, the level achieved could be

Code	Level
01	Pass
02	Honours
03	First class honours
04	Distinction

The following is an extract from a typical list of academic achievements

Code	Description
01	GCE
03	Intermediate certificate
07	Leaving certificate
09	University degrees

Languages

Generally it is sufficient to allow for a maximum of four languages per employee. Some systems require that the maximum number in this type of situation be specified and it is not then possible to exceed this number. Where the system already exists there is no alternative available. If a system is being designed from scratch it may be necessary to decide how many occurrences to allow for per employee. Where a limit is imposed it generally means that space is being preallocated regardless of whether it is to be used. A system catering for up to six entries for academic achievements, for example, would have space assigned within each employees record for

Academic code	Status code	Date of achievement
2 characters	2 characters	6 characters

Total $2 + 2 + 6 = 10 \times 6$ entries
$= 60$ characters per employee

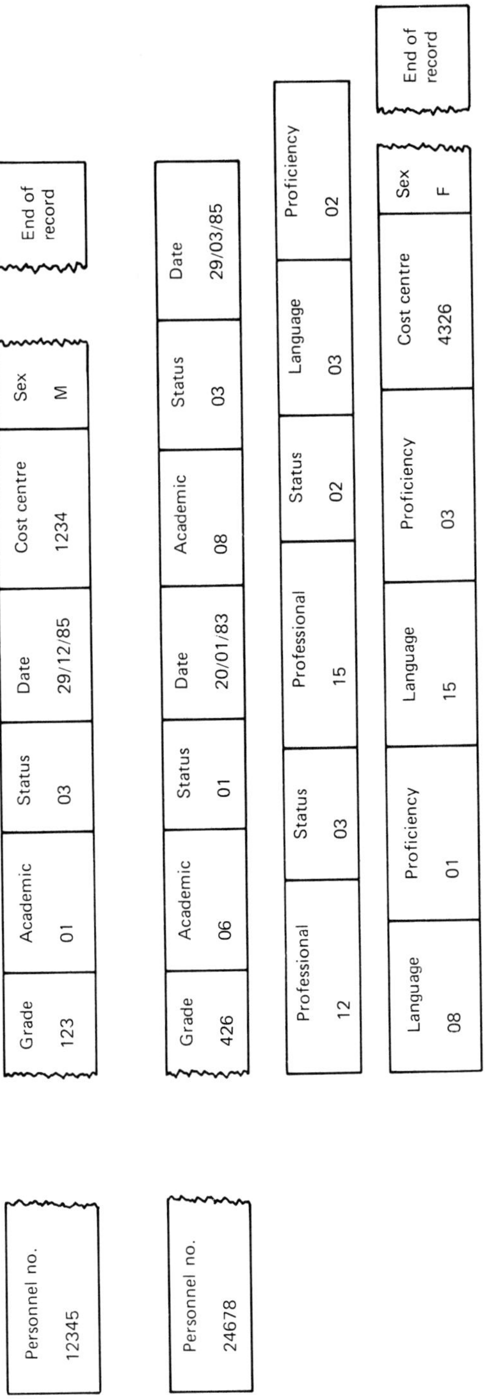

Personnel no.	Grade	Academic	Status	Date	Cost centre	Sex	End of record
12345	123	01	03	29/12/85	1234	M	

Personnel no.	Grade	Academic	Status	Date	Status
24678	426	06	01	20/01/83	03

Professional	Status	Professional	Status	Academic	Status	Date
12	03	15	02	08	03	29/03/85

Language	Proficiency	Language	Proficiency	Language	Proficiency
08	01	15	03	03	02

Cost centre	Sex	End of record
4326	F	

Figure 67   *Record layout catering for a variable number of languages etc.*

For a file of 10,000 employees this represents 0.6 million characters. From this it can be seen that the space allocated should generally correspond to the norm or only slightly above the norm. Exceptional cases can be dealt with in some other way, e.g. by way of a note on the employee's computer record, so that space is not wasted.

An alternative and more efficient system design – from a file size point of view anyway – is one which allows for a virtually limitless number of occurrences but where space is only taken up when there is data present. This layout is shown in Figure 67. In this example qualifications etc. occupy ten characters in the case of the first employee and forty characters for the second employee.

Typical system entries relating to knowledge of languages are

Proficiency codes
01   School – unpractised
02   Read only
03   Basic
04   Conversational
05   Fluent
06   Native
Languages
01   English
02   French
03   German
04   Italian
05   Spanish

Training courses

The system should hold data about courses and who attended the courses. Basically it should be able to answer queries such as 'Who has been on management development programmes?' or 'What courses has John Whiteside attended over the past five years?'. To answer this type of query the system must hold data on all courses – this is referred to as the courses file – and must either hold details on each employee's file of courses attended or hold cross-references from the employee record to the courses file.

The following courses data would be held for each employee for each course attended

Course number
Course name
Course date – start and end dates
Course duration – days
Result – perhaps a narrative indicating the attendee's performance
Rating – indication of how this attendee rated the course.

Courses file
The following details might be held for each course

Course number
Course name
Internal/external
Course dates (start and end)
Number of modules
Duration – number of days
Course leader or organizer
Chief lecturer or organization giving course
Location of course
Remarks. It is useful to have a field available for remarks or comments
about the course e.g. 'First course geared towards the revised
syllabus'.

Training department management and staff may like to have a more
detailed analysis of attendees' evaluation of each course. This involves
each attendee attributing a rating to various features of the course viz.

1 How the course met the objectives set for it.

From: Training and staff development manager

To: Financial accountant   29/4/86
cc Director of finance

Notification of training course

    I wish to inform you that the members of your staff listed below have
been selected for the training course as shown. I should be pleased if you
would arrange for their release from normal duties for the specified dates.
Joining instructions will be sent to the individuals concerned in due course.

Course title: Micro-computers and the accountant
Date: 29/5/86 to 30/5/86
Duration: 2 days
Location: Barnes Harvey & Co., Harvey House
Notes: Half day follow-up to be arranged in July

            John Batesman: Assistant accountant
            Clive Allen: Payroll supervisor
            Harry Roberts: Budget assistant
            Linda Barnes: Credit controller
            Thos. Williams: Production cost assistant

Figure 68 *Course notification – department manager*

2 The content of the course
   • the treatment of each subject (level of detail)
   • the relevance of the subject covered.
3 The administration of the course
   • general organization, timetable and accommodation (lecture rooms etc.)
   • use of visual aids etc.
   • arrangements for lunch, coffee, living accommodation etc.
4 Length of course.
5 Lecturers.

The main points to bear in mind in regard to this type of data is that the format of the evaluation form may have to vary for certain types of course. In some cases the evaluation will have to relate to individual subjects and individual lecturers and it may involve a significant amount of inputting effort. This must be balanced against the benefits which will be expected to accrue from the system. The training system should interface with the word processing or letter production facilities in order to cope with as much of the course administration work as possible – this includes letters to staff who are due to go on a particular course and the corresponding notifications to departmental managers (see Figure 68).

Training aids

The purpose of having training aids on the system is to assist in controlling the use of these items and to record the extent to which they are used. Training aids consist of such items as reference books, manuals, audio cassettes, video cassettes, audio and video recorders and players. They may relate to particular courses or they may be generally available from the training department for use by members of the staff.
   The system would be expected to

• keep track of aids issued to employees
• show who has a particular aid at present and who the last users of that aid were
• provide details of all aids currently recorded as being outstanding against a particular employee.

The system would normally hold the following data on each training aid

1 *Training aid number (reference)*   This is a unique reference for every single item on file.
2 *Category*   This would be a coded category with the description held on the descriptor file. Categories include books, audio cassettes, video cassettes etc.
3 *Title/description*   The name of the particular aid e.g. *French Made Easy – Module 2.*
4 *Status*   In stock or on loan.
5 *Date issued*   i.e. the last date issued.
6 *Date due back*   or date returned if currently in stock.

7 *Narrative 1* A note relating to the aid itself e.g. used in course No. 126.

8 *Narrative 2* This could be a free form note holding information such as 'Hold for John Adams – laboratory'.

9 *Movement* Name and location of employee who has the item on loan at present and those who have had the item on loan previously.

15 Word processing and letter production

There are many ways of looking at how word processing (WP) should b
achieved within the context of a CPMIS. One view is that it should b
divorced completely from the CPMIS and that the best system is to hav

- stand-alone WP facilities catering for the normal WP needs of th
  division and with no or very restricted interface with the personne
  management system
- a facility within the CPMIS which will produce letters.

An alternative view is to have a WP or text-editing system on the sam
computer as the CPMIS and use this both for normal word processin
and to interface closely with the CPMIS for letter production or fo
incorporation of information direct from the system into reports. Th
need for the latter is limited and in practice may prove to be a somewha
cumbersome procedure.

Whichever method is adopted the personnel management system mus
be capable of producing letters to staff and job applicants. The followin
is a list of the types of letter which the system should produce

- recruitment correspondence
- notification of training course booking for participants, departmen
  managers and lecturers
- notification of changes in conditions of employment, and incremen
  advice to employees or their supervisors
- letters drawing an employee's attention to his/her sick leave record

The system should be easy to operate and there should be simpl
procedures for initiating the production of letters. Figure 69 shows hov
the system might work. A number of standard procedures would be se
up which would allow for the selection of details from the personne
database or files. These details would be associated with a letter from
file of standard letters held in a computer file, each of which is identifie

178

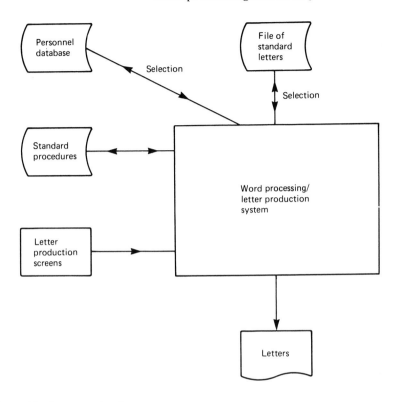

Figure 69   *Letter production process*

y means of a code. The procedure is initiated by identifying it on a
election menu and specifying a range of parameters. These parameters
ould indicate such items as the criteria to be used for selecting records,
he letter to be used, the data to be printed on the letter, and the letter
ignatory. In the case of letters which are normally produced in large
uantities it may be wasteful to tie up relatively slow letter-quality
rinters in producing them completely. The best method may be to have
 number of these letters printed as standard letters and to have the
ystem insert whatever variables are required e.g. name and address,
ompetition name, interview date and time, interviewer's location. In
electing the letter in the procedure the user would indicate to the system
whether it was expected to produce the whole letter or fill in the gaps on
he preprinted version. This option provides more flexibility. For exam-
le in the case of a competition which has attracted a large number of
pplicants, the preprinted stationery would be used. However if only a
w letters are involved the letters can be requested without having to
sert the special stationery into the sheet feeder. Thus these letters can
e mixed with letters concerning contract expiry, sick leave record etc.
   An example of the type of screen layout which could be used to indicate

---

ABC Manufacturing Co.

Personnel management information system
letter production

Facilities available
01   Contract cessation letter   02
03   04
05   06
07   08
09   10
11   12
13   14
15   16
17   18
19   20

Please select facility required [01] and press return

Figure 70   *Letter production – facilities screen*

ABC Manufacturing Co.

Personnel management information system
letter production

Procedure for producing: Contract cessation letter
   Selection criteria:
      Contract due to expire before [31/12/85] (DD/MM/YY)
      Contract types to be included [A] [B] [C] (The system will default to
      all contract types – please replace with spaces if you wish to exclude
      any type.)

   Letter type:
      Letter type to be used [AB27] Preprinted [No] (If you wish to replace
      the default letter type please replace with appropriate reference.)

   Letter date: [12/10/85]

   Press return to initiate this procedure

Figure 71   *Letter production – run procedure screen*

the facilities available, i.e. the letters which can be produced, is shown in
Figure 70. If the user selects the option to produce contract cessation
letters, the system calls up the procedure which displays a screen as
shown in Figure 71. This screen might display default values which can
be used or changed. In the example, which is a screen display with
current date of 12/10/85, the system default values would select all types

A, B and C contracts which are due to expire between the current date and the end of December 1985. If these are not the required selection criteria the suggested values would be changed by the user before the procedure is initiated. The system also expects that the normal letter to use is Type AB27 and that it is reasonable to print the current date on the letter. The system would normally default to printing the full version of the letter but if 'yes' is inserted in the field titled 'preprinted' the system would assume that the stationery used would not be blank sheets but would have the standard part of the letter preprinted. The system would then extract from the personnel database all employees who are contract types A, B or C and who have a contract expiry date which is earlier than 31 December 1985. It will extract letter number AB27 from the file of standard letters and it will produce letters like that in Figure 72.

ABC Manufacturing Co.   Telephone Ext. 2368.

Personnel administration dept.   Ref. AB27/14867/AK

John Stanley
Laboratory technician
Central laboratory

Dear Mr Stanley,

Expiry of contract

In accordance with your terms of employment your contract with the company ends on 20/12/85.

Because of the new local authority project which is due to start in January next the company is in a position to extend your contract for a further twelve months should you so wish. In any event I would ask you to telephone Ms Kathleen Jones at extension 2368 to arrange an appointment for your interview.

Yours sincerely,

J.R. Edwards
Personnel administration manager

Figure 72   *Letter re contract expiry*

To produce letters of regret for unsuccessful job applicants, appropriate parameters which would need to be input are

1 Competition number e.g. 106 – statistician.
2 Application status range e.g. 12 to 15 – four status types which indicate unsuccessful candidates.

This would result in letters which would obtain an applicant's name and address from the recruitment system and would also refer to the competition by name, e.g.

'Re your application for the post of statistician'.

Stand-alone word processing

Apart from word processing activities which are directly associated with the CPMIS there will be a number of other applications within a personnel division which will be amenable to WP. Such applications include

1 Any long documents which require drafting and detailed proof reading. Trade union agreements are a good example. Other examples are job specifications and reports on such matters as staffing levels and the documentation of the CPMIS from the specification of requirements through to procedures manuals.
2 Any reports which are produced regularly and have a formal structure e.g. monthly report on industrial accidents, manpower plans with regular updates, monthly report on the organization's catering facilities.
3 The regular issue of staff information bulletins. Some of these documents have a lot of common text, and others are issued on an annual basis with only the dates changed e.g. arrangements for Christmas, Easter and annual holidays.
4 Returns to government agencies – in particular those which do not require the use of special stationery.
5 Monthly report of the division and minutes of divisional and departmental meetings.

Advantages of word processing

Many benefits accrue to the personnel division from the use of WP and letter production facilities when used in conjunction with high quality printers. Among the benefits are

1 Integration of letter production procedures into the CPMIS. This implies that the total clerical operation is taken into account and a more efficient and integrated solution is obtained.
2 A better service is provided to other departments and to the outside world. This results in the department creating an impression of efficiency and is good for public relations generally.

3 It enables managers as well as typists and secretaries to be more productive. A major benefit of WP is the freedom which it gives a manager or executive to make changes to original drafts. The flexibility which it gives can result in immeasurable benefits. Take the case of an industrial relations executive who has to prepare a draft agreement for discussion with trade unions. He is likely to be working to a tight deadline and as soon as he reads the document he might recognize that a certain paragraph should be at the start of the document rather than towards the end, or his boss might feel that a change of phraseology in certain areas would be better. The flexibility that a WP system offers in a situation like this is one of its major benefits.

4 The production of routine correspondence and standard letters is done more efficiently and eliminates a certain amount of monotony from some jobs.

5 The facilities provided result in a higher level of productivity from typists and secretaries. A substantial amount of any typist's time is taken up with erasing mistakes, making corrections, using correcting fluid and paper, checking spellings, inserting new sentences and paragraphs, proof reading etc. The facilities provided by a WP system substantially affect the time spent on these activities.

6 Facilities for automatic centring of headings and titles also saves time.

7 Most WP systems also have facilities for automatic emboldening, and automatic underscoring of words or sentences, and the operator may have a choice of different type sizes leading to greater flexibility and a more professional-looking output.

8 By creating the text on disk (or diskette) a filing system is automatically available and procedures may be set up for securing and retrieving this data subsequently.

9 Generally speaking people who operate a good WP system will find it more rewarding to work with than the alternatives.

Disadvantages of word processing

One of the main disadvantages which may arise with a WP system is that the personnel department may expect too much of the system and may be disappointed when it does not cater for everything. This situation may indeed arise because the system is not being used properly. This unfulfilled expectation is a danger rather than a disadvantage and arises both from a failure to understand what WP is all about and from the failure to plan properly for its introduction. The planning involves

- deciding how the system will be operated, what applications it will handle and ensuring that everyone concerned knows what to expect
- developing the links between WP and the CPMIS and giving sufficient attention to the procedures surrounding both systems.
- ensuring that all staff are properly trained in using the system.
- ensuring that the hardware acquired is appropriate

- in the case of a shared system, ensuring that everyone is aware of such items as how printing is to be controlled, the standards to be used in allocating file and document names and the back-up and security procedures to be observed.

Some disadvantages which may be associated with word processing are

1 Authors may become careless about the quality of their input on the basis that it is easy to change it afterwards.
2 With a shared system chaos can result unless procedures are rigidly adhered to – this applies to such matters as document naming conventions. In this situation it is easy for someone to despatch a large quantity of an out-of-date standard letter.
3 It may give rise to an increased volume of internal correspondence to the detriment of telephone or face-to-face communication.

16 Manpower planning

Althought it can be lost sight of in the day-to-day operations of the personnel division, the first duty of the personnel function is to develop and maintain a manpower plan which is consistent with and integrated into the corporate strategy of the organization. What is meant by the term 'manpower plan'? In this context it means providing the manpower resources which will enable the organization to achieve its stated aims. This involves determining the number of posts required, the grading of each post, the cost and the skills, qualifications and training required to establish and maintain the appropriate work force. This is an area where the personnel function cannot operate in isolation. It must be constantly in touch with the other functions, the policy-makers and the corporate planners.

How does a CPMIS relate to manpower planning? It will generally be capable of producing a lot of output which is relevant for manpower planning purposes, including standard reports which the system will produce regularly and reports which may be generated on an *ad hoc* basis. Reports generated from the establishment system – analysis of posts and vacancies, reports providing age and service profiles of various grades of staff, and reports classifying qualification, training, skills and experience – are particularly relevant.

Usually the final manpower plan is drawn up outside the CPMIS but using data produced by the CPMIS. As long as the basic data is available the plan can be developed manually or with the aid of a computer. There are manpower planning systems available into which this data can be input and they will produce plans based on whatever rules or criteria are input with the data. They are essentially modelling systems and one could be developed on an in-house computer using one of the many established modelling systems or languages available. If a CPMIS is run on a dedicated mini-computer, data from the personnel system should be capable of being transferred to or accessed from the corporate main-

185

frame, since there is likely to be a modelling system available on it for other purposes. It is likely that data from the payroll system will also need to be input to the model. Since modelling can impose a very demanding load on a computer it may very well be that the resources of a main-frame computer is required anyway.

In this chapter the subject of manpower planning is treated by looking at what manpower planning is, what computer modelling is, some of the reports which are produced by a CPMIS which are aimed at assisting in manpower planning and a brief outline of the elements of a manpower planning model.

Manpower planning defined

Manpower planning covers the areas of recruitment, records, training, and development of staff, but the important part of its definition is that it is concerned with planning and not merely with doing the job. Manpower planning is a strategic activity. It is concerned with the formulation of strategy about what should happen within the organization in relation to its human resources, with looking into the future, and the translation of the human resources element of the organization's development plan into plans aimed at providing an effective work force armed with the necessary qualifications, skills and experience. If it is anticipated that another 500 skilled production workers will be required in five years' time, the organization must now start deciding how this will be achieved – the study of the extent to which these skills are available locally, an examination of the relevant educational facilities available and, if appropriate, negotiating with local technical colleges and institutes with a view to providing suitable courses for school leavers.

The organization may have to consider the establishment of a suitable training facility and workshop and ways of ensuring that existing production workers are in a position to provide on-the-job training for the future recruits. Arrangements may also have to be made for training in supervisory skills so that existing employees will be in a position to occupy the new supervisory posts which will be created in the new environment. A prime example arises in the case of craftsmen where a three to four year apprenticeship introduces a substantial lead time between initial recruitment and the date when the organization has a mature craftsman.

Aims of manpower planning

The aims of manpower planning can be listed as

1 To get the balance right between the utilization of plant and equipment and the utilization of manpower. This involves examining the costing of the use of both elements and coming up with the optimum balance – plant-intensive, labour-intensive or a suitable balance between capital investment and labour costs.

2 To determine what the recruitment needs of the organization are, bearing in mind
 • the planned level of activity
 • the need to avoid both overstaffing and the possibility of not being able to deliver the planned output
 • the need to take into account normal staff wastage, and the desirability of creating an attractive working environment including the provision of promotional opportunities.
3 Having an appropriate management development philosophy. Suitably trained and experienced managers are essential to the well-being of any organization. In order to achieve this position existing managers must be backed up by a team of managers and supervisors who are being groomed to move up the ladder when required. Some organizations concentrate on management, supervisory and senior technical staff in setting up data in a CPMIS. This makes the maintenance of a detailed staff profile more feasible and is of great benefit in the area of manpower planning.
4 The achievement of a satisfactory state of industrial relations. This is essential if the planned level of productivity is to be achieved.
5 Having a suitable training programme. The need for management training has already been mentioned but the training programme should embrace all skills – administrative, professional, technical, research and development, marketing, public relations and production.

Stages in manpower planning

Manpower planning can be analysed over six stages (see Figure 73).

1 Defining or updating the corporate plan. As mentioned above, the manpower plan is a subset of the organization's corporate plan. Accordingly the success of the manpower plan is primarily determined by the quality of the corporate plan. This plan must reflect the corporate strategy and objectives as related to the environment and markets in which it expects to operate and must also integrate the plans of the various divisions and departments within the organization. Once the corporate plan is firm, the human resources aspect of it can be planned and subsequently updated as the corporate plan is modified to reflect changes in the environment.
2 Setting up and maintaining the environment within which manpower planning will operate.
 This requires
 (a) The involvement and support of top management who must give unambiguous backing to the planning process.
 (b) Full integration with corporate planning activities. The manpower planning must be seen to be an integral part of the organization's strategic planning activity. There must also be consistency in terms of the period which the plan covers.

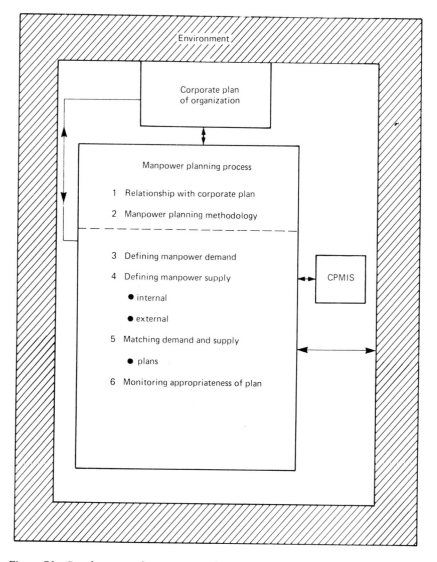

Figure 73   *Development of a manpower plan*

(c) Clear definition of responsibility for manpower planning. This will depend on the size of the organization and its management structure. It is sometimes associated with the department which is responsible for establishment. In the context of a CPMIS it may be appropriate to include the detailed work associated with the preparation and maintenance of the plan among the responsibilities of the personnel services section as described in Chapter 21.

(d) The level of detail expected in plans will have to be clearly defined and in the earlier years of the plan the relationship with the organization's budgetary procedures must be clarified.

(e) The dependence of good planning on the accuracy of data held in the CPMIS must be understood and emphasized. There is no point in using data of which the quality is suspect.

3 Definition of the degree of manpower required i.e. the demand. This stage is concerned with estimating the manpower resources required to meet the needs of the organization having regard to both quantity and quality. There are various ways of doing this

- estimates based on experience
- production plans derived from marketing expectations.
- forecasting based on measures of productivity.

The degree to which each of the above is relevant will vary.

4 Assessment of existing resources and of the state of these resources in the future – manpower audit or inventory, i.e. the supply. This stage is initially concerned with the analysis of existing staff, and the rate of success of this exercise is determined by the accuracy of the personnel records – this again is where the CPMIS is critical. The information required is at a summary level and it is in this area that the value of a computer is appreciated. The information involved is both quantitative and qualitative. Examples of the quantitative information involved are

- number of employees analysed over grade, sex, category, occupations, qualifications and skills.
- number of employees analysed by age, length of service, length of time in department, marital status etc.
- departmental and overall totals for absenteeism, labour turnover (resignations, retirements, transfers) staff training time
- departmental payroll costs.

Qualitative information required will include

- expected capability for promotion of employees
- level of achievement of employees
- effectiveness of present reward system
- views on scope for increased productivity

A CPMIS will be of limited value in providing qualitative information. Both types of information requirements outlined above relate to internal labour supply. The external supply market will also have to be evaluated. This involves examining the characteristics of the local, and perhaps national, work force, taking into account current and future legislation likely to affect employment, and government employment incentives. All of this data will be outside the bounds of the CPMIS.

5 The production of the manpower plan. That is reconciling or matching the demand for labour with the supply available from both internal and external sources. This process will result in a series of action plans, the detail of which will depend upon the timescale envisaged. They will consist of statements of personnel policy together with detailed plans which indicate precisely what action is to be taken and when this action should be taken. These action plans may include

ABC Manufacturing Co.   *Sales/profit model*

The company manufactures a product which sells at £100 each and has an established cost structure as follows:

- materials 20 per cent of sales
- labour (direct) £50 per unit
- manufacturing overheads – variable £5 per unit
- manufacturing overheads – fixed £100,000 per annum
- selling and distribution expenses 10 per cent of sales
- advertising expenses 3 per cent of sales
- administrative expenses (labour) 5 per cent of manufacturing labour costs
- administrative expenses (other) 2 per cent of sales

A simple model to reflect this structure and which would produce a pretax profit would be

Sales	= units input × £100
Materials	= sales × 0.02
Labour	= sales units × £50
Manufacturing overheads (fixed)	= £100,000
Manufacturing overheads (variable)	= sales units × £5
Manufacturing costs	= materials + labour + manufacturing overheads (fixed) + manufacturing overheads (variable)
Gross margin	= sales – manufacturing costs
Selling and distribution expenses	= sales × 0.10
Advertising expenses	= sales × 0.03
Administrative expenses (labour)	= labour × 0.05
Administrative expenses (other)	= sales × 0.02
Operating expenses	= selling and distribution expenses + advertising expenses + administrative expenses (labour) + administrative expenses (other)
Taxable profit	= gross margin – operating expenses

Management can then ascertain the impact which various levels of sales will have on the taxable profit under these rules.

If it is envisaged that 100,000 units will be sold the following calculations will be done prior to producing the summary trading statement.

Sales	= 100,000 × £100	= £10m
Materials	= £10m × 0.20	= £ 2m
Labour	= 100,000 × £50	= £ 5m
Fixed overheads		= £ 0.1m
Variable overheads	= 100,000 × £5	= £ 0.5m
Manufacturing costs	= £2m + £5m + £0.1m +£0.5m	= £ 7.6m
Gross margin	= £10m – £7.6m	= £ 2.4m

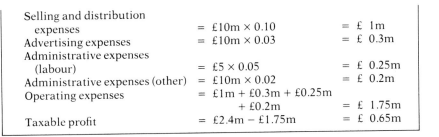

Selling and distribution expenses	= £10m × 0.10	= £ 1m
Advertising expenses	= £10m × 0.03	= £ 0.3m
Administrative expenses (labour)	= £5 × 0.05	= £ 0.25m
Administrative expenses (other)	= £10m × 0.02	= £ 0.2m
Operating expenses	= £1m + £0.3m + £0.25m + £0.2m	= £ 1.75m
Taxable profit	= £2.4m − £1.75m	= £ 0.65m

Figure 74   *A simple sales/profit model*

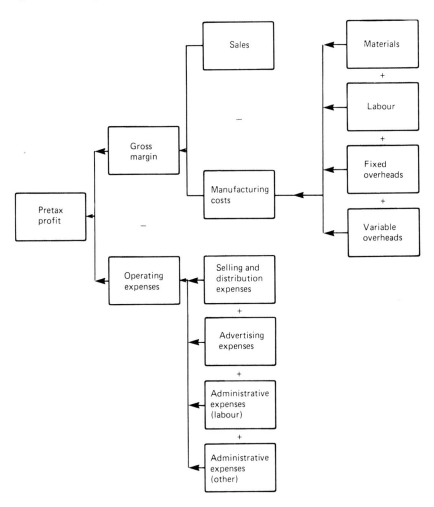

Figure 75   *Model diagram for sales/profit model*

- the need to secure acceptance of new technology in certain defined areas within a given time period – this may require negotiation and agreement on productivity procedures with particular trades unions.
- the need to improve productivity in key areas, and the related need to reduce the rate of labour turnover or absenteeism in certain departments
- recruitment, redeployment and early retirement plans
- career development plans, training programmes, work experience programmes or staff attachment schemes.

6 The constant monitoring and modification of the plan. Forecasts must be constantly compared with reality and adjustments should be made to the plan as soon as the need is perceived. It is usual also to have a formal review of the plan at stated intervals in conjunction with reviews of the overall corporate plan. In this monitoring process the CPMIS will be of great assistance.

Computer modelling

A business planning model is a method of structuring, manipulating and experimenting with a variety of planning options. The various business constraints within which an organization has to live, the options which it can take and the internal implications of these options are represented in a model by various algorithms. This constitutes the business model and it is then subjected to changing variables in order to study the impact. In this way it may be possible to establish the optimum solution in a way which could not easily be ascertained in the real world situation. In applying different variables the modelling process involves a great deal of calculation and interactions and because this is a strong point with computers various computer modelling systems have evolved over the years.

Figures 74 and 75 provide a simple example of a model which calculates a profits before tax figure from a forecast sales volume and various rules. At a sales volume of 100,000 units a pretax profit of £0.65m is derived. If it is required to show the impact of a 10 per cent increase in wage costs, the rule for calculating labour costs is changed by using a multiplier of £55 instead of £50 and this will cater for the revised calculation of administrative expenses (labour). As can be seen this 10 per cent increase in labour costs reduces the profit from £0.65m to £0.125m.

A real model to calculate these figures would of course be more complex. The rules would have to be refined to take into account the impact on costs of different levels of activity e.g. the degree to which costs classified as fixed start to change, the relevance of variable costs such as selling and distribution codes at very different levels of output etc. However the example will perhaps serve to illustrate the principles involved.

Within a CPMIS a simple example of a model is one which is able to provide an answer to the question 'If we implement a general pay

ncrease for everybody of 4.5 per cent from 1 January 1987 and a further
per cent from 1 June 1987 for everyone with five years' service at that
tage, what will the wage bill be for each department?'

There are various computer modelling packages on the market which
are designed to meet general business needs although most of them were
originally designed to provide a financial modelling service for accoun-
ants. Such packages consist of

a model-building language
facilities for running the model
a report generator to produce attractive output reports
a graphics facility to produce graphs, bar charts, pie charts etc.
'what if' facilities to permit the easy input of alternative scenarios
a statistical facility for the analysis of data.

n addition to the established modelling packages the growth in the
micro-computer market in particular has resulted in the development of
multitude of spread-sheet systems. A spread-sheet is an electronic
work-sheet corresponding to a manual work-sheet consisting of numer-
us rows and columns. These rows and columns form a grid with cells
occurring at the intersection of the rows and columns and each cell is
identified by reference to its coordinates. If rows 1 to 3 represent posts,
staff serving and variance respectively and columns represent months
from January, cell 3, 6 should hold the variance between the number of
uthorized posts and actual staff serving for the month of June. Spread-
heets are generally easy to use and the specification of rules for the
alculation of cell values is quite straightforward. They are very useful
or any application which lends itself to the rows and columns format
nd recomputations are done very quickly following changes to specific
ariables.

The statistical analysis facility referred to above is an essential part of
ny package which is to be used for any manpower planning application.
Where data is available from a CPMIS covering a number of years, it may
e analysed to discover relations which may be expected to continue in
he future and in this way it may be possible to arrive at future values for
ariables to be used in the model.

There are various techniques used in analysing this data which are
ormally an integral part of a good modelling system. The main techni-
ues used are

Trend analysis which looks at items such as employment levels over a
defined period.
Smoothing which attempts to isolate irregularities or random variations in order to concentrate on what might be regarded as the normal
level of activity. One of the principal ways of doing this is to use
moving average figures.
Seasonal analysis which is used to obtain seasonal patterns such as
peaks in the car-battery business prior to the onset of winter driving
conditions.

4 Correlation analysis which attempts to find the relationship between variables. This technique can also assist in finding relations where a time delay is involved e.g. high sick leave occurring a few weeks after a high overtime period.
5 Calculations of means, modes, quartiles, standard deviations etc.

Reports

A number of reports produced by a CPMIS either on a regular or *ad hoc* basis will be useful for manpower planning. These are largely based on an analysis of the personnel database and include

1 *Movement in staff numbers* which shows the staffing level by department over a number of years.
2 *Absence analysis* which examines the patterns of absence throughout the organization over time. This is particularly relevant to sick leave or lateness (if this data is captured by the system).
3 *Age analysis* which provides a profile of the staff based on age and sex (Figures 76, 77 and 78).
4 *Service analysis*. This is somewhat similar to an age analysis but provides a snapshot of the organization by reference to the length of service which employees have and the degree of mobility through various grades (Figures 79 and 80).
5 *Skills profile*. This report attempts to provide input to the audit of existing manpower and to help in determining how future demand may be met from internal sources.
6 *Staff turnover reports*. A CPMIS will provide a number of report relating to turnover – examples are provided in Figures 81, 82, 83, 84 and 85. In some of these reports a labour turnover index is used. This is given by

ABC Manufacturing Co.   20/02/86

Age/grade analysis

Grade	Under 20		21 to 25		26 to 30		31 to 35		36 to 40		41 to 45		Over 60		Total	
	No.	%	No.	%	No.	%	No.	%	No.	%	No.	%	No.	%	No.	%
Totals																

Figure 76　*Age/grade analysis*

ABC Manufacturing Co.

20/02/86

Age/grade/sex analysis

Grade	Under 20				21 – 25				26 – 30				Totals			
	Female		Male		Female		Male		Female		Male		Female		Male	
	No.	%	No.	%	No.	%	No.	%	No.	%	No.	%	No.	%	No.	%
Totals																

Figure 77　*Age/grade/sex analysis*

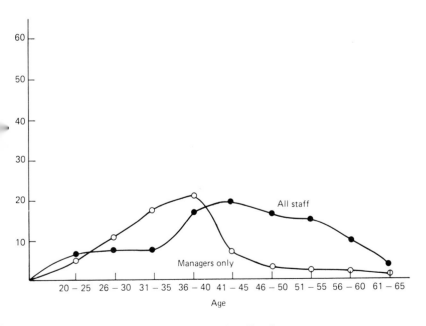

Figure 78　*Graph comparing age profiles of all staff and managers*

ABC Manufacturing Co.   20/02/86

Service/grade analysis

Grade	Under 3 years		3 to 5		6 to 8		9 to 11		12 to 14		Over 40 years		Total	
	No.	%	No.	%	No.	%	No.	%	No.	%	No.	%	No.	%
Total														

Figure 79   *Service/grade analysis*

Figure 80   *Graph comparing service profiles of all staff and managers*

ABC Manufacturing Co.   20/02/86

Staff turnover report for category-managers
Staff who have left the organization since 1/1/85

Cost centre	Name	Grade	Salary	Start date	Date left	Age	Service in organization	Reason for leaving
Personnel admin.	F. Collins	MO3	23,400	15/01/80	31/12/85	32	5.0	Better prospects
Personnel admin.	J. Constable	MO3	24,600	10/02/82	12/06/85	37	3.3	Unhappy
Industrial rels.	R. Woolley	MO1	27,300	19/11/84	31/12/85	38	1.1	Better prospects
Training	H. Fisher	MO5	21,900	12/06/79	17/05/85	29	6.1	Ill-health
Training	M. Moore	MO5	21,700	19/03/82	12/03/85	31	3.0	Own business
Product design	H.C. Dickenson	MO1	29,700	15/03/55	19/09/85	65	30.5	Retired

Figure 81   *Staff turnover report – managers*

ABC Manufacturing Co.   20/02/86

Staff turnover report – grade or cost centre

Grade	Number at 31/12/84	Number at 31/12/85	Number who left	Turnover index
Foreman – class 1	27	23	5	20
Laboratory technician	130	120	20	16

Cost centre

Fabrication	250	240	10	4
Laboratory	190	186	30	16
Manpower services	20	22	1	5
Overall totals	460	448	41	9

Figure 82   *Staff turnover report – grade or cost centre*

$$\frac{\text{Number of leavers during period} \times 100}{\text{Average numbers employed during the period}}$$

The average is calculated by adding the number of employed at both the start and end period and dividing by 2. This obviously ignores recruitment during the period. It is a simple, if crude, measure of staff turnover. It can still be useful despite its limitations, so long as its use is supplemented by other indices such as those which reflect employee survival or stability rates. It should also be pointed out that the production of such reports from a CPMIS is not as straightforward as might appear – account must be taken of various categories of employees (temporary, casual, contract), and employees who are on leave of various types.

The other point which should be emphasized is the need for good data concerning reasons for leaving. Procedures have to be established which allow this data to be captured at time of exit.

A manpower planning model

A manpower model is primarily designed to analyse and plan an organization's manpower supply but it can also be designed to model the demand or manpower requirements aspects. Figure 86 represents a simple manpower system for an organization with six different groups of grade or category of staff. Each of the boxes represents a group of employees. These groupings are referred to in modelling terms as *stocks*. The stocks in the example represent the grade groupings. They relate to the people in these grades at a particular point in time and they could be

ABC Manufacturing Co.

20/02/86

Staff turnover report by age group

Age group	Female				Male			
	Number at 31/12/84	*Number at 31/12/85*	*Number who left*	*Turnover index*	*Number at 31/12/84*	*Number at 31/12/85*	*Number who left*	*Turnover index*
00 to 20								
21 to 25								
26 to 30								
31 to 35								
36 to 40								
41 to 45								
46 to 50								
51 to 55								
56 to 60								
61 to 65								
over 65								
All staff								

Figure 83   *Staff turnover report – age group*

ABC Manufacturing Co.

20/02/86

Analysis of leavers by length of service
period 1/1/85 to 31/12/85

Length of service	Female		Cumulative		Male		Cumulative		Total		Cumulative	
	No.	%	No.	%	No.	%	No.	%	No.	%	No.	%
Up to 3 months	12	5	12	5	25	6	25	6	37	5	37	5
3 to 6 months	20	8	32	13	32	7	57	13	52	8	89	13
6 to 9 months	25	10	57	23	43	10	100	23	68	10	157	23
9 to 12 months	20	8	77	31	38	9	138	32	58	9	215	32
13 to 18 months	18	7	95	38	29	7	167	39	47	7	262	38
18 to 24 months	17	7	112	45	36	8	203	47	53	8	315	46
2 to 3 years	15	6	127	51	30	7	233	54	45	6	360	53
3 to 5 years	16	6	143	57	32	7	265	61	48	7	408	60
5 to 10 years	24	10	167	67	49	11	314	73	73	11	481	71
10 to 15 years	20	8	187	75	48	11	362	84	68	10	549	80
15 to 20 years	18	7	205	82	20	5	382	88	38	6	587	86
20 to 25 years	12	5	217	87	15	3	397	91	27	4	614	90
25 to 30 years	14	6	231	93	18	4	415	96	32	4	646	95
30 to 40 years	10	4	241	97	12	3	427	98	22	3	668	98
over 40 years	8	3	249	100	6	2	433	100	14	2	682	100

Figure 84   *Analysis of leavers by length of service*

Analysis of leavers by reason period 1/1/85 to 31/12/85

Reason	Female		Male		Total	
	No.	%	No.	%	No.	%
01 Retirement	22	9	41	9	63	9
02 Better prospects	29	12	18	4	47	7
03 Ill health	6	3	2	1	8	1
04 Dismissal	2	1	4	1	6	1
05 Starting own business	5	3	11	3	16	2
Totals	249	100	433	100	682	100

Figure 85   *Analysis of leavers by reason for leaving*

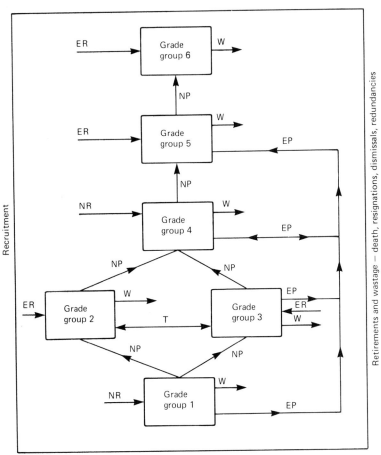

W   = Wastage
T   = Transfers between grades
NR = Normal recruitment (entry grades)
ER = Exceptional recruitment
NP = Normal promotion - to next grade
EP = Exceptional promotion - to any higher grade

Figure 86   *Simple manpower system – stocks and flows*

further subdivided into smaller or alternative groupings on the basis of sex, age, length of service, location etc. Movement into, out of, or between stocks is referred to as *flows*. These flows relate to transfers or promotions between grades, recruitment from outside and departures from the organization. The flows also reflect the natural ageing of the work force.

Figure 86 shows that the modelling system will require data relating to

1 *Current stocks* i.e. a detailed profile of each grade. This includes age, sex, qualifications, service, experience, mobility etc.
2 *Flows*. This means that there must be data on recruits, leavers, promotions and transfers. This includes items such as normal wastage rates by type, normal transfer rates between grades, and normal or historical promotion rates between grades.
3 *Rules* including rules governing promotion (e.g. age requirement), policy on recruitment, normal retirement age, schemes for early retirement, projected redundancy schemes etc.

Once this data is available the model will be designed to use the data and the rules and to project forward over the required period of time. The system will then be in a position to provide outputs such as

• age profile of organization five years' hence
• service and grade profile during the same period
• likely number of internal promotions over the period and the gaps which this may leave in the organization.

17 Query language and report generator

In the context of a personnel system the terms query language and report generator are synonymous. The facility must allow for the users of the system to answer *ad hoc* queries speedily and generally without reference to data processing staff. This is done by means of an interactive session at a computer terminal during which the user formulates the query and specifies how it is to be output. The query is formulated via a query language part of which is an output formatter or report formatter. A report generator plays the same role as a query language but the emphasis is on the report formatting end and it may have more advanced reporting features than a package which is primarily concerned with data retrieval.

A CPMIS will have various facilities built into it as normal features. For example if a manager wishes to ascertain

- the salary history relating to an individual employee
- the vacancies unfilled in a particular department
- the number of staff serving against the established posts in each division within the organization
- what applicants have been called for interview for the post of chief chemist

it will be possible to obtain the information by calling up the relevant facility which will already be part of the system.

Problems will arise, however, if a manager wants to know

- how many employees do we have who are over sixty years of age and earn less than £10,000 per annum
- how many staff will be retiring from the transport department in the next five years
- how many qualified engineers do we have working for us apart from those in the production division.

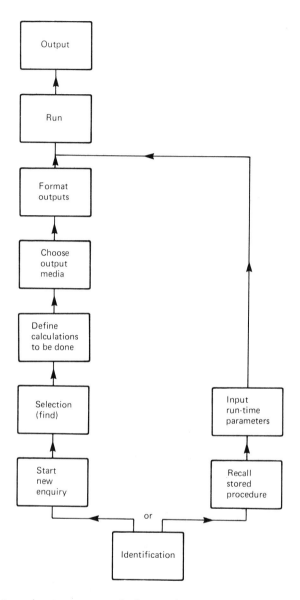

Figure 87   *Query language – stages in the enquiry process*

There will be no specific item on a menu which will provide this facility. If the system is to be worthwhile it must be possible to be able to input something like this

FIND ALL EMPLOYEES WITH AGE GREATER THAN 60 AND ANNUAL SALARY LESS THAN £10,000.

LIST EMPLOYEE NUMBER, NAME, COST-CENTRE, AGE, DATE-OF-BIRTH, SALARY.

The value of such a facility is obvious and the complexity of the system required to handle this type of query can also be appreciated. It is also obvious that the task of developing such a system is enormous if maximum flexibility is to be provided for. Such a system would probably require more development resources than that required to develop the CPMIS itself. Computer manufacturers and software houses have of course recognized this and have developed packages to meet these requirements.

Query languages are available for most computers and the more popular models will have a choice available. The systems vary greatly in terms of facilities, ease of use and of integration with the CPMIS. Since its use is an important factor in the success of the system, evaluation of the query system ranks alongside the evaluation of the personnel system proposal or package proposal and the evaluation of the hardware.

Principles of operation

A query language revolves around the use of a dictionary or directory. The format and contents of dictionaries can vary considerably. They range from a data dictionary which is an integral part of the systems philosophy of a computer supplier, to the directory which is constructed specifically to allow the query language to be used on certain files.

The dictionary describes the data held in the system, the structure relating to how the data is held, relationships between file and record types, and database structures. It will also hold data names relating to each field and alternative names or synonyms. If the query language is just one element in the computer manufacturer's total approach to systems development in which the data dictionary plays a central role, then all of the data required will already have been defined in the data dictionary. This is the case with ICL (International Computers Ltd) whose system development philosophy is built around a very sophisticated data dictionary system. The data dictionary is surrounded by various products including

1 *IDMS*   A database management system.
2 *Application master*   A fourth generation language which allows for the fast development of new systems.
3 *Querymaster*   A query language.
4 *Reportmaster*   A report generator.

Depending upon the nature of the dictionary it is either generated by the data processing department, by the supplies of the package or generated by someone in personnel who has a detailed knowledge of the structure of the system. In any case a user should not have to worry about how this is done. One of the features of a good query system is that the user should only be concerned with specifying the problem — not wondering how the system can be set up to cater for the problem.

When a user sits down at a computer terminal (VDU) the procedure is as shown in Figure 87. The first stage is one of identification – introducing himself or herself to the system, quoting the user name and password and indicating the data which he/she wishes to enquire upon. At that stage he/she lets the computer know whether he/she wants to generate a completely new enquiry or to call up a query which has been input previously and stored so that it can be rerun. In the case of the latter he/she may want to rerun it with a different set of parameters. It may already be set up, for example, to list all employees with annual salaries between £10,000 and £20,000. If he/she now wants to list all employees with salaries between £25,000 and £30,000 and still requires the same output format, he/she may input something like

RUN SALARIES (25000, 30000)

where SALARIES is the name of job to be run and it allows for the input of two parameters.

In the case of a new enquiry the next phase is to specify the selection criteria e.g. 'all employees over 50'. This is done by specifying data items (e.g. AGE), and values (e.g. 50) and linking them via boolean expressions, (e.g. EQUAL TO), logical expressions, (e.g. AND), and other expressions (e.g. CONTAINS). A list of typical items or operators is shown in Figure 88.

The ease with which the selections can be input is determined by how much flexibility the system allows in terms of alternative forms or spellings of data names and expressions. The variety of formats of expressions used can be seen in Figure 88, although some systems do not provide as much choice. With data names it varies very much from system to system. Some cater for a single name per item while others allow a virtually unlimited number of alternatives or synonyms. In the case of the latter the responsibility lies with the person who sets up the system to input an adequate number of alternatives. In practice this can be a tedious operation and there may be a tendency to short-cut this stage but in the longer term the additional work will be rewarded by ease of use. Ideally someone from the personnel area should be able to use the system without having to refer to lists of field names. References may have to be made on occasion to lists of grade codes, allowance codes, conditions of service codes etc. The facility to be able to refer to the field name COST-CENTRE as CC, CCENT, CCENTRE, COSTC, BUDGET-CENTRE, BUD-CENTRE, COST-CENTRE, BUDGET-CENTRE or BC clearly identifies the value of using synonyms.

In some systems it is also possible to use 'conditionals'. With this facility it is possible, for example, to input MALE rather than SEX = M, or PERMANENT to select all permanent employees rather than by inputting something like IF CATEGORY = P. Sets of conditions are used in the selection process by the use of AND, OR and NOT. The following are examples

Operator	Meaning	Examples
= Equal Equals Equal to EQ	Equal to	Cost-centre = 4206 Grade equals 216
Not = < > NE Not equal Not equal to =/=	Not equal to	Category not = permanent Grade not EQ 300
> Greater Greater than GT	Greater than (Not greater than expressed by a prefix of NOT)	Salary > 10000 Age GT 50
> = GE Greater or equal > or = GT or EQ > or equal	Greater than or equal to	Salary > = 10000 Age GT or EQ 50
< LT Less than Less	Less than (not less than expressed by a prefix of NOT)	Allowances less than 5000 Allowances < Salary
< = LE Less or equal < or = LT or EQ < or equal	Less than or equal to	Overtime-earnings LE 5000 Service < or equal 20
Between BT	Value is between two given values (usually inclusive)	Salary between 10000 and 20000 This is equivalent to Salary GE 10000 and Salary LE 20000
STA Starts with Startswith	Starts with	Name STA 'COLL'
CON Contains	Contains	Address CON 'LONDON'

Figure 88   *Alternative forms of operators*

1 SALARY > 20000 AND
   AGE > 60 AND
   PENSIONABLE-SERVICE > 30.
2 GRADE = 300 AND COST-CENTRE BT 2400 and 2800
   OR
   GRADE = 500 AND COST-CENTRE > 3340
3 EDUCATION-LEVEL > 5 AND LANGUAGE-PROFICIENCY (5)
   > 3 AND NOT OVERSEAS

The next stage is to define to the system what calculations should be carried out on the data and what counts should be established. This is done by using work-fields and the usual arithmetic operators are used

+ Addition
− Subtraction
× Multiplication
/ Division
% Percentage.

For example

    REMUNERATION = SALARY + ANNUAL-ALLOWANCES
    NEW-SALARY   = SALARY % 110
 or NEW-SALARY   = SALARY × 1.1

It is sometimes possible to specify the calculations to be performed prior to the selection phase and to incorporate the results into the enquiry. Thus

    NEW-SALARY = SALARY × 1.2
    FIND NEW-SALARY > 20000

allows for selecting all employees who would have an annual salary of more than £20,000 after their salaries have been notionally increased by 20 per cent.

The next stage is to choose the output medium – VDU, main printer, local printer etc. – and to format the output in accordance with the type of output medium chosen. This must take into account such matters as the 80-column VDU display compared with the facility to print over 130 characters per line on printer output. The sort sequence of the output must also be determined. The title of the output must be specified together with the various fields to be printed, field headings, page numbering, spacing between lines, skipping to new page, control breaks and totals to be displayed or printed. At that stage the user may also have an option to store the enquiry for future use. This involves assigning a name to it for subsequent identification and also providing for the input of run-time parameters.

The remainder of this chapter consists of a brief description of two examples of query languages and a list of points to watch out for in evaluating a query language.

A simple system

DEKE is a general purpose enquiry package designed to allow user department staff to obtain answers to complex enquiries on computer files or databases almost instantly. It is a product developed by Dorset County Council for use on ICL 2900 series computers running under the VME operating system. Thus in the personnel context it applies to a CPMIS run on the corporate main-frame.

The structure of the files to be used and the data names and synonyms are defined to the system by the DP department. The user is given a directory listing which is a list of all of the data items in a particular virtual file, which is a user's view of data which may be drawn from one or more physical computer files. Armed with this listing, the passwords required and a concise user manual, the user can come to terms with this truly user-friendly system within a matter of hours. The system is unusual in that it generates a COBOL source program using the information supplied by a user to determine the code to be generated. Once the user has finished specifying the enquiry conditions a batch job is issued which goes through the normal process of compiling and running the generated COBOL program.

The DEKE enquiry process consists of five phases –

Identification during which the user identifies himself or herself to the system and nominates the virtual files to be enquired upon.

Selection during which the user specifies the selection criteria, calculations, output medium and output format to be used within the enquiry.

Extraction/compilation. During this phase DEKE generates the COBOL program and initiates the compilation process.

Processing/reporting. During this phase the program is run and the output is produced as specified.

Finalization. As soon as the enquiry is completed, the output has been produced and the user is finished, the system performs the housekeeping tasks of deleting the generated program and all other traces of the completed enquiry.

To illustrate the use of this system the following query is chosen.

Provide a listing by grade of all staff with an annual salary of more than £20,000. Start each grade on a new page and provide titles for each grade – number over £20,000 and their total salary. Also show the impact of a 4.5 per cent increase in their salaries.

This query is designed to demonstrate a straightforward use of the system. A user familiar with the system would submit this query in less than five minutes and should have results within a few minutes depending on the size of the files involved and the workload on the computer. The screen layouts used in general equate to actual DEKE screens but in the interests of providing a quick overview some item are omitted.

In Figure 89 the user selects PERSONNEL as distinct from SALES,

---

DEKE enquiry system

What data do you wish to look at?   [Personnel]
Give the necessary password   [Secret]
Identification   [JNF]

Figure 89 *DEKE identification screen*

DEKE enquiry system

Please mark the virtual file that you wish to look at
Personnel records   [x]   Training   [ ]
Recruitment   [ ]   Personnel complete [ ]
Personnel summary   [ ]   Pension fund   [ ]
Qualifications   [ ]   Establishment   [ ]
Payroll   [ ]   [ ]

Figure 90 *DEKE virtual file selection screen*

DEKE enquiry system

Please enter your selections or type 'E' to pass to next screen
[Salary > 20000   ]
[   ]
[   ]
[   ]
[   ]
[   ]

Figure 91 *DEKE general selection screen*

DEKE enquiry system

Definition of work fields
[New-salary   ] = [Salary   ] [x] [1.045   ]
[Work 02   ] = [   ] [ ] [   ]
[Work 03   ] = [   ] [ ] [   ]

Figure 92 *DEKE work fields screen*

```
                          DEKE enquiry system
  Please define COUNT01
  [All                                                      ]
  [                                                         ]
  [                                                         ]
  [                                                         ]
  [                                                         ]
```

Figure 93 *DEKE count screen*

```
                          DEKE enquiry system
  Please enter the required output options
  Page limited [100]         Selection limit [2000]
  Single or double spacing? [D]
  Do you want the output sorted? [Y]
  Destination [VDU]          Media [    ]
  Page width [080]           Page Depth [20]
  Copies [    ]              Lines/inch [    ]
```

Figure 94 *DEKE reporting options screen*

```
                          DEKE enquiry system
  Title?        [Salaries over £20,000 by grade      ]
  ----------------------------------------------------------------
  List fields to be printed [Grade * P      ] [No.       ]
  [First name       ]   [Surname      ]   [Salary          ]
  [New salary       ]   [Age          ]   [Cost centre     ]
  [                 ]   [             ]   [                 ]
  ----------------------------------------------------------------
  Please give any control breaks you require [Grade      ]
  [                ]   [              ]   [                 ]
  ----------------------------------------------------------------
  and fields to be totalled [Salary      ] [New salary]
  [Count01         ]        [             ]    [            ]
```

Figure 95 *DEKE report formatting screen*

STORES etc. and provides the password associated with the dat.
Having gained access to PERSONNEL the user is asked in Figure 90 t
indicate the file or view within PERSONNEL that he/she is interested is
Suppose the user knows that the information required can be obtaine
from PERSONNEL-RECORDS. The system then invites him/her to inpu
the selection criteria (Figure 91). The user realizes that he/she has t
print revised salaries showing a 4.5 per cent increase on current levels s
he/she uses a work-field (NEW SALARY) as shown in Figure 92.

Since the number of selected staff in each grade is required he/sh
defines COUNT01 as relating to *all* employees selected (Figure 93). I
Figure 94 the user indicates how the result is to be output. Generally th
screen will have normal default values and any required changes, e.
double spacing required on output, sorted output required, are mad
The screen shown in Figure 95 provides the means of formatting tl
output report, whether it is on screen or on paper. The title which is t
appear at the top of each page is input followed by all of the fields to t
printed. In the example, GRADE ✣ P indicates to the system that GRAD
is the first item on the line, that the report is to be sorted in ascendir
grade sequence (since the sort option was chosen in Figure 94) and th;
on change of grade the system should skip to a new page. The remainir
fields to be printed are then input. The user is then asked to indicate ar
control breaks required. In this case totals are required by grade so tl
user then inputs any fields which have to be totalled at both break ar
overall level. In the example, current salary and the increased salary a;
input and since all selected employees are to be counted this will t
printed automatically.

When the program has finished, the output as shown in Figure 96 w
appear on the screen as requested – there is no requirement to bring tl
output back to the VDU before printing, but this was the option chos€
for this report. At this stage the user can page backwards and forwa;
through the report and this is sometimes done to verify that the que
was specified correctly prior to initiating a print that may consist

---

Next page 002

Salaries over £20,000 by Grade   Date 20/01/86   Time 15:03 page 1

Grade	No.	First name	Surname	Salary	New salary	Age	Cost centre
001	04213	Bob	Morgan	21,306	22,265	32	4107
001	05316	John	Harvey	25,109	26,239	30	2176
001	11217	Kenneth	Stoker	20,976	21,920	25	2260
001	12416	Dennis	Turner	27,308	28,537	28	2356
001	13917	David	Morday	22,147	23,144	49	2356

COUNT01 5 SALARY 116,846   NEW SALARY 122,105

Figure 96   *DEKE enquiry result on VDU*

```
                    DEKE enquiry system
Please specify how your output is to be listed
Device [PERS      ]
Number of copies [2]
Media [      ]
Page width [80]
Page depth [20]
Lines per inch [6]
```

Figure 97   *DEKE post-video print screen*

hundreds of pages. To print the output the user calls up the screen shown in Figure 97 and overwrites whatever parameters should be changed: in our example the report is to be produced on a normal printer in the personnel department and two copies are required.

Datatrieve

DATATRIEVE is a product of Digital Equipment Corporation (DEC) and versions of it run on DEC's range of computers. It is an interactive query, report and data maintenance system designed for use by both data processing and user staff. It is a more extensive system than DEKE and accordingly can be more difficult to master – the more sophisticated and comprehensive the facilities are, the more complex the operating instructions must become. It is a data management tool as well as a means of retrieving data. This means that the person using it can create, amend or delete records or data items. The use of this type of facility must be tightly controlled if the personnel database is to be protected.

DATATRIEVE is a full command language. The command language can be simple to use. Each command name describes its function (e.g. MODIFY, SORT and PRINT) and the syntax of each command is similar to that of English. The following DATATRIEVE statement requests that data on all employees with overtime earnings in excess of £2000 be displayed.

PRINT ALL OF EMPLOYEES WITH OT-YTD GREATER THAN 2000

The system carries out each command as it is entered so the results can be seen immediately. It is therefore possible to continue by issuing more commands, correcting errors, seeking help or stopping. If the system cannot understand the instructions a clear error message is displayed and if parts of a command are not input the system will issue prompts for the missing data.

The HELP facility is comprehensive. The HELP command displays a complete description of all commands, their effects and examples of how to use them. Assistance on individual commands can be obtained by specifying the command involved.

As well as the HELP facility the system also provides a GUIDE mode which is useful for beginners in that it prompts the user for every operation and the user is thus led through the session. Datatrieve commands range from the simple ones which allow the casual user to produce immediate results, to the complex ones which can combine many functions in a simple operation and which can produce complex reports with sophisticated formats. The system can have graphics commands which allow further information to be presented as histograms, bar charts, pie charts, scatter diagrams, or time-series graphs. Complex procedures can be stored and reused. The sort facility allows users to sort records in either ascending or descending order of the value of any field.

Datatrieve provides the following statistical functions which can be used wherever a value expression is required

1 *MAX*   The largest value.
2 *MIN*   The smallest value.
3 *AVERAGE*   The average value.

These facilities are not available in some query languages. The following examples show how useful they are – without these facilities this data would have to be derived some other way.

FIND EMPLOYEES WITH SALARY > 0
PRINT AVERAGE SALARY
PRINT MIN SALARY
PRINT MAX SALARY

PRINT EMPLOYEES WITH SALARY = MAX SALARY OF EMPLOYEES

Statements such as IF THEN ELSE or REPEAT enable users to incorporate complex conditions in data retrieval procedures.

The report writer creates and prints reports in a variety of formats but it is also possible to produce simpler reports using the single statement PRINT. While PRINT does not provide the full formatting and statistical facilities of report writer it is a very useful facility.

The description tables facility – which is similar in concept to the descriptor file described for the CPMIS – is very useful in making reports more easily understood. A description table is a group of code-and-description pairs which the user can create and store under a unique name. Using this facility it is possible to hold a code in the employee record but in printing the record it is possible to print the description held in the description table rather than the code itself e.g. 'Single widowed or divorced' rather than 'S'.

Apart from use of files and records two further terms are used by DATATRIEVE

1 *DOMAIN* which is defined as a specific group of related data – a complete set of records which have the same record definition. In a

simple example this equates to a file.

2 *COLLECTION* which consists of related records that are brought together into one unit. An example of a collection is the group of records resulting from a FIND command to collect all employees born between 1 January 1940 and 31 December 1949.

The main commands used by the system are

1 *HELP*   Provides a summary of each DATATRIEVE command.

2 *READY*   Identifies a domain for processing and controls the access mode to the appropriate file.

3 *FIND*   Establishes a collection or subset of records contained in either a domain or a previously established collection.

4 *SORT*   Records a collection of records in either the ascending or descending sequence of the contents of one or more of the fields in the records.

5 *PRINT*   Prints one or more fields or one or more records.

6 *SELECT*   Identifies a single record in a collection for subsequent individual processing.

```
DTR >   Ready employees
DTR >   Report employees with allowances > 2,000

                    Sorted by cost centre

RW >    Set report-name = 'employees with allowances over £2000'/
RW >    'Monthly report'/
RW >    'July/Aug 1986'
RW >    Set column-page = 70
RW >    At bottom of report print col 1, 'Total employees': ', –
RW >    Count col 35, 'Total allows.', Total allowances using ZZ,ZZZ
RW >    Print name, cost-centre, grade, allowances
RW >    End-report
```

Employee with Annual Allowances Over 2,000
Monthly Report
July/August 1986

Name	Cost-centre	Grade	Allowances
M. Bush	2106	301	2,800
R. Elliot	2107	301	3,500
H. Hopkins	2318	350	2,100
R.V. Cole	3218	280	2,750
A. Rees	4200	281	3,225
Total employees: 5	Total allows:		14,375

Figure 98   *Simple DATATRIEVE report*

7 *DECLARE* Defines global and local variables to be used within a DATATRIEVE query.

8 *DEFINE* Provides a consistent mechanism for creating domain, record, procedure, table and view definitions in the data dictionary. In addition to these commands, which aid information retrieval, commands such as STORE, MODIFY, ERASE and EDIT provide facilities for data maintenance.

A DATATRIEVE query to produce a simple report is shown in Figure 98.

Desiderata of a query language

The primary requirement of a query language is that it should be easy to use. Otherwise people will be reluctant to use it and so the value of the computer-based personnel system will be substantially reduced. This can be overcome to some extent by writing a number of procedures to cater for as many sets of conditions as can be envisaged, which can be stored away and recalled easily by the personnel staff. These procedures should allow variable parameters to be used as they are being run. Appropriate measures should be taken for restricting access to the system and to particular data or features. This is done by the use of passwords and user codes and is particularly important if the system is capable of adding, altering or deleting data. It may also be useful if a log is maintained of the use or attempted use of the system. The system must be capable of supporting the file structures or database of the CPMIS. It must also be capable of using both VDUs and printers for the output of results.

It should be easy to implement the system, easy to set up the dictionary or directory and it should be supported by good documentation and training.

Good report formatting facilities are essential if easily understood reports are to be produced. This involves facilities for

- user defined report headings
- automatic printing of date and time
- automatic page-numbering
- single-line and multi-line formats
- printing of literals
- suppression of leading zeroes
- variable page size
- variable number of columns per page
- variable horizontal spacing
- setting the length of the report
- maximum number of lines or pages
- control breaks
- totalling.

The specification of selecting criteria must be easy to input and this can be facilitated by provision for a number of synonyms for each field.

ABC Manufacturing Co.		20/10/86
Report on employees in each grade		
Grade	*Name*	*Salary*
Architect grade 1	J. Dawson	20,216
	H. Moore	20,420
	R. Palmer	20,420
Senior architect	K. J. Fisher	27,987
	Joseph Watson	27,987
Drawing office asst.	N. C. Baker	15,305
	D. Stephens	12,201
	H. A. Shaw	11,104
Draughtsperson – gde. 1	R. P. Taylor	13,312
Draughtsperson – gde. 2	K. Collins	15,107
	M. Davies	15,309

Figure 99   *Report with suppression of grade title repetition*

String handling is a useful feature for retrieval of certain types of data. Sorting facilities should cater for both ascending and descending sequence. Table handling facilities, if available, can result in file production of reports which are more easily understood.

The system should be able to recognize dates as special format fields for comparisons, calculations and printing. There are various print formats available for printing dates – YYMMDD, DDMMYY, YY/MM/DD, DDMMYY, and DD/MM/YY – so the most suitable must be chosen. If the system has a facility for printing out specific values only when they change the result can be a clearer report format. For example, if a report on employees by grade is produced and the grade is only printed on change of grade it will be easier to absorb than a report which prints the grade on every line (see Figure 99).

The availability of the main statistical functions will also help to make certain outputs more meaningful and this facility is further enhanced if a graphics capability is also available. Every system will have provision for work-fields and counts but it is worth finding out how easy it is to use them and how many such fields are available.

18 Other features and peripheral applications

This chapter deals with items which can be classified into three groups.

1 Special requirements which may be satisfied within the boundaries of the CPMIS.
2 Requirements which exist within the personnel management function but which may be regarded as 'peripheral' to the CPMIS proper and which are probably catered for most satisfactorily by computer-based systems which are largely outside the main personnel system.
3 Facilities which may improve the effectiveness of the CPMIS.

Conditions of service

In a CPMIS it is generally worth inputting conditions of service and associating them with each employee. One approach is to set up a file or files of conditions and to define for each grade the conditions which apply. Conditions relate to such matters as

- hours per week
- overtime entitlements
- shift and other premium pay entitlements
- annual leave entitlements
- entitlements to allowances.

It may be appropriate to store within the system two descriptions of each condition. One would be a suitable abbreviation which would be concise enough to be displayed on a screen. The other would be a detailed description of each condition of service which could for example be incorporated into a letter offering a job to a prospective employee or which could be included in defining the conditions of individual grades as they would appear in the personnel procedures manual or in a supervisors' handbook. Figure 100 is an example of an enquiry on an

---

ABC Manufacturing Co.

Employee conditions of service

Personnel No. 43267   Whiteside John David

Cost centre: Drawing office
Division: Engineering
Post: Draughtsperson   Grade 2   E30203

Conditions

01 Grade 2 roster	02 Tech roster duty allowance
23 Overtime scale 2	34 Annual leave entitlement type 6
38 Public holiday category 3	44 Progression type 4
53 Service leave A	

Figure 100   *Display of conditions of service (abbreviated) – employee*

individual employee showing the abbreviated form of his conditions of service.

The process of assembling all current conditions of service relating to each grade can in itself be a most useful exercise. It may indeed be difficult because it is quite possible that the central records would not be up to date or may consist of files of agreements, letters to trades unions etc., from which it is not easy quickly to ascertain the up-to-date position. Many organizations have experienced the delay in providing the payroll department with the answers to what appears to be a simple enquiry as to an employee's entitlement to some form of premium payment. Even if the data were never input to the computer system, at least the exercise will result in a concise definition of conditions for each grade.

Accidents on duty

The computer may be required to hold details of accidents involving employees on duty. The need to have this data on computer is determined by the number of employees and the nature of the industry. If it is decided to hold the data on computer, the forms used for recording accidents should be designed so as to facilitate its input. Since the computer is best at calculations, analysis and comparisons, the data should be structured accordingly. This allows for the production of both statutory returns and internal statistics and comparisons. Thus it will be possible to answer questions such as 'What proportion of serious accidents occur in the Machine Shop in —?' and 'What impact has the Health and Safety Campaign in — had over the past two years?'

The following is typical of data held for each accident.

- personnel number
- name

- National Insurance classification
- grade
- cost centre/department
- date of accident
- time of accident
- location of accident
- cause of accident
- injuries sustained
- extent of medical attention required
- degree of hospitalization
- absence from work arising out of the accident
- action taken
- various analysis codes used in classifying accidents.

In setting up accident data, consideration should also be given to other departments which may already have systems in operation to hold this data or which may benefit from having access to the output from the system. These potential users include

- health and safety committee
- transport/distribution department
- insurance department.

Facilities booking

The personnel division as a whole may have a need to keep records of forward bookings of facilities such as conference rooms, interview rooms, lecture rooms and other training facilities. The practicality of using a computer to assist in booking the facilities will depend on the number of facilities concerned, how the booking procedure is normally handled and any need to interface with aspects of the CPMIS such as training or recruitment. If it is considered a worthwhile computer application it should be structured so as to provide statistical output as a by-product. These statistics could relate to the level of usage of each facility, which departments used them, the number of meetings held with each trade union etc. To get these statistics from the system the relevant data must be input at the time of booking and it may be difficult to get reliable data. It also necessitates logging all bookings, including such items as maintenance (e.g. painting of interview rooms or scheduled maintenance of the training workshop). To complete the picture the system would also have to take account of 'outside' facilities used by the organization.

Industrial relations information

An information storage and retrieval system catering for information which is of use throughout the personnel division in general and the industrial relations area in particular can be of benefit. This facility could be used to

Requirement: Find all references to paint-shop productivity in meetings with
trade unions.

Select database: Industrial relations
Search chapter: Union meetings
Find paint-shop and productivity or paint-shop and efficiency or paint-shop and
output measurement
3 articles fulfil the specified criteria
1 Meeting with union group 20/10/85
2 Arbitration hearing 26/12/85
3 Meeting with paint union 20/02/86
Please select article:

Figure 101 *Information retrieval example*

1 Provide up-to-date information, or pointers to where such information
is available on issues such as disturbance pay settlements, and
regulations and trends relating to annual leave, maternity leave,
paternity leave etc. This information can be obtained from such
sources as arbitration awards, appeal tribunal awards, ACAS recommendations and legislation.
2 Hold indexes of professional journals, reports of commissions reporting on industrial relations matters etc.
3 Hold details of internal or external (e.g. national) agreements.
4 Hold published measurements such as the cost of living index, index of
retail prices, index of industrial production, and productivity norms
for the industry.

Packages are available – mainly on larger computers – which accept data
in a relatively unstructured format and provide a means of retrieving the
data in a straightforward, easy-to-use and efficient manner. Such packages often automatically accept documents produced by a word processing system and in doing so generate an index which can be used for
subsequent retrieval. This can be very useful for storing such items as
minutes of meetings and union agreements. Figure 101 shows how the
information can be retrieved.

Disputes information

Statistics relating to disputes will be required by management and also
by other bodies – both statutory and trade. Generally once this data has
been 'captured' it is not difficult to summarize and produce comparative
figures. Larger organizations may wish to hold this information on
computer and have the computer produce the statistics. This can be
useful if the computing facilities are available and it helps to establish a
routine in regard to the collection of the basic data.
   The data held for a dispute typically would include

1 Trade union(s) involved.
2 Classification of staff involved
   • grades
   • cost centres
   • personnel numbers.
3 Subject of dispute.
4 Dispute classification – official/unofficial.
5 Nature of dispute
   • work-to-rule
   • overtime ban
   • all-out strike etc.
6 Duration – start and finish.
7 Number of staff involved directly.
8 Number of person-days lost.
9 Production lost.
10 Revenue lost.

Graphics

The availability of a graphics facility can enhance the effectiveness of the management information produced by a CPMIS. The impact of the pie chart in Figure 102 is greater than a tabulation of numbers of staff in the

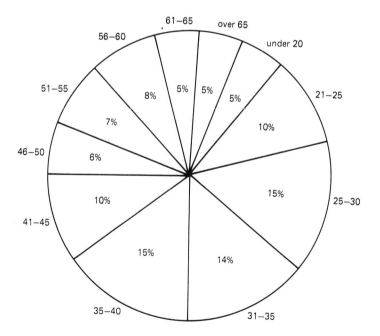

Figure 102   *Age profile pie chart*

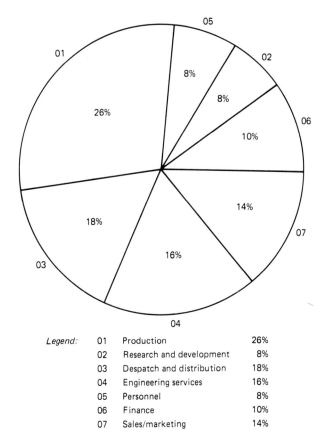

Figure 103   *Salary by division pie chart*

various age groupings. Similarly Figure 103 shows at a glance how the salary bill is spread over the divisions within the organization. Graphical output can be displayed on VDUs which support graphical output but since hard copy is generally required, graphics may require a graph-plotter. Of course a graphics facility is not essential since the output can always be produced in other ways once the basic data is available. It should also be remembered that graphics are not necessarily always better. If yearly intervals were chosen in Figure 102 the result would be meaningless. Similarly if there were 100 different grades of employee in the organization, using a pie chart to show the grade distribution would also result in a form of output which would be impossible to comprehend.

Diary facilities

The need for diary facilities can be approached in either of two ways or by a combination of both. The first method is to hold key dates on each employee's record and to produce listings relating to forthcoming events. Examples of such dates are

- probation expiry date
- training/apprenticeship end date
- increment date
- contract expiry date
- automatic grade progression date
- expected retirement date.

Using these dates the system would be expected to produce reports in advance of forthcoming events, e.g. lists of increments due next month, or reports on contracts due to expire next month. Predefined fields in the employee record will cater for these items and *ad hoc* events can be catered for by having a number of fields which can be associated with a date and a description or narrative. The dates and narratives can be held in the descriptor file, but a more flexible approach is to allow a number of dates and associated descriptions to be attached to an employee record. This data would be displayed on an employee enquiry screen and would also be used to generate reports.

It is even more useful to allow for the holding of a code or initials against each date so that the reports can be provided for the person in the personnel department who is interested in the event (see Figure 104). The benefits of this approach are that the events are attached to an employee,

Extract from an employee record

Personnel no.	Name	Diary date	Description	Initials
40206	J. Acorn	14 06 86	Salary review promised	JHC

Sample report

ABC Manufacturing Co.   15 05 86

Diary review list for JHC

The following items have a diary date occurring during June 1986

Personnel no.	Name	Cost centre	Date	Description
40206	J Acorn	Design	14 06 86	Salary review promised
20849	T F Baker	Budgets	16 06 86	Due back from ABC Overseas Ltd
21907	M T Stanley	Personnel	21 06 86	Getting married
10476	A R Millar	Sales	24 06 86	Special performance review

Figure 104   *Ad-hoc diary dates on employee record*

they can be displayed on the employee enquiry screen, but can also be listed for attention by the person who is interested in the events.

The second method is to set up a personal diary system in the computer. Every user would have a diary facility protected by password, which would allow him/her to hold on the system any type of data or reminder which could be examined on screen. This method has some advantages but overall it is better to have the events associated with employees as described in the first method.

Telephone directory

It is reasonable to consider including in the CPMIS a telephone extension number of each employee. Having done this it may be possible to produce an internal telephone directory. This may be satisfactory in some cases but the following factors should be borne in mind

1 It may be necessary to provide for more than one extension number for an employee.
2 A directory normally provides extension numbers for departments or sections as well as for individual employees.
3 Unless there are workable procedures, the personnel department may find it difficult to keep this data up-to-date.

Labels

A personnel system should be capable of producing labels for despatching enveloped material to all staff or selected groups of staff. This may be catered for by the word processing system or the letter production facilities. Figure 105 shows a screen layout appropriate to the production of labels.

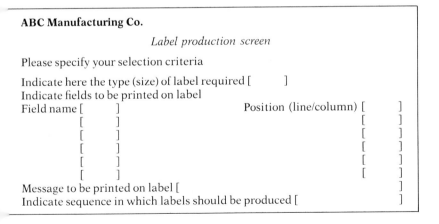

```
ABC Manufacturing Co.
                      Label production screen
    Please specify your selection criteria
    Indicate here the type (size) of label required [    ]
    Indicate fields to be printed on label
    Field name [    ]              Position (line/column) [    ]
               [    ]                                     [    ]
               [    ]                                     [    ]
               [    ]                                     [    ]
               [    ]                                     [    ]
               [    ]                                     [    ]
    Message to be printed on label [                            ]
    Indicate sequence in which labels should be produced [      ]
```

Figure 105 *Label production screen*

The first section of the screen is for specifying the selection criteria, for example

1 GRADE-CODE > 500 AND AGE > 60
2 COST-CENTRE > 4000 AND COST-CENTRE < 5000
   OR COST-CENTRE = 2030
   OR COST-CENTRE = 2640
   OR COST-CENTRE = 2930 AND CATEGORY = 1

The second section provides for the selection of the size of labels required (assuming that the system can cope with more than one type.) The remainder of the screen is concerned with the fields to be printed (e.g. name, address, cost centre) where they should be printed on the screen the sequence in which the labels should be produced (e.g. location) and any special message to be printed on the labels.

19 Proposals for hardware and software

his chapter outlines the process involved from the stage at which it is
ecided to go out to tender or seek proposals through to the issue of a
commendation. It examines the question of determining who should be
vited to propose, provides some guidance on the evaluation of propos-
s and suggests a format of report outlining the recommendations.

eeking proposals

uring the feasibility stage of the project the main options available will
ave been considered and now that the requirements have been defined
 a fair degree of detail it is appropriate to seek proposals for the
evelopment or supply of a system. A decision will already have been
ade as to the approach to be taken – main-frame or dedicated
ersonnel computer; custom-built system, existing package or modified
ackage. No matter which approach is chosen an appropriate proposal
ould be made to the personnel management function. This applies
ually to the development of an in-house system and to a bought-in
stem. Apart perhaps from the financial aspects, the in-house proposal
ould be similar to an outside one. It should include guarantees of
rvice, an implementation timescale, commitment to the involvement
 specified analysts and programmers and most of the other safeguards
hich would be sought from an external supplier.

In this chapter and chapter 20, which examines the process of evaluat-
g proposals, it is assumed that a decision has been taken to acquire a
ackage which will probably require a certain amount of modification to
eet the organization's specific requirements and that it should run on a
dicated computer within the personnel function.

Seeking a proposal covering both hardware and software has a lot of
lvantages over obtaining hardware and software from different
urces. In this way it is possible to have assurances that the combined

227

performance of hardware and software will fulfil the stated require
ments. If separate suppliers are involved there is plenty of scope fo
conflict concerning

1 Delivery times of hardware and software.
2 Suitability of the hardware and system software for the applicatio
software. There may be differences between computer models withi
the same series or slight differences in terms of facilities provided by
version of the system software.
3 Performance of the hardware or software on the particular configur
tion installed; if the transaction response time on the system i
unsatisfactory the software supplier will be blaming the hardware an
vice versa.
4 Other problems, of a teething and long-term nature, may arise an
result in arguments as to who is responsible.

In this situation it is imperative that there should be a single propos
covering both hardware and software and that this should be the subjec
of an agreement/contract with a single supplier. The contract shoul
generally be with the hardware supplier. This may appear to caus
problems because the hardware supplier is not the owner or developer
the personnel system. This can usually be resolved by putting th
hardware supplier in touch with the software supplier and allowin
them to sort out their own contractual arrangements. In this way if the
is a problem subsequently there can be no doubt as to who is responsibl

Proposals from whom?

Some organizations seek proposals from as many potential suppliers
possible. Generally speaking this is a mistake. It gives rise to delays, t
the investment of a lot of time and money by both the organizatio
seeking the proposals and by the proposers. Before inviting proposals th
market should have been examined, i.e. as soon as discussion drafts
the specification of requirements become available (see Figure 106).

Once the requirements have been defined it is relatively easy t
pinpoint the systems which are broadly in line with them and usually
maximum of five or six proposals should be sought. Before deciding o
the final number, the likely candidates should be approached and give
an opportunity to make a brief presentation of their system and
discuss special requirements. In this way it will be possible to rule o
any which are unlikely to figure in the final evaluation. This will allo
more effort to be devoted to the real contenders. It also avoids th
situation where a supplier has to devote time to producing a detailed an
often expensive proposal within a given timescale, to allocating staff
setting up demonstrations and presentations, even though at the end
the day he has no real chance of getting the business.

The invitation

When the decision has been made as to who should be invited to subm
proposals a formal invitation should be issued. This should be sent o

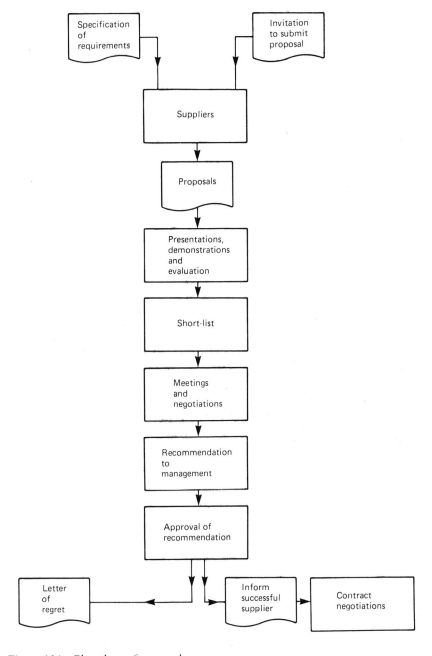

Figure 106 *Flowchart of proposal process*

ABC Manufacturing Co.   *Computer-based personnel system*

Information required in proposal

This document is issued in conjunction with the *Specification of requirements* dated October 1985. It specifies the information required in any proposal and is issued on the understanding that no charge will be made by suppliers for making the proposal.

ABC Management Services
November 1985

General information

1 Description of the organization – ownership, size, products and services provided and presence in the locality.
2 A list of customers who may be approached for references.

System

3 Description of approach to development/implementation.
4 Description of the system proposed.
5 A list of requirements specified which cannot be met or which can only be met with difficulty. In the case of the latter there should be an indication of the effort required.
6 A list of any features of the proposed system which are additional to the requirements specified.
7 The programming language used and details of any standard software products proposed e.g. query language.
8 The names and brief details of experience of personnel who will be involved in the development and implementation of the system.
9 Arrangements for maintenance of the system.
10 If a modified package is proposed, any restrictions which the modification process will impose in relation to access to any future development of the package should be outlined, e.g. will it be possible to implement enhancements which may be provided for users in general?
11 Training and support arrangements.
12 System documentation which will be provided.

Hardware

13 The proposal should be based on n VDUs accessing the system but should show how it can be expanded to cope with a maximum in the x to y range.
14 Based on the estimated volumes and load the proposal should state what average transaction response time can be expected.
15 The proposal should describe how VDUs accessing the personnel system can conveniently communicate with ABC's mainframe computer which is a —.
16 A description of maintenance arrangements, guaranteed response time to calls, policy on holding spares and the availability of a suitable back-up computer.
17 Growth path of hardware.
18 Any special housing, environmental or electrical requirements.
19 Maximum distance for direct connection – VDU or printer to computer.

Costs
20 Costs should be analysed over hardware, software, delivery and installation, training, manuals etc.
21 There should be a clear distinction between initial and recurring costs.
22 In addition to the capital cost of hardware, annual rental or leasing arrangements should be outlined.

Implementation
23 Four copies of the proposal should be submitted so as to reach ABC not later than Friday 17 January 1986.
24 It is expected that a decision will be made as to which proposal is the most suitable by 28 February. On this basis the proposal should include an implementation schedule showing the dates by which it is expected to complete each stage of the project.

Figure 107   *Information required in proposal*

along with the specification of requirements and should indicate the type of information which is required in proposal. An example of the type of document involved is given in Figure 107. The example is self-explanatory but it is worth highlighting a few points.

1 It should be clearly understood that the proposer will not be re-imbursed for expenses involved in preparing and submitting the proposal.
2 Each proposer should be given an opportunity of making a formal presentation of the proposal.
3 It should require very specific details of all costs involved – both initial and recurring.
4 A date should be specified for submission of proposals and an indication should be given as to when a decision can be expected and when implementation of the system is likely to start. This is an area where dates can go badly wrong. At the time when invitations are being sent out it may appear very reasonable to expect a decision within a matter of weeks. This generally takes on over-optimisitc view of the amount of work involved and the delays inherent in the process of reaching a decision.

It will be difficult to get people together for demonstrations and meetings; site visits will have to be arranged and when a recommendation is made the approval process may give rise to further investigations and negotiations. Accordingly the dates quoted should be as realistic as possible and having arrived at what appears to be a realistic date it is usually appropriate to add a further period for unforeseen slippage. Since the supplier is being asked to provide an implementation date, this involves a plan for allocating appropriate staff over that timescale. This entails dovetailing with other projects and unless the quoted dates are realistic it may be unfair to expect the supplier to be in a position to supply similar resources against a different timescale.

Evaluation of proposals

As soon as the proposals are received there should be an initial quick evaluation undertaken with a view to reducing the field further. This should be done by reference to the main criteria which are to be used in the selection process. These criteria are likely to include

- main facilities available as related to the stated requirements
- costs involved as related to the budget
- the ability to deliver within the required timescale.

If the initial screening prior to inviting proposals has been well done it is unlikely that any proposal will be ruled out completely. If, on the other hand, any proposal does not meet the basic requirements it should not be allowed to divert effort from the real selection process and so it should be regarded now as having failed.

Having determined the shortlist the evaluation process can start in earnest. Evaluation should be undertaken by the project team representing both personnel and data processing interests. As a first step it is usual to produce a short synopsis of each proposal – no more than one page on each – which should be circulated to personnel and data processing management. Copies of the proposals should also be circulated to the relevant people.

The process then comprises

- a detailed analysis of each proposal
- meetings and discussions with the potential suppliers
- visits to sites where the proposed hardware and software is in use
- a formal evaluation of each proposal by reference to an agreed checklist.

Analysis

The purpose of the detailed analysis is to understand thoroughly the proposal, to relate it to the detailed requirements and to enable a list of queries and any points of clarification to be prepared for discussion with the proposers. This study should ensure that the system being proposed is understood and that cost and contractual details are clear. In analysing different proposals at the same time one may prompt queries about another and these points can be taken up in subsequent discussions.

Discussions

Contact with suppliers at this stage will comprise a formal presentation of the proposal, demonstrations of the system, and meetings and correspondence regarding queries and matters of detail. At this point there may be some negotiations on charges and contract terms, although in practice these matters tend to come at a slightly later stage when the front runner has been identified.

Site visits
One of the most important aids towards evaluating proposals is to visit sites where the system or the proposed hardware is in use. Each supplier should have been requested to include in the proposal a list of reference sites with the name of a contact person at each. Ideally these sites should be as similar as possible to the organization and to the solution proposed. This will not always be the case, but it is still worth following up the reference. This can be done by means of telephone calls but arrangements should be made to visit the key sites.

Site visits are important for the following reasons.

1 Assessing hardware performance, judging how it can cope with the load, measuring performance in terms of up-time, and seeing how it performs in a particular physical environment.
2 Getting first-hand views on
   - software performance (problems or bugs)
   - response to service calls (hardware and software)
   - relationships with the supplier
   - assistance provided with implementation and the level of post-implementation support
   - the particular personnel who will be involved
   - ease of use of the system e.g. acceptability of screen formats
   - level of training provided
   - standard of documentation provided.

On site visits it is important to talk to the people who actually use the system and not just to the managers – they were probably responsible for making the recommendation and so may have a biased view.

Formal evaluation
A checklist should be drawn up which can help to make the decision. This should list all of the requirements, classifying them into 'musts' and 'wants' or assigning a weighting factor to each item. Then each proposal can be matched against this list and given a score. The weights can then be applied to the scores and a weighted score calculated for each proposal.

Having established the scoring in each case the result may help in making the final decision. If there is a clear favourite this should be reflected in the score. If on the other hand there is little between proposals the final score may be used as a means of settling for one rather than another.

In drawing up the list of criteria it is worth noting the significance of certain factors.

1 If a good system is faulted because it does not have facility X should this have a major influence on the decision? It is better to have a system which has, say, 80 per cent of the facilities specified but which will work, than one which purports to have all 100 per cent facilities but fails to work because it is difficult to use or is badly supported. It is

quite possible that facility X is a 'pet' requirement of an influential member of the selection group so this situation has to be guarded against.

2 The quality of the staff involved is very important. Throughout this phase the main contact will be with a salesperson – regardless of what the job title is. It is important to meet the people who understand the CPMIS and its related software and to get assurances as to who will be working on the project. The questions which must then be asked are

- do they appreciate the personnel requirement fully or are they primarily concerned with installing a technically perfect computer system?
- will they get on with the staff in the personnel function who will have contact with them during implementation and training?
- will the key people be in a position to devote all the time required or will they have a project role with limited user contact and leave that to some junior programmer?

Software houses which sell general ledger systems often employ accountants who are involved in the design and implementation of the systems. Very few software houses employ staff who are qualified personnel management practitioners. It is important to ensure that the people who will be involved in implementing the system have had good relevant experience and appreciate the workings of the personnel management function.

3 The commitment of the supplier to getting in the proposal on time, seeking clarification on points of detail and the overall quality of presentation of the proposal are important points to look for. Generally a careless approach at this stage will be followed by the same approach to implementation. Some suppliers ignore the specified format in which the proposal is required. They will produce their standard proposal from a word processor and generally will not address the specific requirements which should be addressed.

The recommendation

At the end of the evaluation process a brief report should be prepared outlining what has happened and containing a clear recommendation as to the proposal which is most suitable and which should be accepted together with any special conditions which should be met prior to signing the contract. This report should be submitted to senior personnel management and anyone else who is involved in authorizing the decision.

As soon as the recommendation is approved, everyone who submitted a proposal should be informed of the decision. At this stage those who have not been successful will be anxious to know where they failed. It should not be forgotten that they have put a lot of effort into submitting their proposals and deserve the courtesy of a meeting to discuss the position with them.

Format of recommendation report

This section contains some suggestions as to the format and content of the report outlining the recommendation. While, because of its nature, the specification of requirements is a long detailed document, this must be concise and to the point. The sections of the report should cover the background leading up to the recommendation, the proposals received, the recommendation and the reasons for it and any implications arising out of the recommendation or the implementation of the system.

Background

This is a brief summary of what happened since the specification of requirements was sent out to potential suppliers. It lists the key dates, e.g. deadlines for submission of proposals, the suppliers approached, suppliers who declined to submit proposals, and suppliers who reached the short-list.

Investigation of systems

This section summarizes how the investigation process was handled. It should mention the salient features of the main contenders and list the site visits related to each proposal.

Recommendations and suitability of system

At this stage the recommended system should be identified and there should be a few paragraphs outlining the reasons for the choice. There should be a brief reconciliation between the features of the system and the requirements as specified.

Implications of system

This can be a useful way of stressing again some useful points such as

- the need to realise cost savings to counter the expenditure on the system
- the need to examine the impact which the introduction of the system will have or should have on structures within the personnel function
- the need to allocate responsibility and authority to someone within personnel for the smooth implementation of the system
- the amount of work which still remains to be done in order to achieve a satisfactory implementation.

Implementation

This section should describe the main tasks to be undertaken and preliminary target dates for the main phases.

Appendices
The appendices should contain

- a comparative cost summary
- cost details of the recommended system
- any important correspondence which is likely to become an integral part of the contract e.g. guarantees.

20 Signing the contract

Where either, or both, computer hardware and software is being acquired from outside the organization, the signing of contracts will be involved. Computer contracts can be quite intimidating and in this chapter it is proposed to look at features of the different types of contracts and to provide some advice as to how to cope with them. Before doing that it is worth reading some of the clauses which are common to computer proposals and contracts. The clauses listed in Figures 108, 109 and 110 are taken from actual agreements and cover some general contract terms, clauses from typical hardware contracts, and commonly used clauses from software contracts.

Over the years an enormous number of computer installations have failed in the sense that hardware and/or vendor-supplied software has failed to fulfil the expectations of the purchaser. Some of these difficulties have become public as a result of legal proceedings but the vast majority have been resolved by agreement between the parties themselves at the end of months or years of tortuous and often acrimonious haggling or by the intervention of a mutually agreed arbitrator. Where this happens there is no real winner.

Relationships between vendor and customer become strained often to the point that it becomes impossible subsequently to establish the type of working relationship which is necessary for the successful implementation and maintenance of any computer-based system. Word spreads quickly around the business and computer world about unsuccessful systems and the deals which may be necessary to avoid total collapse or litigation will leak out despite the best efforts of the supplier to preserve its image. The mobility of computer staff is an influencing factor in causing computer and software suppliers to adopt a very defensive line in regard to their role in systems which have been less than successful. A salesperson, analyst or programmer who has been working for Company A this week may be working for another software house competing for

1 The customer acknowledges that its senior management has read this agreement, understands it and agrees to be bound by its terms and conditions and further agrees that it is the complete and exclusive statement of the agreement between the parties which supersedes all proposals oral and written and all other communications and prior agreements between the parties relating to the subject matter of this agreement . . . .

2 The recommendations for equipment, programs, education/training, and other services contained in this proposal are estimates based on the data which you have furnished to us and our observations. While we believe our estimates to be sound, the degree of success with which equipment, programs and other services can be applied to data processing is dependent on many functions, many of which are not under the control of XYZ Ltd. Therefore, our estimates as to the results to be obtained from the equipment etc. being supplied must not be regarded as express or implied warranties.

3 Successful application, implementation, operation and management of XYZ products and services are the responsibility of the user. Examples of these responsibilities are – selecting the proper equipment, configuration and programs, developing appropriate systems procedures, incorporating protective measures to safeguard the privacy of data and providing qualified personnel to obtain the desired results. In no event shall XYZ have any liability for consequential damages.

4 This proposal is subject to change or withdrawal by XYZ without prior notice and shall expire sixty days from the date of this proposal unless extended by XYZ in writing.

5 *Overdue accounts*

If any sum payable under this contract is in arrears for more than thirty days then (in addition to any other remedies) XYZ reserves the right to charge interest on a day-to-day basis from the original due date at a rate of 4 per cent above the minimum lending rate or above such other equivalent rate in force from time to time.

Figure 108   *Some general contract terms*

the same business next month. During the discussions and negotiations which take place prior to a decision it is not unusual to be told 'You know, of course, of the terrible problems which Company A had with the personnel system from Company U – they had to upgrade the machine, and they have twenty people rewriting the software for the system which was due to go live nearly two years ago.'

When situations like the one quoted are examined it is generally found that there is a number of causes rather than one single cause. Many of the factors which contributed to the problems are probably the user's (customer's) responsibility. However, as far as the customers are concerned the system is not doing what they thought it would do and, regardless of the fact that they may be at fault, they can be in a position to put a certain amount of pressure on the supplier. Regardless of whose fault it is the supplier will not want to be associated with an unsuccessful

1 The maintenance service provided under this Agreement does not include service in respect of failures in the program product
   (1) Caused by materials or services not provided by XYZ.
   (2) Resulting from Licensee's modification of the program product.
   (3) Owing to misuse of the product, equipment or software or owing to operator error.
   (4) Owing to use of product releases earlier than the release level currently supported.
   (5) Owing to the Licensee requested and specified tests and checks outside XYZ's normal test specifications and procedures.
2 Defects
   (1) Within twelve months from the date of delivery of the software product and in the event that repeatedly demonstrable defects making the product incapable of use shall become manifest in the product, XYZ will at its option either remedy such defects or supply an alternative product for the same application.
   In the event that neither remedy nor supply of an alternative product can be effected, then XYZ will repay to the Licensee such charges as have been invoiced to and paid by the Licensee for the affected product and the Agreement will be treated as discharged in respect of the affected product.
   (2) This clause states XYZ's total liability to the Licensee whether in contract, tort or otherwise, in respect of the product or from any work done under this clause and is in lieu of and excludes all other conditions and warranties implied by statute law or otherwise.
   (3) XYZ warrants the application software to be provided under this Agreement, for a period of three months after live implementation, against all documented defects inherent to improper programming practice. This warranty shall not apply if the programs are misused or if they are amended by programmers other than those in the employment of XYZ or if the operating system is changed within the warranty period. XYZ warrants the application software to be provided to be such as to conform to industry accepted standards.

Figure 109   *Some software contract terms*

system and up to a point will be anxious to devote resources to ensuring that the customers are satisfied. There is a limit to the extent to which this can be done and since many troubles have their origin in user shortcomings, suppliers have to protect themselves and to a large extent this is what has given rise to contract clauses which appear unjustly to favour the supplier.

Regardless of how a customer's rights are protected by law and by the contract these safeguards should only be regarded as being there to protect the customer's interest in a case of last resort. While it is important to ensure that those interests are protected the main emphasis should be on ensuring that the whole project is handled in such a way that the need to resort to the fine print of contractual obligations is not necessary. An unsuccessful system will result in adverse publicity for the

1 In no event shall XYZ have any liability for damages, whether as consequential damages or for loss of business or profits or otherwise, arising out of or in connection with the use or performance of the equipment.

2 Except for any hardware warranties stated in this clause, XYZ disclaims all other hardware warranties whether express or implied in law or otherwise, and the warranties in this Agreement are in lieu of all obligations and liabilities on the part of XYZ for damages arising out of or in connection with use or performance of its product.

3 Product prices include delivery to the door or entrance of the installation site. Costs of transport into the purchaser's site and costs for measures taken in connection with the transport shall be paid by the purchaser.

4 The time of delivery is the time when the product is unloaded outside the address designated by the purchaser.

5 XYZ may, at its option, and without prejudice to any other remedy providing such overdue payment is a minimum of thirty days in arrears and represents not less than 30% of the total contract value, enter in upon the purchaser's premises and take possession of the items listed.

Figure 110 *Some hardware contract terms*

customer as well as the supplier. This publicity can often have severe repercussions for an organization, including an adverse impact on the morale of both data processing and other user personnel.

Failure can also affect the credibility of computers, leading to a setback for data processing plans, which might lessen the organization's ability to embrace the new technology, so making it less competitive in certain areas – especially selling and production. The failure of a personnel system may not have quite as immediate an impact as some other systems but will result in

- substantial waste of resources – money and time
- loss of morale within the personnel function
- the creation of a bad image for the personnel function within the organization
- a reluctance to get involved in further attempts to introduce computers
- perhaps a cynical or distorted attitude by personnel staff towards the introduction of computers in other areas of the organization.

The remainder of this chapter examines the question of the contract in the following ways

1 Avoiding problems.
2 Problems with the contract – general clauses.
3 Problems with the contract – specific clauses.

Avoiding problems

As mentioned above, there is seldom a clear winner when both parties get involved in protracted arguments. Unfortunately this is becoming more common and there has been an increase in litigation and disputes, in particular relating to software contracts. To some extent this has arisen because more and more organizations are looking to software houses to meet their requirements. This move has been influenced by the shortage and cost of key systems and programming staff and by the increased availability of packaged software. This of course means that a greater proportion of the total pool of operational software is now being provided by third parties and while there have been plenty of failures in terms of internally developed, custom-built software these do not lead to litigation. Such failures do not get the same level of publicity and anyway most of them are 'rescued', since it is to the organization's benefit to do so.

The other major factor which had led to this type of problem with software houses is the fact that user departments negotiate directly with software houses to obtain one of the increasingly available application packages. DP departments have experience in dealing with hardware and software suppliers, and so are familiar with the normal contractual terms of suppliers. They may indeed have learned about some of them the hard way, and from their experience should be in a position to ensure that the organization's position is safeguarded. However a user department does not have the same experience, and may get involved with an inappropriate solution to its system requirements in the following way.

The personnel director visits a computer exhibition and sees a micro-based system on display. He has never paid much attention previously to how a computer-based personnel system would work but has pro-visionally provided £15,000 in this year's budget for a system. He is very impressed by the system on display because at the touch of a button he can see

1 An employee's record showing all the usual information
   - name
   - address
   - date of birth
   - spouse's name
   - current salary
   - cost centre
   - languages spoken etc.
2 An age profile of the test company.
3 The cost of implementing a 10 per cent wage increase.
4 A list of all employees who can speak French fluently and a further list of those who have school French only.
5 A list of all single female staff under 30 who earn more than £15,000 p.a.
6 A list of all staff due to retire month by month within the next five years.

He is bowled over, especially since he has just had great difficulty recently obtaining a list of the staff who were due to retire within the next few years, and by the time he had the information decisions on the introduction of an early retirement scheme had been taken anyway.

The salesperson on the stand tells him about the flexibility of the system and that they could provide him with the hardware, software and a VDU for himself and the personnel administration department for the £15,000 he has in his pocket. The salesperson also tells him that Brown Transport Company has just bought the system.

When the personnel director gets back to his office he rings the personnel director of Brown Transport, who confirms that, while he does not know much about the system, they have bought it and will be implementing it shortly.

He then summons his managers to a meeting, tells them of his experience, says it would be nice to have the system up and running before the annual review process starts in two months' time and asks two of his managers to investigate the system further and, if suitable, to arrange for implementation.

The managers then have a look at the system, are impressed, but have a few queries about it.

1 Can we have four screens?
2 Can we hold details of our pensioners?
3 Will it retain salary history?
4 Can it produce letters to employees about their sick leave records etc.?
5 Will it cope with our 3000 employees?
6 Can we have word processing on it?

The salesperson, who in reality knows very little about how the system operates in practice, reassures them on all points and also puts their minds at rest in regard to such items as

• hardware reliability
• response to maintenance calls
• electrical requirements
• performance in a normal office environment
• availability of spares
• the number of maintenance engineers employed
• guaranteed and average response times to calls
• availability of back-up machines
• the names of their big customers.

Within a few weeks the contract is signed. The payment schedule requires that 60 per cent be paid with order, 30 per cent on delivery of the computer and the final 10 per cent two months after delivery. The contract is for an 'initial configuration' with processor, hard disk, floppy disk drive, printer and two VDUs. It also covers the standard personnel package.

As soon as the computer and the system are delivered it becomes obvious that there are substantial drawbacks with the system.

1 Not only is there no room on the system for pensioners, but in order to accommodate the 3000 employees a number of items have to be dropped from each employee's record.

To access details of an employee it is necessary to know the employee's number – access by employee name is not feasible.
Because of the size limitations it is only possible to hold an employee's current salary and the previous two salaries. Consequently it is not possible to dispense with the manual records for salary history.
Because of the demands made on the system by programs used to produce age analysis, salary analysis, etc. it is not possible to use the second VDU while these programs are running.
To use word processing an additional memory board will have to be purchased.
To add two further VDUs the processor will have to be replaced with another model and anyway the VDU will have to be within 100 m of the processor, which is not practicable.

hat has happened is that an inappropriate solution was acquired to eet an undefined problem or requirement. The whole thing was proached in an unstructured fashion and while the supplier could rtainly be faulted, the main fault here must rest with the customer. The first real appreciation which the personnel director has of the oblems is not until he finds that the annual review has to be handled anually and even then, because so much effort has gone into setting up e disastrous computer system, it is a month behind schedule.
The personnel director calls another meeting of his managers. Every-ne agrees that the computer company has provided a terrible service d fails to see how they could have such an enviable customer base. urely any system in this day and age would not expect one to member every employee number!' 'They knew we would want four Us and word processing!' 'They must have known that we would want keep salary history for ever and absence history for six years!'
Since the computer company is saying that the system is doing what it as supposed to do, it is felt that there is no point in negotiating with em, and that the matter should be handed over to the legal department th a view to taking legal proceedings to have the company reimbursed th the 90 per cent of the cost already paid and to claim for considerable mages by way of consequential loss.
The legal department examines the contract and finds that the only ference to the items to be supplied, as outlined in Appendix A, is a list hardware as delivered, plus the existing personnel package as deli-red. They find that it contains all of the clauses necessary to protect the pplier in such cases and no input from the organization to ensure that own position is specifically safeguarded. Accordingly their advice is at there is limited scope for pursuing the matter through the courts d that the organization should cut its losses and negotiate with the pplier for the best possible deal, perhaps even to the extent of andoning the system altogether and making a fresh start with another pplier.
The above example is entirely fictitious but serves to illustrate the type situation which can arise in the absence of a planned approach to the

project. The main lesson to be learnt from this case is the need to defir
what the system is expected to do. This is one of the major them
running through this book – the need to know what the requirements a
and to use the definition of requirements as a means of evaluatir
alternative proposals. In the above example the need to know what tl
options or alternative systems are prior to a commitment is highlighte
as is the need to take some time over the decision and avoid tl
temptation to jump straight in.

In the example verbal assurances on certain points were given to tl
staff investigating the system but such assurances are quickly or co
veniently forgotten when it comes to the crunch. Such assurances shou
be confirmed in writing. There should be confirmation that all requir
ments listed in any specification of requirements can be met and tl
potential supplier should also be asked to identify any requiremen
which cannot be met or can only be met with some difficulty. Having g
these assurances in writing they should become part of the contract. Tl
contract should include a statement to the effect that the significance
the following is recognized and taken into account

1 The specification of requirements.
2 The proposal made to the organization.
3 Any subsequent relevant correspondence (which should be clear
   identified).

Sample contracts should be requested as part of any invitation to subm
a proposal. This should be read carefully and passed on to the leg
department or a legal advisor for comments. At the stage when actu
contracts are drawn up legal advice should again be sought and as so
as the user department and/or computer department is satisfied with tl
items covered by the contract the legal and/or purchasing people shou
take over. Any matters within the contract which still cause problen
should be agreed before signature. This should be possible if it
recognized that it is in the interest of both the supplier and custom
to arrive at a contractual arrangement which will meet the overall cu
tomer need and thereby avoid the subsequent bad feeling, litigatic
and publicity which may follow from a software development or imp
mentation project which collapses.

General clauses

It is obvious from reading through the sample clauses included
Figures 108, 109 and 110 that computer agreements are aggressi
documents. There are good and valid reasons why a computer suppli
should want to protect itself from users who may cause problem
Nevertheless it can be quite a shock following weeks or even months
demonstrations, presentations, discussions and site visits organized l
friendly, helpful, understanding sales personnel who feel that eve
requirement can be met or will present only minor difficulties, to
presented with a document for signature which is cold and stark l

comparison and which appears to discount all previous contact between the two parties.

The clauses which cause most concern will relate to

1 The exclusion of all previous verbal agreements or documents such as
   - specifications of requirements
   - vendor's proposal
   - other agreements or representations whether verbal or written
   - specifications which have been listed in the vendor's publicity material.
2 The reduction or elimination of the normal obligations of the supplier. This may extend to the elimination of warranties normally found in other contracts.
3 The ability of the supplier unilaterally to alter some of the terms of the contract simply by informing the customer in writing.

In the light of these statements it should be remembered that the customer has rights and obligations under contract law. The supplier is liable for any express warranty based on

- promises made by the supplier or his representatives
- models
- samples
- statements of fact

if the customer relied on any of these as the basis for the agreement. The supplier is also liable for implied warranties of merchantability. This means that the supplier's product must meet normal business expectations. If a personnel manager buys a CPMIS as a result of the recommendations of the software house which is selling the package, the software house is obliged to meet the implied warranties of performance. If however, the contract clearly states that the software house is not responsible for implied warranties this clearly supersedes the obligations outlined above, so it behoves the personnel manager to ensure that all commitments are given in writing.

Specific clauses

Schedule A
The subject matter of the agreement is normally outlined in a schedule which forms part of the contract. In general this lists the items of hardware and a brief description of the software to be provided. To ensure that all relevant aspects of both hardware and software are covered, clauses such as the following should be incorporated into the agreement.

The following documents are to be considered as part of these agreements
- ABC Manufacturing Company's specification of requirements dated September 1985
- XYZ's 'Proposal for the Supply of Computer Hardware and the XYZ Personnel Package' dated November 1985

- ABC's letters to XYZ dated 12 December 1985 and 14 January 1986 copies included in Schedule B
- XYZ's letters to ABC dated 15 December 1985 and 29 January 1986 copies included in Schedule B.

Hardware performance

Suppliers of hardware are very reluctant to include performance guarantees in contracts, whether in relation to

- uptime of key elements of the hardware configuration, or
- ability of the computer to handle the expected load.

The latter can cause problems for the supplier because of the difficulty in estimating the expected load which will be placed on the hardware. However, in the case of a computer dedicated to the personnel division it is possible to be reasonably precise as to what the configuration will have to handle. Accordingly, clauses such as the following should be included in the agreement; alternatively there should be a reference to the written confirmation of the acceptance of these standards by the vendor.

> 1 It is anticipated that the equipment will be in use from 08.30 to 22.00 for seven days per week. Within the stated times, and with the exception of three hours per month required for preventative maintenance, it is agreed that the equipment will be available to ABC and in full working condition for not less than 90 per cent in any seven-day period and for not less than 95 per cent in any calendar month.

This clause should go on to describe the implications of failure to meet these standards. The penalties will vary depending upon such matters as value of the contract and would include such items as

- holding stocks of spares on site
- presence of engineering support on site during normal working hours
- immediate replacement of equipment.

> 2 An average response time throughout the day of two seconds with a maximum response time of four seconds at peak is guaranteed. Maximum response time is calculated as the highest average in any fifteen-minute period in the day. This guarantee is based on the following load
> - concurrent use of the CPMIS and word processing
> - maximum transaction level of 4000 per day – average expected is 2000
> - maximum transaction level of 200 in any fifteen minute period
> - a total of up to 12 VDUs accessing the system in the following manner
>   3 in update mode
>   2 using the word processing system
>   2 using the query language for *ad hoc* reports
>   5 in general enquiry mode.
> The load assumes that volumes will not exceed those stated in Section 6 Volumes of the specification of requirements by more than 10 per cent.

Achievement of the type of performance outlined in (2) above is dependent upon the quality of the software as well as the hardware. In this instance it is assumed that the packages referred to – CPMIS and WP – already exist and the vendor is already aware of how they should perform.

Hardware quality

It is not normal to have to include a clause in order to ensure that the hardware to be provided is new and in good condition but it is worth considering the inclusion of a clause to cover this. Occasionally it may happen that a particular component of the configuration is out of stock or is not available for some other reason and there may be a temptation to replace this item with a used model. Another example is where the casing of an item of hardware is damaged even though this does not affect its performance. The resulting problems can be avoided by a clause which states

> XYZ warrants that all items of hardware will be new and of original manufacture and will be installed in a condition which is free of any damage. XYZ also warrants that all hardware items will be in good working condition when delivered and installed and will perform in accordance with the published specifications.

Price

As a general principle the customer should seek to have all hardware and software prices fixed. The degree to which this can be achieved will vary. Agreements in respect of hardware tend to be more fixed than those for software but there is still likely to be a clause which allows for price variations arising out of

- taxation changes
- changes in import duties
- foreign currency fluctuations.

One measure which may provide some measure of stability is to try to insist on having prices quoted in native currency.

In software contracts an agreement which fails to specify a fixed price is dangerous. Where a package such as a CPMIS is being acquired the basis should be fixed price and the same should apply to any modifications or extensions which are required. Prices based on time and materials are weighted in favour of the suppliers. This, however, is a matter of business policy or arises as a result of the way in which the business arrangement was negotiated and so it is not really amenable to change at the stage where contracts are being exchanged.

Acceptance procedures

An agreement normally states something like

> Installation date shall be the date of passing the XYZ tests or one month after

commencement of operational use of the equipment or any part thereof or the date specified in ... whichever is the earliest.

It is unlikely that any tests will be referred to except the technical tests of the supplier. Having the customer's tests accepted as an integral part of the agreement will be difficult. The main reason for this of course is that it is very difficult to specify what these user tests should consist of. If bench-mark tests have been carried out on similar hardware during the negotiations leading up to the decision to purchase, the agreement should allow for the running of the same bench mark on the new equipment. In this case there must be agreement on the environment in which these tests will be carried out and on the methods of measuring the results.

The agreement should also describe what action should be taken where the results of the tests are unsatisfactory, for example

> If the operating performance of the equipment fails to meet the specification as described in ... or if the results of the agreed bench mark as defined in ... are unsatisfactory as defined in that document, XYZ shall modify, upgrade or replace the equipment until the performance expected is achieved.

The inclusion of such a clause may be difficult to obtain. As with all such amendments to standard agreements the extent to which modification of terms is achieved will be influenced by the balance of power between the vendor and vendee. A small company will find it very difficult to effect changes to the standard agreement terms of a large multinational computer supplier.

With software contracts it is generally easier to insist on user acceptance tests. However, it is only reasonable or practicable to specify acceptance criteria if there is a good definition of the software requirements. A system is generally accepted after it has undergone a series of user-generated system tests or by default – after a certain period of live running.

A software contract must always allow for the correction of 'bugs' or problems which are discovered within a stated period and it is important that the agreed payment schedule should reflect this. The best way of ensuring that attention is given to those last few minor problems is to have the final payment dependent upon all notified problems being cleared.

Payment terms

The payment terms defined in a computer contract are normally very much weighted towards paying as much as possible early on. Attempts will be made to justify this, especially in the case of hardware, on the basis that resources must be committed to delivery as soon as the order is placed.

The following are typical payment terms

Hardware
25 per cent on order

75 per cent on acceptance of equipment
Software packages
35 per cent on order
45 per cent on delivery
20 per cent on acceptance – in this case acceptance means hand-over to customer.

These terms do not provide any form of threat to the supplier in the case of problems arising after hand-over. The terms should be adjusted to ensure that money is held over until the customer is completely satisfied. In the case of a hardware/software deal it is important to ensure that it is accepted by the vendor that the hardware is useless to the customer until the software is working satisfactorily. The payment terms should be arranged accordingly.

Cessation of trading

A customer must be safeguarded against the situation where, for whatever reason, the supplier ceases to trade. Such an event will give rise to problems in terms of support, equipment maintenance and the availability of spares. There is no way that a customer can be fully cushioned from the impact but just as at the evaluation stage some thought will have been given to the perceived viability of the supplier, some thought must be given at the agreement stage to how the customer's interest can be protected. This is especially so in the case of software. If an organization purchases a CPMIS from a software house and only has access to object code it may not be possible to maintain the system subsequently. Accordingly the agreement should state that all key documentation and program source code should be deposited with a third party – normally a bank. Where there are any possible doubts about the future availability of spare parts it is worth having a clause inserted which provides that the supplier will retain sufficient spares during the life of the system to ensure that the equipment will perform satisfactorily.

Where software is to be developed for the customer the agreement shall ensure that the customer gets ownership of programming work-in-progress, as well as completed programs, if the vendor does not finish the system for whatever reason.

Multiple sites

In the case of application packages such as a CPMIS, the vendor of the package may restrict its use of the system to the customer's installation and may also place a restriction on the making of copies. Where there is the possibility of wanting to use the package at different sites and computers within the organization or group of companies the situation in relation to multiple sites should be specifically referred to.

Summary

The following is a brief summary of the main things to remember in negotiating a suitable contract.

1 Standard computer contracts for both hardware and software are aimed at protecting the interests of the vendor.
2 If contractual terms have to be invoked it often means that the installation or project has failed and it is in everyone's interest to prevent this situation from arising. One of the best ways to avoid this situation is to be a good user and this means being very clear from the start as to what is expected from the vendor.
3 Unacceptable clauses should be rejected and replaced by ones which take into account the rights and expectations of the customer.
4 After technical aspects have been agreed the draft contract should be passed on to the legal department or a legal advisor for professional advice.
5 The possibility of using the customer's standard contract should be examined. In some circumstances this procedure may be acceptable to the vendor.

21 System implementation

This chapter traces the system from the time the decision to proceed along a particular course has been taken – the signing of the contract or the acceptance of an internal proposal – to the time when the system goes live. Although the foundation for success will already have been set down by defining clearly what the requirements are and matching proposals against those requirements, the implementation phase is also one of crucial importance. At this stage project management becomes critical and various decisions will have to be taken which can have a big impact on both time-scale and success.

Planning errors and mistaken implementation policy can result in a never-ending cycle of parallel running, in mammoth exercises aimed at setting up historical data covering many years to the neglect of current data, in personnel staff ignoring the system or failing to get maximum benefit from it and in difficulty in moving away from methods and procedures related to the old system.

Involvement and participation

The importance of involving everyone within the personnel division in the process leading up to computerization has already been emphasised. This involvement also continues through the system implementation phase and becomes more intense as staff are trained and become actively involved in the definition of procedures and in coding and inputting the initial data. As well as the personnel staff two other groups must also be consulted and involved in the project. One of these groups consists of the management and staff in the areas which will interface with the personnel system. Typical of these areas are the budget department – who will be interested in establishment and personnel budgets generally, the payroll department, and internal audit. The second group is the employees of the organization as represented by their trade unions or staff associations. As soon as the idea of a personnel system is being considered an outline of what is proposed should be discussed with employee representatives so that there will be no misunderstanding as to the scope and function of the system. With all of the talk of the computer acting as 'big brother' it is natural that there should be a certain amount of unease concerning the use of a computer by the personnel function.

The establishment of bodies to examine the impact and dangers of computers in relation to the right to privacy and the introduction of legislation to cater for this area emphasizes this concern. Personnel records have often been mentioned alongside police records, medical records, income tax and national insurance records, banking and credit company records. Any feeling of unease or suspicion must not be allowed to exist and the only way to do this is to be completely open and frank. In the early stages of the project personnel management may not be able to be precise as to what the system will do and eventually the scope of the system may be related to the budget and the packages available. However, right from the start, the objectives for the system will be clear and these should be discussed. It may be established at the beginning that the system will be concerned with personnel records as they are known in the organization at present, and personnel files containing such items as employee evaluation and disciplinary records will continue to be held manually.

As soon as a decision has been taken as to the choice of system or approach and a form of implementation schedule is available this detailed information should be disclosed.

The main areas of concern to employee representatives are

1 The type of data being held. Full details should be provided as to what will be held – age, marital status, absence records, training records etc. – and categories of data which will not be held e.g. disciplinary records.

2 Access to the system. They should be given an outline of the password and other access restriction mechanisms which the system will have. Generally a dedicated personnel computer will be looked on more favourably than a computer which is accessed by a number of other departments. All plans for restricting certain levels of access or functions to particular individuals will also alleviate concern in this area. Dial-up access to a computer system from a terminal via a telephone line can be a source of worry. This is a common feature now especially as many computer suppliers provide a level of maintenance support by dialling up the computer and there may be a feeling that unauthorised people would also be in a position to gain access in this way.

3 Confidentiality. Apart from the question of restricting access to the system via a VDU, computer systems can result in other confidentiality headaches. Under a manual system data is held on individual cards or files. These are generally maintained in locked cabinets and access to them can be both difficult and noticeable. With a computer-based

system a print-out showing dates of birth, illness record etc. can be mislaid, or a visitor to the personnel department may see a print-out on a desk listing individual salaries or details of an employee may be observed over the shoulder of a person making an enquiry on a VDU. Personnel management must show themselves to be aware of potential breaches of confidentiality and demonstrate that reasonable measures will be taken to avoid them.

4 Dissemination of data. An assurance should be given that data concerning individual employees will not be given to third parties unless this is required by law or unless it is established practice or is agreed to by the employees concerned.

5 Verification of data. An employee should have the facility to verify the data being held about him/her on the system. In practice this can be a very useful way of ensuring that the organization's personnel records are correct.

Data protection legislation

At this stage it is worth listing the general principles behind legislation governing data protection in the United Kingdom. These are

1 The information shall be obtained and processed fairly and lawfully.
2 The data shall be held for a specified and legitimate purpose or purposes.
3 The data shall not be used or disclosed in any way which is incompatible with those purposes.
4 The data held shall be adequate, relevant, and not excessive for these purposes.
5 The data shall be accurate and where necessary kept up to date.
6 The data associated with a person shall not be kept any longer than is required for the specified purposes.
7 An individual shall have access to information held about him/her and shall be entitled where appropriate to have it corrected or erased.
8 Appropriate security measures must be taken to provide against unauthorized access, alteration, dissemination, disclosure, accidental loss and accidental or unauthorized destruction of data.

Preliminary work

As much groundwork as possible should be done at the earliest opportunity. This includes such matters as ensuring that there is a single identification number for each employee, that this is assigned by the personnel function and that it is universally known as the employee's personnel number. Once assigned this number should never be changed. This is not as easily achieved as it might seem. Possible barriers to achievement are

1 The payroll department already allocates payroll numbers in accordance with their own rules and either find it difficult to change from this

because of the significance of the number within the payroll system or for some other less concrete reason. It is important that the personnel number should not have any in-built significance. There are still some payroll systems around which incorporate attributes such as grade, cost centre or location into the employee number. This of course gives rise to difficulties when an employee changes grade, cost centre or location.

2 Because of traditional requirements of the revenue authorities it may be practice to allocate a new number to a woman on marriage.

3 There may be a number of payroll systems in operation in the organization – each with its own format and size of employee number. In this context it is easy to overlook the senior executive payroll and the pensioners' payroll.

Prior to computerization the personnel function should already be responsible for assigning the personnel numbers and the numbers should ideally be allocated as the next one in sequence. Relevant attributes should be attached to the employee rather than the number but the number should incorporate a check digit as described in Chapter 22.

It is also important at preparation stage to verify the accuracy of the data in any computer-based system which will be used to set up the initial data in the personnel system. This may be the payroll system. Any data which affects an employee's pay will be correct and if there is a good budgetary control system in operation such items as cost centres will also be accurate. Data which has not been used regularly may not be up to date. This data may include date of birth, marital status, grade, number of dependants, date of joining organization, date of entry to pension scheme etc.

Computerization may provide the impetus to rationalize data held. Items which may need to be rationalized include

1 *Salary scales* If there is a large number of scales it may be possible at least to reduce them. It may also be possible that there are very slight differences between salary scales in the personnel records and the actual salaries maintained by the payroll system. These minor differences can arise from slightly different methods of applying general salary reviews in both systems e.g. the rounding procedure in one system may round up to the higher pound on a calculation which results in 50p, while the other system may round to the lower value. These differences will cause problems subsequently in reconciling annual salaries in both system.

2 *Allowances* It may be possible that a number of allowances will be almost identical in value. It may also be possible that two employees nominally receiving the same allowance will in fact be receiving slightly different amounts. A rationalization process may result in a much smaller and more manageable number of allowances at very little cost to the organization.

Impact on the organization of the personnel division

There are two ways of looking at how the CPMIS will affect the organization of the personnel management function and each way is to a large extent influenced by both the scope of the system and its role as envisaged by senior personnel management. Other influencing factors are the size of the personnel function and its structure prior to computerization.

The first, and most straightforward approach is to install the system simply to improve the efficiency of the operation of the function – the new system simply replaces the old. It is usually overlaid on existing structures and the person who was responsible for keeping the manual system up to date is now regarded as having the assistance of a computer. Generally speaking this is a somewhat restricted view of the role of the computer-based system.

The second approach is one which takes the view that not only will the computer allow the department or division to become more efficient but it will enable it to provide a more complete service and play a more positive role in the organization. This approach examines all of the functions as they currently exist and determines how they will exist in a computerized environment. This is different from overlaying the computer on the functions. The process critically examines each function and also considers whether the grouping of functions appropriate under the old system will continue to be the best grouping. The computer is not seen simply as a tool for speeding up the updating of records, but as an important element in the total personnel service. Responsibility for it should rest at a high level in the division and the unit or section responsible for it should be staffed with good people. This section should be regarded as a personnel services or a manpower information department. Figure 111 suggests an alternative structure to that previously described in Figures 20 and 23. In this example responsibility for the CPMIS rests within the manpower department. The manpower planning and information department is responsible for providing a service to departments throughout the division including the administrative department. The emphasis is on providing manpower information. Individual departments are responsible for updating the records which are relevant to them, but the computer unit is the one responsible for coordinating activities and information and generally running the computer operation. The staff in this unit must understand the operation and needs of the whole function. They must understand the structure of the CPMIS and they should be able to provide a service in terms of such matters as the use of the enquiry language and the integration of word processing with the system proper.

The CPMIS will also change the nature of some jobs. One of the objectives of it will be to provide a better service to the personnel professionals – recruiters, negotiators, welfare officers etc. However, in order to provide this service these professionals may have to contribute something to the smooth running of the system e.g. recruiters may have

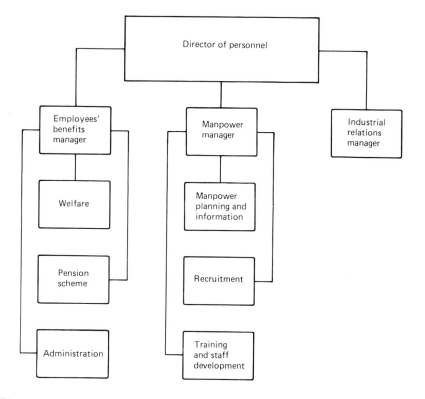

Figure 111 *Organization of personnel division – post-computerization*

to be more precise about details of offers of employment which have to be input to the system or staff counsellors may have to insert codes on a form recording reasons for leaving which are ascertained at exit interviews.

Once the system is running smoothly, regular establishment reports, the preparation of which previously consumed a lot of time, will now be available at the press of a button. This in itself may highlight the need to change the organization structure.

The project team

The installation should be managed by a project team representing management services, data processing and personnel. If external suppliers are involved they should also be represented on the team. All sections within the personnel function should be represented. The team should have regular meetings to plan activities, allocate responsibilities and review progress. At one of the first meetings of this group a detailed implementation plan should be agreed. This should clearly show all of

Task	*Start date*	*Finish date*	*Responsibility*	*Notes*
1 Electrical installation	20/4	30/4	FW	Completed
Cabling for VDUs, printers				
2 First floor		30/4	FW	Completed
3 Second floor		30/4	FW	Completed
4 Branch office		27/5	FW	
5 Training dept		1/8	FW	May not be done until after holidays.
6 Obtain consumables	20/4	20/5	FD	
7 Extend gas system		30/5	FD }	With Engineering Services
8 Instal fire detection unit		30/5	FD }	With Engineering Services
9 Enhance air cooling system		30/5	FD }	With Engineering Services
10 Instal computer	3/6	4/6	XYZ	
11 Generate operating system	4/6	5/6	XYZ	
12 Load initial version of CPMIS	5/6	6/6	XYZ	
13 Instal temporary VDUs and printers	5/6	5/6	XYZ	
Instal permanent VDUs				
14 First and second floor	1/7	1/7	XYZ	
15 Branch office	1/7	1/7	XYZ	
16 Training dept	20/8	20/8	XYZ	

Figure 112 *Implementation schedule – hardware installation*

Task	Start date	Finish date	Responsibility	Notes
1 Agreement of system specification		30/4	GMD (GLC)	Agreed – copies to be kept up to date (GMD)
2 Agreement on WP/system interface	18/6	29/6	GMD (GLC)	
Specification of programs to transfer data from payroll system				
3 Initial set-up		18/5	GLC	
4 Ongoing update		28/5	GLC	
Availability of data transfer programs				
5 Initial set-up	21/5	22/6	GLC	
6 Ongoing update	19/6	15/9	GLC	
7 Formal review of how system is operating	3/12	14/12	GLC	*December '86.*

Figure 113   *Implementation schedule – personnel system (software)*

Task	Start date	Finish date	Responsibility	Notes
1 Set up test system		25/6	GMD	Ongoing
System testing – program by program and overall integration				
2 Phase 1		3/7	GMD	Descriptor files, grades files, salary scales file, post file etc.
3 Phase 2		8/7	GMD	Individual employee records
4 Final phase		28/7	GMD	All programs – integrated testing
5 Get understanding of WP system	18/7	1/8	GMD	
6 Test integration of WP and personnel system	1/8	3/8	GMD	

Figure 114   *Implementation schedule – testing*

Task	Start date	Finish date	Responsibility	Notes
1 Design agreement and documentation of procedures	20/4	25/6	GMD	Setting up of posts, changes to cost centres, salary and allowances changes etc.
Preparation of user manuals and help sheets				
2 Phase 1		1/7	GMD	Basic system recruitment, training and WP.
3 Phase 2		27/7	GMD	
Training (systems and procedures)				
4 Phase 1 (initial)	5/6	1/7	XYZ (GMD)	Introduction, concepts etc.
5 Phase 2	3/7	13/7	GMD	Core system and procedures
6 Phase 3	3/9	14/9	(XYZ)	Recruitment, training etc.
Training query language				
7 Limited use		1/7	XYZ	Basic facilities-introduction
8 Extended use		12/7	XYZ	Special features
9 Specific use	1/10	5/10	GMD	How to rerun existing routines.
Training word processing				
10 Limited use	18/7	22/7	XYZ	
11 Extended use	17/9	21/9	XYZ	
Computer operating procedures and security copying etc.				
12 Phase 1	7/6	10/6	XYZ	Live data input
13 Phase 2	20/6	21/6		

Figure 115   *Implementation schedule – procedures and training*

#	Task			Initials	Ongoing
1	Verify payroll data prior to take on. Process changes to correct the data		30/5	CT	Ongoing
2	Prepare data for essential descriptor and other background files		30/4	GMD	Done – to be maintained.
3	Complete set-up of parameter file and essential data in descriptor file	7/6	10/6	GMD	
	Prepare descriptor data				
4	*Phase 2*	1/6	15/6	CT	
5	*Phase 3*	1/6	21/6	GMD	
6	Complete set-up of of descriptor file phases 2 and 3	21/6	23/6	GMD	
7	Prepare grades file input	1/6	21/6	ED	
8	Complete set-up of grades file	21/6	23/6	ED	
9	Prepare salary scales and allowances input	15/5	21/6	DJ	
10	Complete set-up of salary scales and allowances files	21/6	23/6	DJ	
11	Prepare post data for input	23/5	21/6	ED	
12	Complete set-up of post file	21/6	23/6	ED	
13	Transfer data from payroll	3/7	6/7	XYZ	
14	Check out transferred data	7/7	14/7	KOM	
15	Basic system live	16/7	–	–	16 July basic system live
16	Start using system for absence input reporting	10/9	–	CT	
17	Start using recruitment system	17/9	–	RP	
18	Set up balance of pension scheme data	17/7	26/10	BH	
19	Set up training courses data	15/10	–	FA	
20	Set up training aids data	15/10	–	FA	
21	Start using training system	29/10	–		29 Oct. Training system live
22	Set up training data – qualifications etc.	29/10	16/11	FA	Relates to input of data – gathering of data will have commenced much earlier
23	Use WP system fully	22/9	2/11	GMD	
24	System fully live	2/11	–	–	2 Nov. System fully live

Figure 116 *Implementation schedule – data*

the various activities (the interrelationship between activities should have been considered), the target start and completion date for each activity and a clear indication of who is responsible for each activity. It is important to have this plan from early on in the project even if it has to be modified along the way. A typical implementation schedule is shown in Figures 112, 113, 114, 115 and 116. The schedule is divided into five sections dealing with the main activities which take place during this phase. Each of these five activities is now described in outline.

Hardware installation

The installation of the hardware should not cause many problems so it is normal to allow a limited amount of time to get the computer installed and operational. There will normally be a lead time of some weeks between the date of order and date of delivery. This time can be used to prepare for the installation. This involves getting ready the area in which the processor, disks etc. will be located. If any special environment is required the installation of special air conditioning will have to be organized. Requirements relating to electrical supply and fire detection and fire fighting equipment will have to be attended to. If the computer is to be located close to where people are working attention may have to be given to noise suppression. A visit should be arranged for the supplier's engineering staff so that the proposed site is approved and they can specify the requirements as to power supply, temperature etc. What is referred to in promotional literature as 'a normal office environment' can turn out to be more demanding than envisaged. A visit to another site with similar configuration will show how much noise and heat is generated.

As soon as the computer decision is made and the type of cable required for VDUs and local printers has been defined, cabling can start. At this stage consumables such as computer stationery, printer ribbons, disk packs and tapes can be ordered. Special furniture such as desks or stands for VDUs and printers should be ordered as should such items as sheet feeders and acoustic hoods for printers. The schedule should also take account of any items of equipment to be provided by the suppliers on a temporary basis pending the delivery of any items which have a longer lead time than the main elements of the configuration. The computer is generally regarded as having been commissioned when the main elements (e.g. processor, disks, printer, console and a number of VDUs) are working, the operating system has been generated and the supplier's tests have proved to be satisfactory. If a personnel package is being acquired some aspects of the system should ideally be demonstrable before the computer is regarded as operational.

System testing

The nature of system testing or verification activities are determined by the amount of development work required to provide the organization with the system which it wants. If a lot of modification is required to a package then a detailed system specification will have to be prepared and agreement reached on it between the supplier and the user. Similar agreement must be reached on such matters as the interface between the word processing system and the CPMIS, on the conversion programs required to transfer data from any existing computer-based system and on any programs which will provide the interface with the payroll system on an continuing basis.

An essential part of the system testing is the creation of a test system which is completely separate from the live system. The test system can be used to process transactions for fictitious employees. It should consist of a small number of employees and should be generated so as to test every conceivable set of conditions. Even after the system is live the test system must be retained so that modifications can be fully tested before being included in the live system. The test system is also very useful for training.

Responsibility for testing must always rest with the personnel function. Programmers and system designers will have tested the system on a program-by-program basis and as a whole but ultimately the user has to be convinced that the system as developed does what it was expected to do.

Training

Training in the use of the new system and of the procedures surrounding it is a crucial part of implementation. Training should be a gradual process and ideally should be carried out by personnel staff. The training foundations should have been laid through the involvement of staff at an early stage. This would have included meetings on the scope and format of the new system and demonstrations of it or of a prototype. Following this a brief course which introduces the fundamentals of computers and allows participants to use a keyboard would be beneficial. As soon as the background files and some reasonable test data have been set up a further series of demonstrations is helpful. These sessions should be interactive – the staff should be encouraged to open discussion on how the system will affect their work.

The next training phase concentrates on smaller groups or is done on a one-to-one basis. It is related to the job which each person has to do and to the procedures to be followed. As a rule there will be fewer problems in getting people to use the system than in getting them to adapt to new procedures. Some staff will take to the system more easily than others and additional training and encouragement will have to be provided for those who are slow to adapt.

After the first phase of the system is live further training will be required in elements still to be implemented such as word processing. A brief refresher course some weeks after staff start to use the system will be useful and may also generate ideas for streamlining or enhancing the system. Training in the use of the query language used should also be provided. The nature of this training depends on the type of query language used and the policy to be followed in regard to who can use it and it what form. One approach is to have a few key people who understand the language and its use. These people provide a service to their colleagues and they may also provide a means of using the facilities without having to understand either the language or the structure of the CPMIS in detail. Training can be organized in three phases

1 *Limited use*   This is an overview which provides a number of staff with an appreciation of what the system can do and enables them to generate simple enquiries.

2 *Extended use*   This phase aims to provide a more detailed knowledge of the system and the structure of the personnel data for the few staff who will become the experts in its use. The training in both phases 1 and 2 is normally provided by the supplier.

3 *Specific use*   This training is by the staff who have become the experts for staff who will want to use the system for specific purposes. The experts will have generated a number of rerunnable jobs or procedures which will meet as many as possible of the *ad hoc* queries as can be visualized. The training is concerned with teaching staff how to access and run these predefined procedures.

Procedures

As early as practicable the following procedures must be defined, agreed and documented.

1 Administrative procedures.
2 Procedures for using the computer system.
3 Computer operating procedures, security copying etc.

The first two items may be catered for in a combined procedures/user manual. Such a manual can be of substantial size and once the basic procedures are understood it will only be used for occasional reference. Such manuals should be supplemented by help sheets which provide a very brief summary of the key things which a person must remember in order to use the system. These sheets can be made specific to particular users, e.g. director of personnel, training manager or the clerk responsible for absence data.

The computer operations manual should deal with such matters as

- switching on and off the computer
- back-up (security copying) procedures
- maintenance arrangements
- supplier contacts in the event of problems
- hours of service and arrangements for extended service
- operation of fire detection system
- ordering of computer consumables
- change control procedures.

Procedures generally should define the role of the 'systems controller' in relation to such matters as the allocation of passwords, the control of printing and requests for print-outs, and the reporting of faults on VDUs.

The development of procedures involves the design and introduction of new forms. Proper attention to the principle of good form design is essential if these are to be effective. It can easily happen that 'interim forms' or forms designed and printed quickly can be introduced as a temporary measure but last longer than anticipated. This happens because they are not allowed for in the procedures timetable, and are eventually required in a hurry. It can also happen because the system is changed while it is being implemented and this affects the contents or format of forms so that a cheap, less than professional version is introduced. Once the system is live all such forms should be reviewed and redesigned if necessary.

File set-up

File set-up activity involves the gathering, classification, coding and inputting of the initial data required by the system. This data populates both the background files and the main employee file.

Background files

At quite an early stage the type of data required in background files will be obvious – grades, conditions of service, cost centre or department, types of absence, types of illness etc. The rules governing the significance of this data, and the level of detail required will have to be decided upon early on e.g. what rules determine the classification of academic qualifications and what levels of proficiency will be used in classifying knowledge of foreign languages. The computer programs required to allow this type of data to be input and maintained are also likely to be available from an early stage in the development/implementation cycle. This should be true even if a package has to be substantially modified or if a custom-built system is being developed.

Getting all of the data together may not be as straightforward as it would at first appear. Some of it may have to await decisions which involve a number of managers, and getting them together for the necessary discussions may in itself take time. All of the individual files or groups of data should be identified and dates should be assigned for completion of data gathering and input. These dates should take into account the interrelationship between the different types of data and the sequence in which the data will be required by the system. The interdependence of data during the various phases of implementing the system is shown in Figure 117. An indication of the type of data included in the background files is provided by the schedule in Figure 118. This schedule indicates the dates on which each particular item will be available and the person who has been given responsibility for it. It will prove to be a useful method of checking progress at the regular progress meetings.

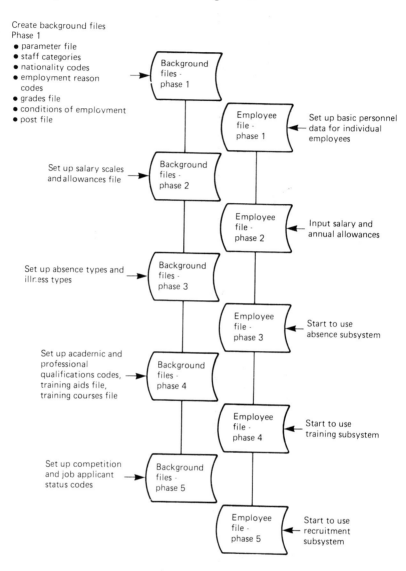

Figure 117 *Interdependence of data*

Employee files

In approaching the transfer of employee data to a new computer system an organization will normally find itself in one of three states

1 Any available personnel records are held in a manual system or systems. Usually the records are held on some form of indexed card system supported by each employee's personnel file which contains all correspondence with the employee, probation reports, annual apprai-

Background files	Priority	Responsibility	Date promised
1 Prepare parameter file data	–	GMD	6 April
2 Prepare descriptor file data	–	–	–
Absenteeism types	6	CT	6 April
Illness types	15	CT	13 April
Post types	3	GMD	6 April
Post occupancy types	4	GMD	6 April
Alterations to staff	5	GMD	6 April
Staff category	1	GMD	6 April
Occupation codes	18	FA	4 May
Schemes	14	CT	13 April
Professional qualifications	21	FA	11 May
Academic status	22	FA	11 May
Competition status	9	CT	6 April
Company codes – transferred service	8	BH	6 April
Nationality codes	7	CT	6 April
Ethnic origin codes	23	CT	4 May
Language codes	19	FA	4 May
Language status codes	20	FA	4 May
Application status codes	10	CT	6 April
Employment conditions	2	DJ	6 April
Reason for leaving	11	CT	13 April
Pension scheme – reason for exit	16	BH	13 April
Casual employment reasons	12	CT	13 April
Salary movement reasons	13	DJ	13 April
Training aids categories	17	FA	4 May
3 Prepare grades file data	–	DJ	13 April
4 Prepare division/cost centre data	–	GMD	13 April
5 Prepare location file data	–	GMD	13 April

Figure 118   *File set-up – background data*

sal reports etc. Other data may be held in quite separate files – illness records, training records and payroll records.
2 A computer-based or some form of mechanized system has been in operation, but its limits have been recognized and it is being replaced.
3 The organization's payroll system has been computerized and provides a limited service in terms of statistics and analyses. In this case the payroll data is ancillary to the main personnel system which again is usually based on indexed cards. Other satellite systems are used for training records, absence etc.

The organization with a totally manual operation is likely to have a small number of employees, and will probably consider a micro-based system for handling its personnel records. The move to the computer system will be less traumatic than in the case of the larger organization. The definition of cost centres, organization structure, salary scales etc.

can be done relatively easily and effort can be devoted to inputting the employee records. Because of the small size this should not prove to be too difficult if the manual records are in good shape. If there is any suspicion about the quality of these records they should be brought up to date before any attempt is made to input them to the system. In this way the system is assured of having good data right from the start.

The importance of having good data in the system cannot be over-emphasized – the first time an inaccurate report is produced by the new system confidence in it will be shaken and it can take time to re-establish confidence. This is particularly the case in the larger organization which is likely to be in one of the states outlined in (2) and (3) above. Either way, the approach to setting up employee data is likely to be a mixture of using whatever data already exists in computer form and updating it with the data which is held in non-computer form. This approach has a lot to recommend it – primarily in that it reduces the amount of effort required and enables the system to become operational more quickly.

The following tasks must now be undertaken

1 Verify that the data held in computer form can in fact be input to the new system. This is generally possible but a number of inconvenient steps may be required before it can be achieved. For example, the peripherals on one computer may be different from those on the other. If one computer uses 7-track tape and the tape decks on the second computer are designed to take 9-track tapes the use of an intermediary computer installation capable of handling both types will be necessary.

2 Ensure that the data in the computer system is accurate and up to date prior to any conversion process.

3 Specify a conversion program which will convert the data from the old system into a format which will be compatible with the new system. Given a good understanding of the data in the old system and the structure of the new system it may be possible to generate a lot of data for the new system. This does not have to be confined to a straight transfer of data between the systems. If the basic data is available and the rules for generating other data are known these can be incorporated into the program. Table 9 shows examples of the types of data which can be set up in this way and the types of conversion process which can be used.

4 Ensure that all manual records are accurate and up to date. Prepare the records for ease of input by increasing legibility and inserting codes.

5 Input the computer-based data into the new system and then update the files with the data from the manual records.

Because of the volatile nature of the data, arrangements will have to be made to perform these tasks within the shortest possible time scale. Once the inputting process starts, the sooner it is finished the better, and to achieve this the operation will have to be carefully planned. Sufficient resources must be allocated to the task and it will help if experienced

Table 9

Old system	Conversion process	New system
Employee name (30 characters)	Separate into the the two elements	Employee first name Employee surname
Grade code (3 digits)	Covert into a 4-digit field by adding a zero in the junior position	Grade code (4-digits). (In exceptional cases the fourth digit will be changed to indicate a subgrade associated with a particular set of conditions of service.)
Category (1 digit)	Transfer as in old system except in the case of code 7 and 8 which should be converted to and output as code 9.	Category
Cost centre (4 digits)	No change	Cost centre
Membership of pension scheme (1 character)	If code = 1 output Y otherwise output N	Membership of pension scheme
Date of birth	No change	Date of birth
Date of birth	If sex = M add 65 years If sex = F add 63 years	Retirement date

data preparation operators are involved. The data can be input in the normal data preparation way by using a key-to-disk or equivalent system. This has the benefit of allowing the work to go ahead independently of the CPMIS and allows the operators to achieve an extremely high throughput rate. It also has the benefit of allowing the keying of data to be verified before it is processed, thus ensuring a very high level of accuracy. The disadvantage is that the normal records must be either sent from the personnel department to the data preparation department or a data preparation bureau, or they must be photocopied or transcribed on to forms for input. Both of these approaches may raise questions of confidentiality. Trying to cope for a period without all of the records available and the amount of work involved in either photo-copying or transcription can also be problems.

An alternative method of using data preparation professionals is to bring them to the personnel records, instead of taking the records to them. People skilled in keyboard operation can achieve very fast speeds – although they may feel that an on-line system slows them down. Apart from the speed of operation there are two further, and perhaps more important benefits to be derived from using this approach *viz.*

1 It causes minimum disruption to the personnel division. Noboby is being diverted from normal work to become involved in what is a relatively routine operation.
2 Personnel staff involved in a high level of keying activity may become bored, and will be keen to have frequent interruptions from the keyboard. A data preparation operator will be familiar with this environment and in general will welcome the opportunity of becoming involved in a user department.

Implementation policy

At an early stage an implementation policy should be formulated. The aspects of implementation considered below are

1 Parallel running.
2 Phasing of implementation.
3 Treatment of history.

Parallel running

The running of both the new and the old system in parallel has been a common feature of computerization. In some application areas it is probably a necessary feature and a typical application is payroll. Very few payroll systems go live without some period of parallel running. This is important in order to ensure that all calculations are being done correctly and that all balances – tax, deductions, national insurance etc. – have been taken on correctly. Since payroll is the system with which personnel staff will have had most contact, there may be a natural expectation that parallel running is a normal feature of implementing a CPMIS. However, parallel running generally should be avoided if at all possible. It generates a substantial amount of activity. Two systems have to be kept running and the outputs of both have to be compared. All of this diverts effort away from the real task of ensuring that the new system is successful.

It is easy to get stuck in the 'parallel running activity trap' where no real productive work is done. The emphasis should be on the new system and the old system should be discarded as quickly as possible.

To rule out a parallel running phase requires a certain amount of courage and confidence. This confidence can only be sustained by proper system testing. The investment of time in system testing certainly pays off and in the long run time spent on testing will be considerably less than that diverted to the parallel operation.

Phasing of implementation

There is no point in trying to do everything at once. This would place a strain on everyone concerned but more particularly upon those responsible for managing the implementation. It is generally better to implement the core of the system initially, then to extend the data held in the basic system, to extend the range of facilities available and then to add on any subsystems such as training and recruitment. This allows the system to settle down and to resolve any bugs which may be uncovered by live running. It also provides opportunities to provide some further training for staff and to evaluate the effectiveness of user and procedure manuals.

As each element of the system goes live the old system should be dropped as soon as it is practicable. As long as records relating to the old system are available some staff will be inclined to continue to use them in preference to adapting to the new system. The declaration of a formal live date for each segment will help to reinforce the view that times are changing. It may also be appropriate to emphasize the dawn of a new era by means of a reception for the staff to mark the launch of the new system or alternatively a wake to mark the demise of the old system.

History

It is usually a mistake to attempt initially to input a lot of historical data to the system. This again can divert effort from getting the system operational. Some organizations regard the setting up of salary history as an essential part of the initial set-up phase. This may be worthwhile where salary history can be transferred from another computer-based system but if it has to be input manually there is little benefit to be gained and the effort involved could be more usefully deployed.

Once the system is up and running there should be nothing to stop the salary history data from being input then. Some other historical data may need to be input reasonably early on in order to produce meaningful reports. For example, if the sick pay rules of the organization relate to the number of sick absence days over a period of years, the computer system will have limited usefulness in this area until this history is available.

The live system

When the system goes live – or when the first phase of it is live – a report should be issued which provides an outline of the work done, the current status of the project and most importantly the change in the nature of duties and responsibilities. The last point is important because there is always a tendency for staff who have been involved in the development and implementation of the system to continue to be involved and for the staff involved in the day-to-day operations of the personnel department to become too reliant on this support. The report should accordingly stress the implications of the move from a developmental to an operational situation. For this move to be successful all procedures will have been properly documented and adequate training will have been essential. For example, up to now the computer system may have been switched on and off by systems development staff or a personnel project person from the software house and this function will now have to be performed by either computer operators or someone in the personnel area. The same applies to such matters as taking back-up copies of files, arranging off-site storage, reporting faults on equipment, ordering supplies, producing *ad hoc* reports, allocating passwords etc. It does not mean that support should no longer be provided but the change in the mode of operation needs to be emphasized.

The regular project meetings should continue but their frequency will need to be examined. If they have been taking place weekly, a move to a fortnightly schedule followed by intervals of a month may be appropriate. There can be no hard and fast rule about this. It is very much a matter of the benefits which accrue from the meetings and of reviewing the position from time to time.

Modifications

Even after the system becomes operational 'bugs' may appear. This is particularly the case in a new or custom-built system. Regardless of how comprehensive the program and system testing was, some bugs may have survived and it is only by encountering a set of unforeseen circumstances in the live situation that a program is seen to handle the situation incorrectly. These bugs will have to be corrected as quickly as possible and any contract with the software supplier should cover this point.

There is a clear distinction to be made between bugs and modifications. Bugs arise where the system is failing to do what it was specified to do. Modifications are system or program changes required. In the ideal world, if the requirements are well specified and the system meets those requirements and is well designed, there should be no need for modification unless the environment in which the system operates changes significantly. However, demand for modifications will undoubtedly arise and what is important is that there is a procedure for dealing with them. If there is not such a procedure the system will be in continuous state of development and may never become stable.

A major danger is that one person who uses the system may request a change to meet his or her particular needs. Since this user may not understand how the total system is designed to work there is a danger that the change requested may have implications of which he/she is unaware. The change might cause problems for the other aspects of the system and other users may request their own changes to try to cope with the new situation. In this way a never-ending cycle of problems may arise.

The demand for modifications will arise because of

1 Shortcomings in the system as it exists.
2 Changes which are seen as being beneficial to the operation of the system e.g. changes to screen layouts or a reports which combines data from several other reports.
3 Change for the sake of change.
4 New requirements.

Policy in relation to modifications should take account of all of the factors outlined above. The policy should be administered by the person who has had responsibility for the specification and implementation of the system. This person should be in a position to appreciate both the need for the change and the implications of the change throughout the system and the procedures.

The following items are suggested as the elements of a policy on system modifications for a CPMIS.

1 There should be a freeze on modifications to the system – unless they are absolutely essential – until the live system has settled down properly.
2 An aspirations file or wish list should be established in which all suggestions for changes or improvements can be logged. This provides the means of keeping a record of all needs expressed. All should be recorded and at this stage no attempt should be made to evaluate their worth or implications.
3 There should be a thorough evaluation of each request for change. This should be done by people who understand the total system and can visualize the implications of each change.
4 The project team should meet to discuss the requests and the output of this meeting should be a list of decisions relating to each item on the aspirations file, a priority rating on each item which has been approved for implementation and an implementation timetable.
5 Modifications should be implemented in blocks or groups rather than individually. In this way the time which will have been devoted to making the program changes, adding new programs, testing individual programs, system testing and altering system documentation will be considerably less than if the changes are implemented in a piecemeal fashion.
6 From this stage onwards the implementation of modifications should be governed by strict change control standards. These relate to the use of test versions of programs, test files, back-up copies and access to live programs. The approach may vary slightly depending upon whether the system is a bought-in package or an in-house developed system. These procedures are established essentially to guard against such possibilities as illegal access to live programs and files or the risk of losing data.

Test version of the system

During the testing phase a test system will have been generated. This system runs alongside the live system and contains its own version of programs and its own files. This enables the system to be tested adequately, to ensure that programs are working before they are moved across to the live system and it is very useful during staff training. The test system should not be discarded as soon as the real system goes live. It will still be very useful for ascertaining how the system treats a given set of conditions, for training new members of staff and most importantly for retesting the system when modifications have been made to it.

Another valid reason for retaining the test system is the need to have something available for demonstration purposes. This may be needed for internal purposes but more particularly for demonstrating to visitors the facilities available in the system. Invariably personnel people in other organizations will want to compare notes and examine the various options available to them when they are looking at the feasibility of introducing a CPMIS. Demonstrating a live system can lead to problems with confidential data so it is much better to have a version available which can be used without disclosing details about either the organization or individual employees. It also means that the person demonstrating the system may not have to ascertain current user identification codes and passwords.

Post-implementation review

From the time the system goes live it will be subject to a number of informal reviews of such matters as outstanding bugs, the modification list, security controls, response times and file sizes. There is also a need for at least one planned formal review of the system. This should take place some few months after the system has settled down. It should relate the state of the system now to the original feasibility study and the decision to introduce the system. The main purposes of the review are to appraise the degree of success achieved, to see what lessons can be learned from the project generally, to ascertain what, if any, aspects of the system are less than satisfactory and to examine what can be done to rectify any such problems.

Areas of attention in the review are

1 How well the system satisfies its original expectations. In doing this it must be remembered that there will sometimes be complaints from users that the system does not meet certain requirements. It is important to distinguish genuine shortcomings from 'pet needs' or 'hobby horses' or features which were deliberately left out for budgetary or other reasons.

2 How the actual development and running costs of the system compare with the budgeted costs.

3 The extent to which projected savings were achieved, e.g. reduction in staff numbers or decrease in need for casual staff to meet peaks.

4 The extent to which management reports are produced directly by the system, without need for amendment or adjustment.
5 How accurate and up to date the data held in the system is and the corresponding accuracy of the reports produced.
6 The speed with which management and operational reports are produced. This also includes the turn-around provided on *ad hoc* requirements.
7 The general level of satisfaction with the system as expressed by both personnel management and the staff who use the system as part of their everyday work.
8 The general level of satisfaction with the hardware, including degree of up-time, faults on peripherals (e.g. VDUs and printers), quality of printed output and screen displays, performance of sheet feeders on letter quality printers etc.
9 The level of satisfaction with the training provided, system documentation, user manuals, procedures manuals, actual procedures and forms in use.
0 The adequacy of security and back-up arrangements.

Once the review has been completed a report should be issued describing the situation and outlining any action which is required.

22 Glossary of terms

Access time The elapsed time between the start and completion of computer instruction to retrieve data – generally from backing storage (e.g. disk).

Address A storage position or location inside a computer. In normal usage it refers to a number which represents the specific location of the unit of memory at which a particular item of data is stored. It is also used in relation to the location of records on backing storage devices.

ALGOL ALGOL is a high level language generally used for mathematical and scientific applications. It defines algorithms as a series of statements and declarations in the form of algebraic formulae and English statements. The name is an acronym for ALGOrithmic Language.

Algorithm An algorithm is a systematic sequence of instructions or rules, expressed in mathematical terms, which is used to solve specific problems.

Artificial intelligence This refers to the use of computers to try to perform functions normally performed by humans – learning and decision making. A common example is the use of computers to play games such as chess.

BASIC This is a high-level language which is becoming increasingly popular especially in programming home computers, micros and minis. It is relatively easy to use especially for simple tasks. The term BASIC is an acronym for Beginners' All-purpose Symbolic Instruction Code. A simple program to accept two figures – annual salary and allowances – to add them and print or display the result is shown below

```
10  INPUT SAL
20  INPUT ALLS
30  REMUN = SAL + ALLS
40  PRINT REMUN
50  END
```

Baud A measure of the speed of data transmission, approximately equivalent to bits per second. A line with a baud rate of 4800 is equivalent to 4800 bits per second or about 600 characters per second.

Bug A bug is an error within a computer program. Grammatical or syntax errors are generally eradicated at the program compilation stage so a bug is normally a logic error. It either prevents a program from processing or it produces erroneous results. Program testing should identify and remove bugs – this process is also known as debugging.

Byte A bit (*B*inary dig*it*) is the lowest form of representation within a computer. It is in the form of 0 or 1. A byte is a collection of bits (usually eight) which together represent a character or number. It is thus the smallest unit which has any real meaning and the term is often used interchangeably with character – a megabyte of memory is capacity for one million characters of data.

Check digit A check digit is a number which is added to a series of numbers for checking purposes. The check digit is derived from the number to which it is attached – it is recalculated each time the number is entered into the system to attempt to highlight input errors. It is primarily designed to trap transposition or transcription errors and depending on the formula used, will trap in excess of 90 per cent of such errors. It is more useful in batch systems than in on-line systems. Since payroll systems tend to be batch systems the personnel number may need a check digit. There are various formulae available but the following is a typical example

Personnel number	3434

Calculation of modulus 11 check digit

1 A weight is assigned to each digit in the number according to a predefined pattern	Number	3	4	3	4
	Weights	5	4	3	2
2 Multiply each digit by the weights		15	16	9	8
3 Find sum of the products					48
4 Divide by 11			4 remainder 4
5 Subtract *remainder* from 11			11 − 4 = 7
6 The check digit is					7
7 The new personnel number is now		3	4	3	4 7

COBOL This is a high-level language which is very popular for programming of business applications. COBOL is an acronym for COmmon Business Oriented Language.

Compiler A compiler is essentially a translator or converter. It is a program which converts a program written in a high level language such as COBOL or BASIC into code which can be executed by the computer. This is known as the conversion from *source code* to *object code*. With many personnel packages the vendor supplies object code rather than source code. In this way the vendor protects the package as it is almost impossible to make changes to the object code. If source code is provided a programmer would be in a position to modify the programs. A compiler is different from an *interpreter* which converts a program written in a high level language into machine code on a line-by-line basis interactively at run-time. A compiler converts the whole program prior to execution whereas the interpreter does it as the program is being executed.

Configuration   The hardware (machine) components which together form a complete computer system. This consists of the processor (CPU) and the various peripheral devices such as printers, tape decks and disk drives.

Database   The term database has been used to describe a number of concepts but its correct definition is a collection of data structured in such a way that it can serve a number of application systems but no one system determines its structure. The data is maintained and retrieved by a highly complex software system called a database management system (DBMS). Typical DBMS packages are

ADABAS
IDS
IDMS
IMS and
TOTAL.

Vendor of many simple file-handling systems frequently refer to their products as database systems and the term is also used to refer to a variety of file-handling systems widely used with micro-computers.

Data dictionary   In the corporate database context the data dictionary is a central repository for the data definitions of the organization. It is the data processing department's own database and provides a means of automating the functions within this department all the way through from the initial investigatory work to operational database systems. The term is also used interchangeably with directory in the context of query languages, where it has a less comprehensive role.

Diskette   See floppy disk.

Entity analysis   This is the process of finding out what the business needs in order to operate, expressed in terms of the type of things it needs and the relevant facts about these things. These 'things' are referred to as entities e.g. employees, customers, competitions, orders, training courses, training aids and job applicants. The relevant facts are referred to as attributes e.g. employee name, date of birth, marital status, nationality and sex. Entities can be subdivided into three types

1 *Real*   Tangible objects or things such as employees or interview rooms.

2 *Activity*   These are activities of interest to the business about which data should be kept e.g. accidents or illnesses.

3 *Conceptual*   These are intangible entities such as cost centre or post.

Expert systems   Expert systems, also known as knowledge systems, are systems which store data relevant to a particular subject, which is input by experts in that subject, so that non-experts can be guided by a procedure to a correct solution.

FORTRAN This is a high level programming language which is very popular for programming scientific and mathematical applications. FORTRAN is an acronym for FORmula TRANslation.

Function analysis This is analysis of the functions which make the business operate, e.g. recruiting staff, paying staff.

Hardware Hardware consists of the various physical components that go to make up a computer system. It generally consists of

1 *Input devices* used to get data into the machine e.g. card readers, tape decks and VDUs.
2 *Output devices* used to take data from the processor and output it in a form which is either legible to humans or to machines for further processing, e.g. printers, VDUs, microfiche (COM).
3 *The central processing unit (CPU)* which stores and processes the data. The memory of the CPU is now generally measured in megabytes.
4 *Auxiliary (or backing) storage devices* which provide mass storage of data. Such devices are normally disks or tapes and is measured in Mbytes or Gigabytes (i.e. thousands of millions). A typical disk on a micro-computer might be 10 Mbytes while individual disks with capacities of hundreds of Mbytes are common on main-frames.

High level languages High level languages are problem-oriented rather than machine-oriented and enable the programmer to write programs in English-like statements. These languages are compiled or translated for execution by the computer and programs written in such languages are generally more transportable between computers than programs written in low level languages. Typical high level languages are COBOL, FORTRAN, BASIC, ALGOL, PASCAL, and PL/1.

LAN Local Area Network. A network is a means of linking together a number of computers and computer devices. A LAN is a privately owned network which provides reliable and high-speed communications channels for connecting the equipment within a limited geographical area. Any information processing equipment can be connected in this way over a geographic area such as an office, an office building, a building complex or a campus. There is a wide variety of LANs in existence ranging from small systems linking a few micro-computers to very complex systems operating at very high data transmission speeds – typically millions of characters per second. LANs facilitate the exchange of information and the sharing of resources within a local work environment and provide standards for communications between the equipment of different suppliers.

Light pen This is a device which looks like a pen, is sensitive to images displayed on a VDU and can be used as an input medium.

Low-level languages   Low-level languages are machine-orientated and tend to relate to the instruction set associated with a specific computer. Such languages are efficient in terms of execution speed but the program code is complicated and difficult to maintain.

Modem   A modem is a device which enables computers to communicate with one another over long distances generally over standard telephone lines. It achieves this by converting serial binary data into audio tones that can be passed over the telephone line. The term modem is derived from its main components – the MOdulator which converts the data into the audio tone and the DEModulator which converts the tone back into binary data which the computer can understand. Alternatively the function of a modem can be described as one of converting a digital signal to an analog signal and vice versa. An acoustic coupler is a low cost and convenient form of modem. It is used where occasional access to a computer is required, often from different locations. No special wiring is required and the procedure is to lift the telephone, dial the computer and as soon as the answer tone is received the telephone handset is placed into the device. The terminal is then automatically connected to the computer. It is a convenient way of accessing a time-sharing computer and typical users are travelling salespersons who need to transmit orders taken or to enquire about a customer's credit rating from a hotel-room, or a journalist who wants to transmit copy to the newsroom computer. In the personnel context modems may connect outlying offices to the central computer. A terminal linked to the computer via an acoustic coupler can be useful in providing access to personnel data from locations such as venues where wage negotiations take place.

Mouse   This device enables the user to communicate with the computer without using a keyboard. The cursor can be moved around the display screen by moving the mouse on a flat surface.

PASCAL   PASCAL is a high-level programming language. It is a highly structured language which allows programs to be written more efficiently.

PL/1   PL/1 is a high-level programming language which is used for both commercial and scientific applications.

RAM   RAM stands for random access memory and is that part of the computer's memory which is used for data, program instructions and sections of the operating system. This type of memory can be directly addressed and the contents are lost when the computer is switched off.

ROM   ROM stands for read only memory. The contents of the memory are fixed and cannot be altered – they are burnt in during manufacture. When the computer is switched off the contents remain unchanged. ROMs are widely used in programmable video games and in home computers. Small computers use this type of memory for storing the BASIC interpreter which converts program statements written in BASIC into executable machine code. PROM, programmable read only memory, and EPROM, erasable programmable read only memory, are further variations of ROM.

Software   Software is the term used to describe all programs which enable the computer hardware to operate effectively. Software can be broadly divided into

1 Systems software comprising operating systems, assemblers, compilers, database management systems, utilities such as sorts and communications software.
2 Applications software embracing off-the-shelf packages, application generators and custom-built systems. These include systems such as personnel, payroll, general ledger, stock control, financial modelling and airline booking systems.

Teletex   This is an automatic text transmission system. It is based on internationally agreed standards which provide a service substantially faster than telex for the transfer of documents or messages.

Teletext   Teletext is quite different from teletex. It is a system of transmitting information to the television screen and the common examples are the BBC's *ceefax* system and ITV's *oracle*.

Index

Absence, 8, 124, 136
  annual leave, 139
  sick leave, 140
Absence analysis, 141
Absence codes, 112
Absenteeism types, 101, 113
Academic achievement, 101, 170, 172
Acceptance procedures, 247
Access restrictions, security, 103, 252, 253
Access routes, 114
  comparison of menu and command, 118
Access time, 276
Accidents on duty, 101, 219
Acoustic hoods, 33, 262
Action codes, 116
Actuarial requirements, 150
ADABAS, 278
Address, 276
Ad-hoc queries, 1, 7, 203
Age analysis, 194
Age profile, 195
Air conditioning, 262
ALGOL, 50, 276, 279
Algorithm, 276
Allowances, 254
  annual, 127
  history, 132
  temporary, 127
Annual leave, 139
Analog computers, 18
Application generators, 4

Application Master, 205
Application packages, 4, 40
  advantages of, 40
  disadvantages of, 41
Application programs, 38
Application software, 38
Application status, 101, 156
Application systems, 40
Arrears, calculation of, 136
Artificial intelligence, 276
Aspirations file, 273
Assemblers, 38, 54
Attribute fields, 97
Auxiliary storage devices, 279

Background files, 265
Backing storage, 20
Badge readers, 27
BASIC, 50, 276, 279
Batch processing, 41
Baud, 277
Bench mark tests, 248
Benefits of CPMIS, 77, 88
Bit, 19
Bug, 272, 277
Business planning model, 192
Byte, 19, 277

Calculator punch, 13
CARDBOX, 16
Casual employees, 126
CEEFAX, 281
Central processing unit, 18, 279

Cessation of trading, 249
Check digit, 100, 254, 277
Checklist for evaluation of proposals, 233
COBOL, 14, 50, 209, 277, 279
  writing a program in, 52
Coding systems:
  academic achievement, 172
  action, 116
  cost centre, 95
  entity, 117
  grade, 97
  leave/absence, 112
  location, 98
  professional qualifications, 171
  proficiency (languages), 174
  reason for leaving, 201
Collator, 13
COM *see* Computer output on microfilm
Command-driven systems, 116
Command languages, 54
Compiler, 38, 50, 277
  program compilation process, 51
Competition number, 153
Competition status, 101, 113, 154
Computer modelling, 192
  manpower model, 198
  techniques of, 193
Computer operations manager, duties of, 62
Computer operations manual, 264
Computer output on microfilm, 27, 34
Computer service bureau, use for a CPMIS, 13, 84
Computers:
  history, 12
  types, 15, 18
Computer systems, flexibility, 107
Conditions of service, 101, 113, 218
Confidentiality, 9, 103, 252
Configuration, 278
Console, 27
Contracts, 237
  negotiation, 250
  problems with, 240
  general clauses, 244
  specific clauses, 245
Conversion of data files, 268
Copy, 54
Corporate plan, 187
Cost-benefit analysis, 75

Cost centre, 95
Cost of living index, 221
Courses, 170, 174
Courses file, 175
CPMIS:
  approaches available, 9, 79
  benefits of, 77, 88
  definition, 6
  flexibility, 9, 107
  general requirements, 103
  impact on organization, 255
  implementation of, 251
  modifications to, 272
  on a micro, 81
  on a mini, 82
  on a mainframe, 83
  reports, 194
  requirements, 9, 124
  review of, 274
  scope of, 7, 79
  system testing, 262
  test version of, 274
CPU, 18, 279
Custom built systems, 40, 83, 84

Data:
  accuracy of, 254
  dissemination of, 253
  historical, 271
  interdependence of, 266
  verification of, 253
Database:
  administrator, 61
  personnel database, 84
Database systems, 4, 16, 47, 278
  features, 48
  comparison with conventional systems, 48
Data capture devices, 26
Data dictionary, 278
Data Description Language (DDL), 49
Data files, 45
  types of, 45
  file elements, 45
  file organization, 46
Data item, 49
Data Manipulation Language (DML), 49
Data preparation, 268
  bureaux, 29
Data processing manager, duties of, 59
Date processing organization, 56

head of function, 59
  organization chart, 58
  typical structures, 57
Data protection legislation, 253
Data recorders, 27
Data transmission, 35
DATATRIEVE, 213
dBASE III, 16
DBMS, 16
DDL, 49
DEC, 15, 213
DEKE, 209, 213
Descriptor file, 111
Diary facilities, 223
Dictionary, 205, 278
Digital computers, 18
Direct input devices, 27
Directory, 205
Diskettes, 23, 25, 26, 278
Disk *see* Magnetic disk
Disputes, information on, 221
DML, 49
Document readers, 27
Documentation *see* Procedures, 27
Dorset County Council, 209
Duplex files, 106

Editors, 53
Electrical supply, 262
Electronic office, 12
Employee categories, 102, 113
Employee files, 266
Entity analysis, 278
Entity codes, 117
Environmental requirements, 262
EPROM, 281
Establishment, 8, 161
  link with recruitment, 153
  management information, 166
  outputs from system, 166
  post file, 163
Evaluation of proposals, 232
Expert systems, 278

Facilities booking, 101, 220
Feasibility study, 64
  cost-benefit analysis, 75
  purpose, 74
  report, 67
Files:
  background, 265
  conversion, 268

courses, 175
employee, 266
maintenance, 54
File set-up, 99, 265, 267
Fire detection, 262
Fixed price contracts, 70, 247
Floppy disks (diskettes), 23, 25, 26
Flows (in modelling), 198, 202
Forms design, 265
FORTRAN, 14, 50, 279
Fourth generation languages, 5, 54
  use in a CPMIS, 83
  see also Application generators
Function analysis, 279

Grade analysis, 162
Grade codes, 97
Graphics, 101, 222
Graph plotters, 27, 34

Hard disks, 22
Hardware, 279
  acceptance procedure, 247
  installation, 262
  maintenance agreement, 103
  payment terms, 248
  performance, 246
  proposals for purchase, 227
  quality, 247
  resilience, 106
Help facilities, 118
High level languages, 49, 279
  features of, 49
Historical data, 271

IBM, 13, 14
ICL, 13, 14, 205, 209
IDMS, 14, 205, 278
IDS, 278
Illness statistics, 141
Implementation, 235, 251
  involvement and participation, 251
  phasing of, 271
  policy, 256
  preliminary work, 253
  schedule, 257
  system implementation, 71
IMS, 278
Indexed sequential files, 47
Index of industrial production, 221
Index of retail prices, 221
Industrial relations, 8

Industrial relations information, 101, 220
Information retrieval, 220
  example of, 221
Input/output devices, 26, 279
Interpreter, 38, 50
Interview schedule, 158
Invitation to tender, 228
Involvement, importance of, 251
Internal audit, 251

JCL, 54
Job applicants, 155
  record, 157
Job control language, 54

Keyboard devices, 27
Key punch, 13
Key-to-disk, 27, 28

Labels, 225
Labour turnover index, 194
LAN, 279
Languages, 172
Language proficiency codes, 174
Leaving, reason for, 201
Legal advisor, involvement of, 244, 250
Letter of regret, 182
Letter production, 124, 178, 179
  link with recruitment, 159, 178
Letter re contract expiry, 180
Light pen, 279
Live system, 271
Location codes, 98
Log file, 106
LOTUS, 16
Low level languages, 280

Magnetic disk, 22
  cylinder concept, 23
Magnetic tape, 20
Magnetic ink character recognition, 27
Magnetic tape encoders, 27
Mainframe computer, 15
  use for a CPMIS, 83
  disadvantages of, 84
Management information, desirable attributes, 166
Manpower planning, 8, 185
  aims of, 186
  definition of, 186
  development of, 188

  models, 192, 198
  reports, 194
  stages, 187
Manpower summary, 162
Media recorders, 27
Menu-driven systems, 114
Merge, 53
MICR, 27
Micro-computer, 4, 15, 16
  use for a CPMIS, 79
Microfiche, 34
Microfilm, 34
Mini computers, 15
  use for a CPMIS, 82
Modem, 280
Modelling, 192
  manpower planning model, 198
Modifications to system, 272
Mouse, 280
MULTIPLAN, 16
Multiple sites, 249

Network controller, 61

Object program, 50
OCR, 27
Occupation code, 155
On-line processing, 9, 43
Operating systems, 38
  function of, 39
Operations manager, 62
Optical character recognition, 27
ORACLE, 281
Organization structure,
  personnel, 88
  post-computerization, 256

Packages:
  use for a CPMIS, 83
  see also Application packages
Paper tape readers, 27
Parallel running, 270
Parameters, 108
  in command-based systems, 117
  parameter file, 111
  run time parameters, 109
Participation, importance of, 251
PASCAL, 279, 280
Password, 38, 104, 264
Payment terms, 248
Payroll:
  as a batch system, 41

payroll-associated CPMIS,
  advantages, 80
  disadvantages, 81
  personnel data in, 2
Payroll number, 253
Pensionable service, 144
Pension records, 8, 124, 144
  actuarial requirements, 150
  administration system, 149
  benefit statement, 148
  relevant data, 145
Peripherals, 19
Peripheral applications, 218
Personnel database, 84
Personnel management function, 88
Personnel number, 4, 93, 253
Personnel records, 8, 124
  information held, 125
Pie chart, 223
PL/1, 14, 50, 279, 280
Point-of-sale terminals, 27
Post code, 164, 166
Post file, 163
Post-implementation review, 274
Preserved pension, 146
Printers:
  daisy-wheel, 33
  dot-matrix, 33
  line, 32
Privacy, 252
Price, fixed, 247
Procedures, 264
Processing techniques, 41
Professional qualifications, 170
Programmer:
  duties of, 60
  application, 60
  systems, 61
Programming, 70
Program specification, 61
Program testing aids, 54
Project meetings, 121, 256, 272
Project team, 256
PROM, 280
Proposals from Suppliers, 227
  evaluation of proposals, 232
  flowchart of process, 229
  seeking proposals, 227
  selecting suppliers, 228
  recommendation, 234
Punched input, 27

Query language, 3, 106, 203
  DEKE, 209
  desiderata of, 216
  principles of operation, 205
  stages in enquiry process, 206
  use of operators, 207
Querymaster, 208

RAM, 280
Random access, 23
Random organization, 47
Reasons for leaving, 102
  codes, 201
Real-time systems, benefits of, 44
Recruitment, 9, 152
  competitions, 153
  enquiries, 157
  job applicants, 155
  reports, 159
  system in operation, 156
Report generators *see* Query language, 9, 106, 203
Reportmaster, 205
Reporting levels, 95
Reports, 194
Reproducer, 13
Resilience, 106
Response time, 113, 246
Retrieval systems, use of, 3, 220
Retrospection, 131
Retrospective pay awards, 132
Review, system review, 71, 274
ROM, 280
RPG, 50

Salary History, 130
Salary increase, general, 132
Salary records, 126
Salary scales, examples, 128, 254
SCL (System Control Language), 54
Security, 103
Selecting suppliers, 228
Service analysis, 196
Set, 49
Sequential files, 46
Sheet feeders, 262
Sick leave, 112, 140
Signing the contract, 237
Site visits, 233, 262
Skills profile, 194
Software, 38, 281
  proposals for purchase, 227

Software development aids, 54
Software programmer, 61
Software resilience, 106
Sort, 53
Sorter, 13
Source program, 50
Specification of requirements, 68, 86
  format and scope, 87
  importance, 86
Spreadsheets, 4, 16
Staff associations, involvement of, 252
Staff level enquiry, 165, 167, 168
Staff number, 93, 253
Staff savings, 74
Staff turnover report, 197, 198, 199, 200, 201
Stocks, in modelling, 198, 202
Storage:
  backing storage, 20
  disk, 22
  magnetic tape, 20
SUPERCALC, 16
Support facilities, 121
  development, 121
  implementation, 122
  operational, 122
System control language, 54
System description, 91
System feasibility study, 64, 74
  objectives of, 67
  contents of feasibility report, 67
System implementation, 71, 251
  see also Implementation
System manager, 104
System proposal, contents of report, 60, 68
System review, 71
System software, 38
System specification, contents of, 69
System study report, 67
System summary, 88
System testing, 70, 262, 274
Systems analyst, duties of, 60
Systems controller, 264
Systems development process, 63
  communications in development process, 66
  development methodology, 64
  life cycle, 65
  reasons for failure, 63
  standards, 64
Systems programmer, 61

Tabulator, 13
Tape cartridges, 22
Tape cassettes, 22
Technical support programmer, 61
Telephone directory, 225
Teletex, 281
Teletext, 281
Temporary employees, 126
Terminal restrictions, 104
Test system, 274
TOTAL, 278
Trade union agreements, 101
Trades unions, involvement of, 251
Trading, cessation of, 249
Training aids, 92, 170, 176
Training and development, 124, 170
  academic achievements, 172
  languages, 172
  professional qualifications, 170
  training aids, 176
  training courses, 174
Training courses, 170, 174
  courses file, 175
Training in use of system, 263
Training records, 8
Transferred service, 146
Translators, 38

User-friendliness, 103, 114
User manual, 118, 264
User number, 104
Utility programs, 38, 53

Validation, example of, 110
VDU, 9, 27, 29
Verifier, 13
VME, 14, 209
Volumes in specification of requirements, 98

Winchester disks, 23, 25
Wish list, 273
WORD, 16
Word processing, 16, 101, 124, 178
  advantages of, 182
  disadvantages of, 183
  facilities, 17
  link with recruitment, 159
  stand-alone, 182
  types, 16
Word processor, use for a CPMIS, 82
WORDSTAR, 16